150290
Leach Library
Londonderry, NH 03053

P9-DHQ-942

LEACH LIBRARY
276 Mammoth Road
Londonderry, NH 03053
432-1132

**Leach Library**
276 Mammoth Road
Londonderry, NH 03053
Adult Services 432-1132
Children's Services 432-1127

# BRIGHT FROM THE START

# BRIGHT FROM THE START

The Simple, Science-Backed
Way to Nurture Your Child's Developing Mind,
from Birth to Age 3

## JILL STAMM, PH.D.

WITH PAULA SPENCER

GOTHAM BOOKS

649.122
STA

08 May 13
Amazon
2600(1716)

GOTHAM BOOKS
Published by Penguin Group (USA) Inc.
375 Hudson Street, New York, New York 10014, U.S.A.
Penguin Group (Canada), 90 Eglinton Avenue East, Suite 700, Toronto, Ontario M4P 2Y3, Canada (a division of Pearson Penguin Canada Inc.); Penguin Books Ltd, 80 Strand, London WC2R 0RL, England; Penguin Ireland, 25 St Stephen's Green, Dublin 2, Ireland (a division of Penguin Books Ltd); Penguin Group (Australia), 250 Camberwell Road, Camberwell, Victoria 3124, Australia (a division of Pearson Australia Group Pty Ltd); Penguin Books India Pvt Ltd, 11 Community Centre, Panchsheel Park, New Delhi – 110 017, India; Penguin Group (NZ), 67 Apollo Drive, Mairangi Bay, Auckland 1311, New Zealand (a division of Pearson New Zealand Ltd); Penguin Books (South Africa) (Pty) Ltd, 24 Sturdee Avenue, Rosebank, Johannesburg 2196, South Africa

Penguin Books Ltd, Registered Offices: 80 Strand, London WC2R 0RL, England

Published by Gotham Books, a division of Penguin Group (USA) Inc.

First printing, August 2007
10  9  8  7  6  5  4  3  2  1

Copyright © 2007 by Dr. Jill Stamm
All rights reserved

Excerpt from *The Little Prince*, by Antoine de Saint-Exupéry, ©1943 by Harcourt, Inc.; renewed by Consuelo de Saint-Exupéry. English translation ©2000 by Richard Howard. Reprinted by permission of Harcourt Inc.

Gotham Books and the skyscraper logo are trademarks of Penguin Group (USA) Inc.

LIBRARY OF CONGRESS CATALOGING-IN-PUBLICATION DATA
Stamm, Jill
  Bright from the start: the simple, science-backed way to nurture your child's developing mind, from birth to age 3/Jill Stamm, Paula Spencer.
    p. cm.
Includes bibliographical references.
ISBN 978-1-592-40285-4 (hardcover)
1. Child psychology. 2. Toddlers—Development. 3. Toddlers—Psychology. 4. Child rearing. I. Spencer, Paula. II. Title.

BF721.S578 2007
649' 122—dc22          2007012342

Printed in the United States of America
Set in Adobe Garamond • Designed by Elke Sigal

Without limiting the rights under copyright reserved above, no part of this publication may be reproduced, stored in or introduced into a retrieval system, or transmitted, in any form, or by any means (electronic, mechanical, photocopying, recording, or otherwise), without the prior written permission of both the copyright owner and the above publisher of this book.

The scanning, uploading, and distribution of this book via the Internet or via any other means without the permission of the publisher is illegal and punishable by law. Please purchase only authorized electronic editions, and do not participate in or encourage electronic piracy of copyrighted materials. Your support of the author's rights is appreciated.

While the author has made every effort to provide accurate telephone numbers and Internet addresses at the time of publication, neither the publisher nor the author assumes any responsibility for errors, or for changes that occur after publication. Further, the publisher does not have any control over and does not assume any responsibility for author or third-party Web sites or their content.

*This book is dedicated to my daughters,*

*Jenny and Kristin*

# About This Book:
## What Babies Really Need
## Is Easy as ABC

Every day I hear questions that reveal just how much parents care about raising a child with a bright future:

*Should I really read to my baby? What kind of toys do babies need? Can teaching a baby sign language really boost IQ? How should my caregiver be stimulating my baby? Should I enroll my toddler in foreign language lessons? Is all TV bad, or only some TV? Should I pipe classical music into the nursery?*

These are fairly new concerns. While mothers and fathers have always dreamed of their children growing up happy and successful, until very recently most of us, because we believed that intelligence was only inherited, did not spend our time and resources concerned about *our role* in influencing IQ. A child's potential was therefore thought to be pretty much predetermined. Today, we know differently.

Thanks to new technologies that make it possible to safely "see" inside a living, working brain, the medical world now knows that a huge amount of the brain's functioning and capacity develops after birth—and that a baby or toddler's early experiences can greatly influence his or her future learning potential.

Every baby living in the twenty-first century, whether born with impairments or bound for Harvard, deserves parents who have an awareness of the basics of how a young brain naturally grows. It's the foundation for all of the other things we've long been taught to pay attention to in babies and young children, including physical milestones, social-emotional development, and speech. As a parent, being mindful of brain development from birth can significantly impact your child's future success in academics and in life.

This book will help you separate the myths about early brain development from the facts and show you simple but effective ways to nurture your baby's remarkable growing mind.

## FIRST, BEWARE OF THE HYPE!

We're living in an exciting age of discovery about the infant brain. Cutting-edge neuroscientific research is challenging some old assumptions and helping to prioritize the importance of others. Knowledge about young children's minds is no longer based only on behavioral observations or on studies of injured brains and postmortem tissue. Now we have dramatic, concrete evidence about how typical brains develop. Scientists themselves are amazed by what they're discovering, particularly about how early the brain wires up for learning—far sooner than was previously assumed.

Unfortunately, as news of these findings has trickled into parents' lives, accurate and practical applications have been slower to follow. Media outlets, for example, are full of headlines about every latest brain-science study. Maybe you caught a segment on your favorite morning TV show about love-deprived Romanian orphans or noticed moms in an online chat group discussing the music-intelligence link. *Time* and *Newsweek* have devoted splashy cover stories to the infant brain. And what parent hasn't seen the loads of products in every baby store and catalog that promise to "create engaging learning opportunities," "stimulate cognitive development," or provide "brain-building fun?" *Edu-tainment* has become a $600 million business, with more than $100 million alone devoted to "developmental" videos and DVDs produced specifically for infants and toddlers.

The trouble is, headlines and ad slogans are often misleading. Many of the things we're currently doing for babies *aren't* accomplishing what we think they are. And we don't necessarily know what they *are* doing. What we do know is that families are spending a lot of money and energy on these efforts. Meanwhile, other activities with clear-cut evidence to support them are missed or discounted because parents aren't yet aware of their importance.

I see many different reactions to the "baby brain boom." For every mom or dad who feels stressed about keeping up with all the latest brain-building trends, there's one who hears words like "brain science" and "infant stimulation" and simply tunes out. Others still believe that "it's all in the genes" and how you interact with a baby doesn't much matter. I'm often asked, "A good preschool or kindergarten is the main thing, isn't it?"—which reveals the popular line of thinking that learning happens mostly in the school years.

Whether a parent undervalues the importance of brain development, overcompensates, or falls somewhere in between, there's a nagging sense of guilt: *Is this enough? Is it right? What if my child falls behind? Tell me, Dr. Stamm, what is it that I am supposed to be doing?*

Finding accurate, practical answers has been surprisingly tricky for parents. Few pediatricians have the time to dispense brain-development advice alongside their recommendations for feeding, sleep, and safety. Baby-care guides tend not to dwell on brain science or they don't include the topic at all. Though you can find lists of developmental milestones and expectations for different ages and stages, these always emphasize changes in the child, not the environment that's influencing her. News reports barely have time and space to explain the experiments, let alone interpret their findings in a way that helps you make sense of the latest crazes and decide how you want to spend your time, money, and energy with your baby. Although there is no end to suggestions about parenting techniques, important explanations about *why* you might want to do one thing over another are not available. The urgent sales descriptions you read on all those brainy toys and potty chairs with lights and sounds were written by advertising agencies wanting to sell products, not by neuroscientists who understand firsthand the facts about brain function.

## THE BRAIN TRUTH: WHAT BABIES AND TODDLERS REALLY NEED

This book will help to ease your concerns by bringing neuroscience from the laboratory into the nursery. I'll explain how scientists are discovering new information about infants and toddlers, the implications that can be drawn from such knowledge, and how you can use these science-backed insights to shape your own interactions with your child.

What the science tells us is this:

1. What babies need is **simpler** than you might think.
2. But they need it **more consistently** and **earlier** than we often provide it.
3. My recommendations for early care are **within every parent's ability** to provide, regardless of your resources.
4. In fact, they're as **easy to learn** as ABC. The cornerstones of what a bright, happy baby or toddler needs are Attention, Bonding, and Communication.

Let's look at each statement more closely:

### What Babies Need Is Simpler Than You Might Think

Sometimes parents interpret the new brain evidence to mean that if you do more and more of the "right things" with your child, she can become a genius. That's not what the scientific findings suggest at all. The data does not support the idea of brainy videos at six months, baby software at twelve months, and Chinese lessons at age two. Far from it. It turns out, a very young child's future success depends less on "academics" (however the word is often interpreted for the three-and-under set today) than on such critical factors as whether your baby loves her babysitter, how often she hears bedtime stories, and how much time you spend on the cell phone or in front of the TV yourself. That's right: Laptime is more critical than lapware!

The science suggests that there are ways to purposefully work with an infant or toddler that will encourage that child to attend better and longer, to be more emotionally connected to others, and to communicate better—each of which is truly important for future success. Chances are very good that you're doing many of these things already.

You may be surprised to find that some of the suggestions are simple. *But don't conclude that just because something is simple, it's not important!* In fact, many of the simplest lessons from neuroscience provide the strongest foundations for healthy brains. All of the information in this book is rooted in the current brain science.

I want to help you become aware of the importance of simple things you can do, simple things you can change, and simple things that science shows really matter.

### They Need Simple Things More Consistently and Earlier than We Often Provide Them

Consistency of loving care is one of the best examples of a simple thing that's vitally important. Babies don't need flashcards, but in the first three years they do need wonderful, consistent care from families who love them in order to help them thrive in kindergarten and beyond. That may sound too ordinary and not very directly connected to success. Yet it is. Certain biological effects directly result from such elemental factors as who cares for a child, and how knowledgeable that person is, as well as what happens day-in and day-out in that child's life. Without a well-laid groundwork of security and attention, later classroom learning may be more difficult.

Focus on a child's learning abilities used to begin at kindergarten, or later. Then during the 1960s, the value of early-intervention programs such as Head Start led to a boom in preschools that began at age four. Yet low test scores continue to be a problem in public elementary schools. Why are so many kids *not* ready for school? Are they born slow? Do they have low IQs? Is it deprivation? Poverty? Researchers are increasingly aware that what happens *before preschool* is critical.

School readiness does not mean *having already developed* the academic content of schooling. It does not mean being able to recite the alphabet, count to one hundred, or know the four sounds that the letter "A" can make when you are three, four, or five years old. Parents often exert a lot of effort and worry (and feel a lot of pride) over the acquisition of such skills, but the reality is that they will be taught by experienced teachers in due course and there is little advantage to being able to do them sooner. "School readiness" instead refers to coming to kindergarten with a ready brain—a healthy, active, nurtured brain that is capable of learning.

*My Recommendations for Early Care Are Within Every Parent's*
*Ability to Provide, Regardless of Resources*

Throughout the book, I'll provide lots of vivid, concrete examples of how you can incorporate science-based knowledge into your daily routines with your baby and toddler. I call them "Bright Ideas." Don't worry—I'm not pushing a program of fancy gizmos and drills. Nor are special lessons and classes required. Many of the recommendations are things parents already naturally do, such as singing and talking to your baby. Others are simple twists on ways to play and interact. All of my suggestions involve the most straightforward equipment: basic baby gear, household objects, common toys—and, of course, you.

I'll explain the "why" behind the importance of such activities, giving you clear reasons to engage with your child in these ways. In fact, you'll see how easy it is to create an optimal environment for secure, healthy development.

This advice isn't just for parents. Anyone who spends a lot of time being responsible for a young child should know this powerful information. If your baby or toddler is cared for some of the day by a babysitter, a nanny, or child-care center employees, they should also know the information contained in this book. I strongly encourage you to share this book with them.

*What Your Baby Needs Is as Easy for You to Learn as ABC*

Three overarching concepts should guide everyday interactions between you and your child: Attention, Bonding, and Communication.

**Attention** refers to the ability to use the brain's energy to pay attention, which we have recently learned is partly wired as early as age one. Face-to-face interactions and certain kinds of play can help children attend better and longer. Many technologies, on the other hand, threaten a child's attention span or steal time from more valuable live interactions. For kids under age two, TV, videos, and computers are posing a special risk.

**Bonding** develops security, the cornerstone of normal brain development. Touch, for example, is now known to release brain chemicals that impact attachment. Discoveries about how bonding influences very primal parts of the brain means that choosing infant child care should involve different considerations from choosing care for a toddler or preschooler.

**Communication** includes understanding speech, learning to talk, and activities that will later influence learning to read. Given what's been learned about the fascinating principles the brain operates on, there are many ways you can "prime the pump" for speaking and reading.

Supporting your child in these three areas provides the foundation that's necessary for successful future learning and development. You'll learn everyday ways to do this. Little things really do add up.

## MORE WAYS THIS BOOK IS DIFFERENT

It's reassuring that cutting-edge neuroscience is confirming—and elevating the importance of—many of the most elemental, "old-fashioned" basics of childrearing. This is good news that I hope will build your confidence, rather than add anxiety or guilt.

To that end, you'll notice some distinguishing traits about this guide:

- **I explain the *why*-to-do as much as the what-to-do.** Although I offer lots of brain-benefiting advice and games you can play with your baby, I must say I don't believe in making up snappy programs of dos and don'ts that promise to raise your baby's IQ by *x* number of points if you faithfully do *y, z, p*, and *q*. That's not realistic. Nor is it what the science tells us about what makes a bright child.

  I want you to understand *why* your child needs the various kinds of interactions I'll describe. I want you to know what makes your child's brain "tick." With a backdrop of easy-to-learn and easy-to-remember basics about early brain development, you will be able to make sense of the latest information and better ignore the hype, the latest new trend, or the opinions of your fellow playgroup members or the lady next door. You can decide how you want to spend your time and energy with your child, from birth to age three.

- **My advice is rooted in the basic principles of how brains grow and operate.** The newborn brain prefers an environment that mimics what it already knows. I agree with pediatrician Harvey Karp, M.D., who has defined the first three months of a newborn infant's life as the "Fourth Trimester." This refers to the idea that a newborn's nervous system, digestive system, temperature control system, and so on, are not quite "ready for prime time." *What parents can best provide in this special first period of life outside the womb is to create care routines that mimic the environment inside the womb.* Each of Karp's five S's of quieting a crying baby (Swaddling, Side-lying, Shushing, Swinging, and Sucking) accomplishes the task of mimicking the womb. From a brain development perspective, what these suggestions draw attention to is that there are ways to slowly introduce the baby to life in the outside world. The idea that brains recognize the familiar is at the root of these suggestions! It has a calming effect on the brain to know, at each and every stage of life, what to expect next. It is a good idea that, in a world that is literally ALL NEW, an infant can be "reminded" of easier days in the womb with the effortless comforts of not having to work hard in order to:

- Get nourishment
- Maintain perfect body temperature
- Be comforted by the sounds of a regular heartbeat
- Achieve effortless movement
- Be soothed by a warm, secure environment

Providing what a child needs and is ready for at each stage of his early life is the basis of many of the ideas to follow in this book. The brain's main function is to keep us alive. That fact, combined with other main "operating principles" of brain function, can influence many decisions you make as a parent. The brain is:

- A survival organ
- A pattern-seeking organ
- A pleasure-seeking organ
- A novelty-seeking organ

- An energy-conserving organ
- A meaning-seeking organ

As you will see in the chapters that follow, tapping into the ways a healthy brain functions can provide an internal guide for you as your child's first teacher.

- **My advice is organized according to key cognitive changes—not physical development.** This means that you won't find information packaged in the usual physical milestone-based groupings of birth to three months, three to six months, six to twelve months, and so on. Instead, I purposely focus on the phases of cognitive (learning) changes that accompany neurological (brain) development. This means I use the following age periods:

*Infant—Birth to 6 months:* This is the period during which vision develops to nearly adult capacity; by six months, eyesight is well established and propped sitting aids in a new perspective from which to view the world, which creates a shift in what your child can learn.

*Baby—6 to 18 months:* This is the period of the emergence of language, which includes first words, first short sentences, early concept development. The auditory system is rapidly wiring to both comprehend and produce language. This is also a time of broader social interaction. With increased social opportunities, a child's personality noticeably emerges. Independent mobility (both crawling and walking) opens a world of exploration that was unavailable as an infant.

*Toddler—18 months to 3 years:* This is the period during which opportunities to play and interact with other children (as well as adults) in playgroups or initial nursery and preschool groups influence a child's cognitive growth in both receptive and expressive language development. A child's initial knowledge of concepts becomes elaborated as she has more and more experiences.

Most importantly, I have found that just because parents know what various milestones a child is supposed to achieve, it doesn't mean that they know what to do to encourage the child's development. Therefore, my advice is focused *not* on the actions that your child can or cannot do at specific times, but rather on adult behaviors *that you and your baby's caregivers can do* that will eventually result in your child achieving various milestones in her own good time.

- **You can take away as much depth from this guide as you prefer.** Each chapter maps out the basic new insights and how to apply them. If you want to learn even more about the research behind these findings, look to the Appendix. The References section includes the scientific references for each chapter as well as detailed descriptions of some of the fascinating studies written in a user-friendly tone (Brain Briefs). You'll also find more information about the brain itself and a resource list of further recommended readings and Web sites.

## YOUR BABY'S BRIGHT FUTURE

You can use your new understanding of early brain development to guide your choices of:

- How you spend time with and respond to your child
- What activities to do with him or her and *why*
- What kind of child-care environments to select

These are the choices that shape a developing brain and add up to a truly healthy, happy, and bright baby.

# Introduction

"Your baby is a girl. She's not going to live. You can take a good look if you want to."

Those were the words that welcomed me to motherhood. Although I didn't know it at the time, they would also mark my entrance into my current professional life.

My ideas about children's brains aren't merely those of an interested observer; I've also lived them as a parent. I understand the promise and the power of a baby's brain from a dual perspective that few people are fortunate enough to experience. (Although there was a time when "fortunate" was not the word I might have chosen.)

I think of myself as a learning expert whose life's work is studying the latest scientific research on early brain development and translating it into user-friendly child-rearing advice. I co-founded the nonprofit New Directions Institute for Infant Brain Development for this purpose. The Institute is now a member of Arizona's Children Association as a component of a family of agencies focused on the welfare of children and families in Arizona. I lecture nationally on early learning and cognition. Thousands of parents, educators, caregivers, as well as business and community leaders have attended my workshops to learn these simple messages. Many people assume that because I started an organization focused on infant and toddler brain development, that I must have received my degree in Early Childhood. My interest in very young children is from a *learning perspective*. I hold a Ph.D. in Learning and Instructional Technology, and my specialization is in understanding how people learn. As a clinical associate professor at Arizona State University, I teach courses in how people learn, including how very young minds wire up for learning. In 2001, I patented a system called Brain Boxes™ for teaching parents and other care providers about the science of early development. This product is designed to engage a child in interactive activities linked to brain processes that support later learning skills. The Brain Box prototypes for ages birth through five have been tested in workshops and child-care settings for five years, and I have recently made a home-based product called Baby Brain Box, which concentrates on a baby's first year of life. This play-based box combines toys and books with instructional cards that describe how to engage a young infant's mind. (See www.babybrainbox.com for details.)

In addition to my academic training, I also have a mother's knowledge of the brain's potential. My younger daughter, Kristin, is a Ph.D. candidate in neuroscience at the University of California, Los Angeles. She studies brain development in children at UCLA's Ahmanson-Lovelace Brain Mapping Center, a premiere center of neuroscientific research, and one of the institutes where the world's largest brain-mapping project is taking place.

What a kick for me! How exciting to be able to share an interest in cutting edge research with my child. I could never have imagined such an interesting twist to our family's early concerns about a child's brain. Those concerns began with Kristin's older sister, Jenny, my baby who was not expected to live. Jenny is multiply handicapped as a result of extreme prematurity. I can honestly say that both of my children have been successful, albeit in very different ways, which makes me both proud and a little astounded.

I was a twenty-eight-year-old fifth-grade teacher in Scottsdale, Arizona, when I conceived Jenny in 1974. After working with children my entire young career, I was elated to be expecting a child of my own. Having recently finished all my coursework for a Ph.D. in education, specializing in curriculum development, all I had left to do was to write my dissertation.

I remember walking into my class one day, and I had the same thought many expectant mothers do: *I can't believe my body is going to stretch much farther!* Except I was only five months pregnant, with nearly half of pregnancy's stretching still to come.

The next day, I went into labor. Although I didn't know it at the time, while my own mother was carrying me, she'd been given DES (diethyl stilbestrol), a synthetic estrogen then routinely used to prevent miscarriage and since found to cause certain kinds of birth defects. As a result, where in most women the womb is a roomy organ that expands to accommodate a growing fetus for nine months, mine couldn't. My uterus was divided almost exactly in half and the half occupied by my healthy, normal, perfect daughter had reached its physical limit. She was born almost four months prematurely.

Shell-shocked and scared though her father and I were, of course we "took a good look at her." A first glance didn't offer much consolation. Jenny's long eyelashes seemed to be the only normal-sized part of her. She was the length of a ruler, twelve inches, and weighed one pound, nine ounces.

I could cradle Jenny's head like a tennis ball in my palm, with space left over—that is, if I'd been allowed to hold her. That was impossible. At one minute after birth her Apgar score—which measures a newborn's heart rate, muscle tone, breathing, reflexes, and skin coloration—was one. Most healthy full-term newborns score between eight and ten. At five minutes, Jenny's score was still one. After ten minutes, still one. She was limp, blue, and motionless—but faintly and steadily, her heart was beating.

Jenny lived by the pure coincidence of where she had been born. She was the fourth American baby ever placed on a respirator, because at Good Samaritan Hospital in Phoenix, the neonatologist Dr. Joseph Daley had decided that saving tiny preemies was his mission. He had calculated that Jenny's size and age, along with the fact that she had educated, healthy parents, might give her a fighting chance of leading a normal life. (IQ was then thought to be mostly hereditary.) Today, micro-preemies weighing barely two pounds routinely live and some even thrive. At the time of Jenny's birth, though, such thinking was quite radical. She was born barely ten years after President John F. Kennedy's son, Patrick, died two days after birth because his lungs were immature; he had been only six weeks premature, compared with Jenny's fourteen weeks.

Miraculously, once connected to the respirator, Jenny started to "pink up" right away. The baby who wasn't supposed to live twelve hours kept living—for a day, then a week, and then another. As the machine continued to breathe for her, day after day, I confess I wasn't sure this was such a miracle.

*Why are we keeping this child alive?* I would wonder during our five-times-a-day visits to her isolette, where she lay so still and tiny. So many tubes, bright lights, alarms, and buzzers, monitoring, measuring.

*What would be her long-term prognosis?* I'd ask as I delivered the breast milk I diligently pumped so that she might have a few drops for the external feeding tube that now ran directly into her stomach.

The surgery to insert this feeding tube had been done with absolutely no anesthetic. *How could they?* This was a helpless baby, my baby. *And what about the pain?* Confidently, doctors assured me that they had to do this, that she might not have survived the anesthetic. "She won't remember it. Don't worry," they said.

But I did worry. It would be nearly twenty years later that neuroscientists would discover the true effects of such trauma on the formation of early brain structures. Damage at such early stages, they would learn, does in fact play a significant role in the later development of all other regions of the brain.

In 1974, no one knew that these kinds of early experiences could impact the brain for life.

Nor did anyone know what to expect once her lungs were finally mature enough for her to be weaned off the oxygen. Jenny was four and a half months old by the time she finally breathed on her own. She would be later diagnosed as multiply handicapped. We would discover her vision was poor (due to the high concentrations of oxygen used to keep her alive) and her limbs would later become stiff and difficult to control (the end result of cerebral palsy she sustained following fifteen minutes of oxygen deprivation between birth and respirator). "You are not going to find advice as you go; these are the first babies in the history of the world to be kept alive in this way," warned a doctor improbably surnamed Sunshine. "You'll just have to wait and see."

When we brought her home, Jenny weighed four pounds.

The buffer through this blur, worry, and confusion was our neonatal intensive care unit (NICU) nurses. Because they spend the most time with preemies, they often are a cheerleading squad for families across those endless months. Our nurses liked Jenny. They had seen something in her—personality? Grit? Promise? "She'll make it," they confided.

I had no choice but to believe them.

A lifetime of caring for and learning from Jenny has followed. Yes, I said "learning *from*," for we taught one another in equal measure.

There was a passage from a well-known book that echoed often in my mind as I began to contemplate the enormity of the challenge ahead.

"I am responsible for my rose," I would repeat to myself in the months after we brought Jenny home. "I am responsible for my rose," I would chant over and over, as if making sure to remember. The line is from *The Little Prince*. A fox advises the prince:

> "It is the time you have wasted for your rose that makes your rose so important."
>
> "It is the time I have wasted for my rose," said the Little Prince, so he would be sure to remember.
>
> "Men have forgotten this truth," said the fox, "But you must not forget it. You become responsible, forever, for what you have tamed. You are responsible for your rose . . ."
>
> "I am responsible for my rose," the little prince repeated, so that he would be sure to remember.

Not that I could possibly forget I was responsible for her. I suppose I was trying desperately to convince myself that taking responsibility for her might somehow matter.

I sat in the house looking at my tiny skinned pup of a child, not bothering to wipe my tears since there was no one there to see me. Our hospital vigils over, her daddy had gone back to the bustle and distractions of his long workday. The NICU nurses who had cheered Jenny on were back at the hospital, saving new lives. The doctors had little more to offer. The stark reality was that it was going to be up to me.

Up to me to "waste" enough time to find out how to connect to this tiny person.

Mostly, at first, I prayed for her to grow. When she was about a year old, weighing only eight pounds—finally the whopping size of the newborn I'd once anticipated—we took Jenny for her first extensive developmental testing in California. The neonatologist seemed pleased by her growth and relative robustness.

"You know, she won't turn her head equally from side to side," I pointed out. "What's that all about?"

He didn't seem overly concerned. "I think she'll be fine," he assessed. He recommended bringing her back two months later for more tests, to see how she matured.

Parents in our situation don't mis-hear a word like "fine." We climb aboard it and we sail.

Two months later, though, it was more like, "abandon ship!" The same cheerful man now soberly reported that Jenny had made no signs of neurological progress. His message was clear . . . she would never walk, never talk, never read, never, never, never.

Flash forward thirty years. In one sense, the doctors were right, Jenny is confined to a wheelchair; she has never walked.

But talk? Oh yes, Jenny Stamm can talk. She laughs, asks questions, makes jokes, teases, argues, chats with friends, freaks out when she's cross, and never forgets an item on our grocery shopping list. You can tell that she's a teacher's daughter. You bet she can talk!

Through trial and error, and endless observation—what else did I have to do with my days but observe her?—I began to notice more interesting things. There was the business of not turning her head from side to side. (Later I learned that, because she'd been taped into position in her isolette for so many months, her brain had failed to internally map the use of her limbs into a coordinated, connected motor plan.) She still had a strong infant startle reflex, suddenly jerking her arms and legs up to her chest in response to a loud noise, something she should have lost long before. Eventually, I noticed that even though she could say individual words, she could say them only when she was lying on her back with her head and shoulders supported and propped. What was the explanation for that? Yet I could also see clear signs of intelligence. She could make connections between events, for example. A few days a week, I would have my neighbor come over to watch Jenny while I took our energetic dog for a run. By age two, when Jenny saw me get out the dog's leash, she would fuss, recognizing that I would be leaving soon for a while.

Jenny was cute as a button—curly blond hair, blue eyes, and an adorable miniature body that didn't work for dink. At two and a half, she began to say single words. Each day as I laced her soft, white, high-top baby shoes onto her feet I would slowly and clearly repeat, "Tie . . . a bow." Jenny could say the word *tie*. She could say *bow*. She could not say, "Tie a bow." We worked on this for six months. Every day. Several times a day. Each time I put on her little white shoes, I'd say, "Can you say, tie . . . a bow?" She would try. She'd tense up her whole body in anticipation of her effort—and what frequently came out was, "Bie tow . . . bie tow . . . bie tow." And then she would hit herself in the head. She knew what she wanted to say. She just couldn't.

Finally, one day it happened. Jenny tensed and out came, "Tie a bow." Clear as a bell. That was the start. The start of the slow, arduous task of teaching Jenny to talk. Born that day was the Stamm mantra: "Never, never, never give up on a child." Years later I would use this hard-won wisdom to help parents of typical, normal children and encourage them to find the time needed to connect with their kids.

Watching my daughter's slow development fostered a fascination with how malleable brain development can be in response to repeated effort and experience. Her development would remain so slow that I could literally "watch" learning happen.

If Jenny showed me how the brain wires up in slow motion, Kristin, five years younger, arrived on fast forward. Following a risky, but successful brand-new procedure to reshape my uterus, my next pregnancy was totally normal. Full-term, robust, perfectly healthy, she was like a balm that soothed every hurting part of me. Kristin whisked through her infant milestones right on schedule, according to the developmental charts I'd long ago stopped paying any attention to. Her brain came on-line in the lightning-quick way that nature intended.

After these very different experiences I can assure parents who feel anxious and worried about how to care for their precious babies' brains. "Be patient. You can do this," I tell them. "I have experience with how easy 'normal' can be once you've done it the other way."

I realize that there is so much that we collectively, and I specifically, do not yet understand about the development of the brain. And often, what we do know from the latest neuroscience findings is not yet ready to translate into practical suggestions for parents; the information is sometimes still at a theoretical stage or the level of the research about a particular topic is too small (looking at the neuronal, cellular level) or too large (looking at how traditions in various cultures impact language usage). In this book, I have relied heavily on what I've learned as a teacher of young children, on my experiences in trying to prepare others to become teachers through university training, and on my experiences as a mom who, because of the unique challenges presented by Jenny, learned to pay very, very close attention to how my children (both of them) learned. These personal experiences have provided a unique filter through which I have absorbed and translated for parents the main messages of every neuroscientist I have ever met, listened to, read, and studied.

*Kristin and Jenny*

# PART ONE

## The Brain Truth

# 1

## Five "Wows"
## Every Parent Should Know

- EXACTLY WHY ARE THE FIRST YEARS OF LIFE SO CRITICAL?
  AND HOW DO SCIENTISTS KNOW THIS?
- IS MY CHILD BORN WITH A CERTAIN IQ OR CAN IT REALLY BE BOOSTED?
  - WHAT DOES A GROWING BRAIN NEED?

We now have evidence that shows that early experiences are literally brain-shaping. Thanks to the latest neuroscience—combined with related research in pediatrics, psychology, and child development— we now have clarification about what very young children need most, and when they need it. This new work is confirming age-old wisdom: The very kinds of basic nurturing that most loving parents routinely provide turns out to be most important of all. You can help wire a healthy brain by:

- Spending one-on-one time loving your child
- Playing with your child
- Responding quickly and predictably to your child
- Touching and cuddling with your child
- Providing routines that establish patterns of caring response
- Talking to your child
- Reading and singing to your child

Sounds easy enough, right? In fact, it's easy as A, B, C: Attention, Bonding, and Communication, three proven gateways to a bright beginning. Only recently have researchers been able to show why these very regular behaviors are critical to normal development. Fortunately, there are things that you and every adult who cares for your child can easily do—knowledge that I hope will make you feel less stressed-out, guilty, or confused about your role in your baby's development.

## THE FIVE BRAIN-DEVELOPMENT "WOWS"

*"The real voyage of discovery consists not*
*in seeking new landscapes but in having new eyes."*
—MARCEL PROUST

Before I show you ways that you can influence your child's early learning, it's useful to know some of the impressive major discoveries about brain development that have led to the focus on those ABCs.

On the outside, of course, your baby changes almost imperceptibly from day to day. If you could look inside her brain, however, you would see growth occurring at a miraculous rate. And it's happening faster, and earlier, than anyone inside or outside the scientific community had previously imagined. During the first month of life alone, connections between the 100 billion brain cells present at birth increase twenty-fold, creating more than 1,000 trillion lines of communication that help a baby make sense of her world. Numbers like this are really too big to comprehend. But you don't have to know the first thing about neurobiology to understand that 1,000 trillion of anything represents a huge amount of energy being put to work within a tiny head. Imagine that a more visible body part, like your baby's feet, grew at the same astonishing pace that her brain does—attaining seventy-five percent of adult size by age two. You can bet we would all pay a lot more attention to feet!

Over just the past ten to fifteen years, imaging technologies such as PET (positron emission tomography) and fMRI (functional magnetic resonance imaging) have finally allowed us to see what happens inside a growing, working brain. These technologies produce "action shots" that graphically illustrate which areas of the brain change in response to different kinds of stimulation and use. This work, done mostly in

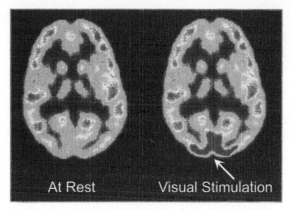

*Figure 1. Neuroimaging: How we know what we know.*

adults until very recently, has given us a new dimension of insight into how brains operate and has dramatically influenced our thinking about what very young children likely need to flourish and when they need it. The brain scan above, for example, shows the difference in brain activity during something as simple as receiving visual stimulation. The arrow shows activation in the occipital lobe (in the back of the head) where we process visual input. Blood flows to those areas working to process incoming information.

### Wow #1: Intelligence Can Be Shaped After Birth

The old thinking was that biology is destiny. IQs were thought to be born, not made. Certainly, some kids seem naturally smarter than others, right from the get-go. But we now know that the sum total of a baby's intellectual capacity is not fixed at birth. A child is born with an IQ range that can vary by as much as twenty or thirty points. While genes and physical health set the stage for some of a child's future behavior, we now know that a child's IQ and ability to function well also depends on the environmental experiences that she is exposed to on a *consistent* basis.

Think of healthy brain development as a dance between biology (what your child was born with) and early care (what happens after birth). The two are so intertwined scientists are now examining factors in the environment that can either hinder or facilitate the way that genes operate. We used to think genes functioned in a static way—if you had a gene for something, you showed that trait (like eye color, for example). However, we now know that some genes can be dormant; whether or not they get "turned on" depends on experience. This is a dramatic new finding! Your baby's consistent early experiences may actually protect *against* the turning on of certain genes involved with unwanted traits, such as hyperactivity, compulsivity, and aggressive behavior.

An amazing example of the power of life experiences to alter the "destiny" inscribed by our genes can be seen in rhesus monkeys. Those born with one particular variation of a gene grow up to be extremely aggressive when they are poorly bonded to their mothers during infancy, yet other monkeys who also have this gene variant do not become aggressive when they have developed a secure relationship with mom. Despite the monkeys in each situation having the same version of the gene, they have different levels of the chemical that's produced by the gene. This indicates that life experiences in the early years can actually change how certain genes function. What's more, because female monkeys go on to mimic the same kind of attachment relationships with their babies that they themselves experienced, it's possible that behavioral tendencies that were long believed to be directly transmitted through one's genes (like aggressiveness) may be transmitted through social learning instead. Stephen Suomi, M.D., Ph.D., head of the Laboratory of Comparative Ethology at the National Institute of Child Health and Human Development, calls this "the buffering effect of good mothering." Talk about the power of experience! We don't yet know for sure if this type of animal research is directly applicable to human behavior, but such new findings highlight basic neurobiological principles that likely hold true for us too.

**What this means for your child:** The classic debate of nature vs. nurture and which shapes intelligence and personality is essentially over. The two are intertwined. A child can grow up to be bright independent of his parents' intelligence levels, and a child who is born bright can sustain or exceed that intelligence depending on life experiences.

*Wow #2: The Majority of the Brain's Basic Wiring*
*Occurs in the First Few Years of Life*

Anyone who spends a lot of time with the very young—parents,
school and kindergarten teachers, child-care workers—can sense
this stage of life is truly amazing. Many of us involved in education
long felt we ought to pay more attention to kids in these early
though few of us could explain *why*. As a result—and also becau
medical community couldn't see the brain the way it could see an
sure other body parts through x-rays, ultrasounds, blood tests,
like—an emphasis on very early development remained a bit of a
thought. Now, of course, we can see why it deserves primary fo

When your baby was born, most of his major organs w
formed, although in miniature. The heart, for example, already
same parts and operating principles in place that it needed to b
than two billion times in a lifetime. The lungs, the liver, the k
all were up and running from the start, their essential circuit
been formed before birth and then growing in steady pace a
the rest of the body.

Not so for the brain. The brain begins life outside
remarkably unfinished—only about a quarter of its eventua
Yet before your child's second birthday, it will have ramped
fourths of adult size, and will be almost at its adult weight
(ninety percent) by age five.

This doesn't mean that ninety percent of the informat
will ever know is learned in the first five years—far from it!
in these earliest years, the way information flows throug
structures and gets processed is largely established. These
structures will be used and reused as learning continues th

Part of the tremendous growth in the first few years is
folding of one's genes, but part of it is the result of early li
A baby's surroundings begin to exert influences on the
brain, right from the start.

Although most of the brain cells (*neurons*) were p
birth, they're poorly connected. The majority of the conn

neurons, called *synapses*, must be created after birth. As the brain matures, each neuron sends out multiple branches to communicate with more neurons. There are two kinds of these connecting "branch lines"—some send information out (*axons*) and some take information in (*dendrites*). Most of brain growth in the first few years is thought to be due to the growth of dendrites, the lines bringing forth information. These synapses work something like phone lines between cells, allowing them to send messages to one another. One's individual pattern of connections forms the basis of all movement, thoughts, memories, and feelings.

The newborn brain is like a communication network in a city where the main lines in each neighborhood exist, but time and experiences are required to create specific connections from house to house. Each brain begins to make its own unique associations with wires that literally grow themselves as needed.

**What this means for your child:** Learning begins long before kindergarten. Every waking hour of every day, new neural connections are formed and modified through verbal and physical interactions that a baby has with parents, siblings, and other caregivers. He cries and is picked up, and a connection is made: *When I do this, that happens.* Each time you pat his back, feed him, or walk into a new place, new connections are made. The brain literally evolves in response to experience and to the environment. In fact, forming, refining, and eliminating neural connections is the main task of early brain development. It's the magical process that underlies all types of learning.

The particular network of wires that your child grows is unique to him. No one else on the planet—not even an identical twin—can replicate the exact combination of his blueprint of heredity and his experience.

*Fact #3: How the Brain Grows Can Be Influenced by How It's Used*
Children can be born into a mind-boggling array of living situations. They may be bundled into bearskin blankets in the arctic cold, or they may be carried skin-to-skin in slings through tropical jungles. They may hear one of hundreds of languages with countless dialects. Those native tongues may be expressed in ways that are loud, harsh, and drunken, or

in voices that are soft, lilting, and friendly. A baby may be sheltered purposefully from life's cruel realities or tossed out to "sink or swim" in a beggar's barrio. From the start, a child's brain begins to adapt to the place and space into which it has landed.

No single, specific blueprint for brain growth could cover what's required to survive in all possible environments. The brain starts with only a general mandate: "Grow connections as needed." Brains are built to change in this manner in order to *stay alive*! Survival depends upon continually adapting to new input and changing conditions. This survival instinct is unconscious but powerful. The rapid speed with which a young brain adapts allows for a baby to gain maximum advantage within whatever climate, culture, or family system she happens to be born.

During early development, far more connections are formed than will eventually be needed—trillions more! The brain of a typical two-year-old, for example, has almost twice the number of connections that your brain has. Daily routines such as feeding, bathing, and playing strengthen particular synapses, while those connections that are not reinforced by repetition eventually wither away. This natural process is called *neural pruning*.

Since we're conditioned to believe that more is better, many people assume that building synapses should be the name of the game. After all, nobody likes to think of "losing" anything! But neural pruning is a neat trick of human survival that allows a baby to adapt to many possible different conditions and settings. The connections that are frequently used remain and are further strengthened through continued use. At a cellular level, such repeated use of pathways allows energy traveling between neurons to flow faster and more efficiently, thereby freeing up energy to enable a person to gain expertise in those ideas, sounds, and concepts she works with most often.

It helps to imagine pathways in the brain as a network of roads. Before neural pruning begins, when we need to get from location A to location B, there are many different routes on small roads we could take to get there. With experience we learn which route is the easiest and fastest, and we go that way more often, no longer using those other smaller, less efficient roads to get from A to B. The road used most frequently is widened over time into a bigger road, and then eventually becomes a super-highway, making a trip from A to B quick and easy.

The number of synaptic connections peaks in the first few years of life. They plateau in early childhood, and then are pruned by about forty percent in late childhood and adolescence. To give you some idea of how much activity is taking place, just between ages four and ten, about a trillion synapses are lost in the visual-processing part of the brain alone. How is it that so many skills are developed during this period when so many connections are being lost? It's due to the fact that at the same time neural pruning is feverishly taking place, so is another process called *myelination*. Myelination speeds up and makes more efficient the communication between the brain cells in the connections that remain. Myelin is a fatty substance that grows to surround the nerve fiber, allowing the electrical impulses that travel along the fiber when brain cells communicate to flow more easily and quickly. Myelination occurs at different times in different parts of the brain, and seems to coincide with the emergence or improvement of various physical skills and cognitive abilities. In other words, the brain is designed to learn more easily at certain points in time. Myelination occurs most rapidly during the first two years of life—when the brain is processing so much brand-new basic information: language, temperatures, colors, sounds, smells,textures, cause-and-effect, what a face is, and so on. But myelination continues into adulthood, with the maximum speed of neural processing being reached during the teenage years.

The images on the next page show slices of the brain that have been magnified to show individual neurons and connections between neurons. The picture on the left shows some of the neurons that are present at birth. Notice there are few connections between them.

The center shows the explosion of neuronal activity by the time a child is six years old. No wonder first-graders are so active and hard to settle! Everything is connected to everything else in their world.

A six-year-old's brain is alive with neural connections. Notice the thicket of neural trees with many bushy dendrites. Learning is nearly

| At Birth | 6 Years Old | 14 Years Old |
|---|---|---|

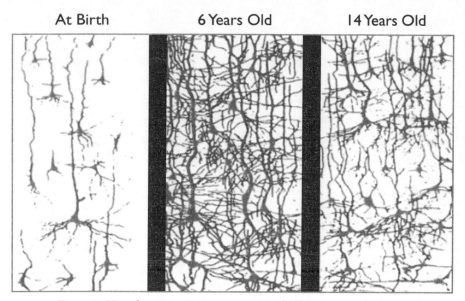

*Figure 2. Neural pruning: Brain connection at birth, 6 years, and 14 years.*

effortless at this age, although traits such as self-control must wait for inhibitory pathways to be sculpted later within this over-connected mass. We all know how it goes:

> The little boy next door stops by to ask you about the fishing pole he saw by your car yesterday. He begins a long tale that starts with the one time he went fishing with his grandpa and progresses to the fact that his grandpa has kidney stones . . . and then to his aunt who complained that she was going broke paying for his bills . . . and then to the money he got for his birthday that he was going to save, but decided instead to buy a kite . . . and on and on.

By about age fourteen (on the right), the brain has begun to prune away connections that are rarely used and that have not formed into permanent circuits. (If you happen to have a young teen in your life, you might joke with them that here's scientific proof that *they are losing it!*)

An example of the kind of knowledge that's lost: When you were in fourth grade, it was important to know the name of the girl who sat next to you in class. Now, years later, you have moved out of your hometown and long ago have lost the need to know this girl's name. That kind of information can be pruned away with no "cost" to your brain.

**What this means for your child:** Which connections are formed and which connections are ultimately retained are initially shaped by one's early experiences. As a parent, you have the power to influence some of the kinds of "roads" that are laid down and which of those will be taken most often in your baby's brain. Key factors: Repetition, routine, and positive reinforcement.

*Wow #4: Early Brain Wiring Is Resistant to Change*
Here's still more proof why infancy and toddlerhood deserve extra attention: Those brain structures that wire up earliest provide a kind of "organizing template," influencing future growth and development. The first parts of the brain to get organized are also the least likely to change. For example, the very earliest brain systems to be wired, prenatally, and within the first months of life, are those that regulate blood pressure, heart rate, and body temperature. Obviously you wouldn't want those vital biological systems to vary radically from one moment to the next.

The brain structures involved in processing emotions are also wiring very early. This fact is critical to know because these structures help set up one's emotional reactivity, the ability to appropriately tailor emotional responses to the situation at hand. Although the emotional system is more adaptable than are the brain regions that sustain key body functions, it's still fairly resistant to change.

**What this means for your child:** This notion that the earlier a system is set up, the more resistant it is to change is both good news and bad news. The good news: The effects of having a strong emotional start are likely to persist, which has positive repercussions for much of the brain development that follows. If a child has a strong emotional start, he's likely to be resilient and able to cope with stressors later in life. All of the systems that process the information necessary to establish a stable, lifelong base of the very best kind for learning flourish in a predictable environment provided by parents who:

- Create interesting experiences
- Assure a strong sense of security
- Lovingly hold and touch their child frequently
- Share interesting things to look at and hear

The bad news, however, is that the reverse is also true: If children live in chaotic, non-supportive, abusive environments, the effects of this will likewise be resistant to change.

### Wow #5: It's Never Too Late!

If you have a child who is already close to age three or older, I want to pause right here and encourage you to "Take a breath!" Sometimes I see parents, upon hearing about how critical the early years are, tense up or lament all the things they fear they did not do "right." (*Maybe I should have read to my baby more . . . I knew I should have insisted that Rachel take music lessons . . . If only I had not allowed my sister to be Ryan's daily babysitter just because she needed the money after her divorce. . . .*) Whatever your regrets, let them go. One of my favorite quotes is from Maya Angelou, who sums up an important lesson: *I did what I knew. And when I knew better, I did better.* Each of us does the very best we can with the information we have, and chances are that your child is flourishing. It's not *every little choice* that determines whether your child will thrive, but the *overall pattern* of love, security, and stimulation that you provide.

The science makes it very clear that your child's brain does not stop growing and learning at age three. It's *never* "too late" to influence the wiring of the brain. It's never too late to improve the quality of a child's life. It is not too late at three or at five; it is not too late at fourteen. It is *never* too late.

The brain has a remarkable, lifelong capacity to reorganize itself in response to the information it receives from the environment. Researchers call this *neural plasticity*, and it takes place at all ages. Neural plasticity consists of several different processes that researchers are just beginning to understand, involving both *increases* in the number of connections between neurons as well as *physical changes* in the shape and structure of those connections. Across the lifespan, neural plasticity is thought to underlie all types of learning and memory, and it is thought to explain how the brain recovers various functions following a traumatic injury.

The older one gets, however, the longer this "rewiring" in response to experience can take; a less-than-ideal start in early childhood can mean a life journey filled with unanticipated problems or even costly professional advice and therapies. Many kinds of interventions are sometimes very successful, from retraining the brain of a dyslexic child to help him read better to physical therapy for perceptual-motor irregularities. But they take time, effort, and money.

**What this means for your child:** You have more than a narrow three-year window to "make or break" your child's odds of success in life (or entry to Harvard). A child of any age benefits from the ABCs. The main value of early attention to these essentials in the first three years of life is prevention. If you are fortunate enough to start with a normal, healthy child in your life, the basic things you do to prevent some of life's bumps can have powerful repercussions. As a slogan in a recent California media campaign about the importance of the first years to early brain development nicely put it, "Your Choices . . . Shape Their Chances." The most important thing a parent can provide is a loving, stable relationship that leads to frequent, meaningful, and responsive interactions with their baby or toddler. Prevention saves time, money, and heartache—and it's not difficult to achieve.

## The Blossoming Brain

Brain growth takes place in three dynamic general directions in a predictable way. This progression of growth happens simultaneously: from Back to Front, from Inside Out, and from Bottom Up. Understanding this progression gives you a new window through which to look at your

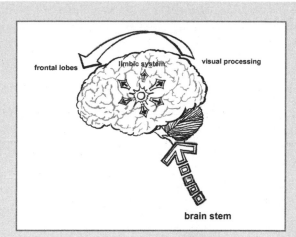

*Figure 3. The arrows illustrate how the brain develops simultaneously from back to front, from inside out, and from bottom up.*

child's development. The reason bonding is so critical in the first year, for example, is because this is when the centrally located and innermost emotional centers of the brain develop. There's no point in working on cognitive skills like logic with a baby when that part of the brain has yet to come online. What's more, the well-being of later-developing systems of the brain (like those involved in academic learning) depend on there first having been healthy development in earlier-developing systems, like emotional security.

1. *From Back to Front:* The parts of the brain responsible for vision wire up early and are located in the back part of the brain (known as the *occipital lobe*). The visual system of a six- to eight-month-old is pretty much like that of an adult. This is why, as I'll show you, so much of early learning is visual.

   Coming more forward in the brain, the hearing system wires up fairly quickly as well. The areas above one's ears (the *temporal lobes*) are important early in life but have a wider window of opportunity for development than the visual areas, staying quite changeable and receptive to learning the sounds of new languages for the first few years of life.

Next, moving forward into the motor and speech areas of the brain is an area of language production. We know that children are capable of hearing and understanding language and word meanings far earlier than they can speak or express their thoughts. As children grow in the first year of life and gain practice in making sounds and babbling, the connections in the motor areas become more established and babies gain better control over the muscles of their mouth and tongue. Children vary a lot as to how soon they start to speak, so there is not one "normal" speed of language acquisition.

Finally, all the way forward in the brain, behind one's forehead, the regions responsible for skills such as planning, abstract reasoning, and understanding the consequences of one's behavior wire up. These areas, called the *frontal lobes*, are not fully developed until high school and beyond. This provides some insight into why toddlers don't understand why they shouldn't touch a hot stove, school-age children have trouble with logic, and even high school teens whom parents expect to "know better" don't always make good decisions. Their brains are not fully able yet to prioritize or to necessarily understand the consequences of their actions. Yes, we really do grow "older and wiser!"

2. *From Inside Out:* Central structures of the brain (part of the limbic system) that process and regulate our emotions develop before the outer part (the *cortex*). These central structures, which "tag" incoming information with an emotional importance, are mostly formed in the first few years of life. The degree to which they form in a healthy way will influence the strength and quality of connections to the outer cortex, which controls the processing of incoming information for thinking and planning, for sensory processing, and for memory storage—basically the kind of brain work that's used in school learning. In other words, how the brain is wired to process emotions in the

earliest years directly sets the stage for how the child functions later in a formal academic setting.

3. *From the Bottom Up:* The parts of the brain responsible for basic functions, such as heartbeat, breathing, and temperature control develop early and are located in the *brain stem* regions. By contrast, the abilities to maintain focus of your attention, control your emotions, and coordinate fine motor movements develop later as the outer cortex wires up.

## HOW YOUR BABY'S BRAIN IS LIKE A BAGEL

Here's a quick, concrete image to help you visualize how your child's brain is formed. When I give presentations to groups, I bring out the following props: a pencil, a bagel, and six layers of tissue paper. Using these common items to represent different brain areas helps new concepts "stick" in listeners' minds without having to remember all those scientific labels. I've had students come up to me years later and refer to "the bagel part of the brain"—and we both understand this shorthand perfectly!

- **The pencil**, at the base, represents the relative amount of neural tissue dedicated to the functions of the *brain stem*. This area is responsible

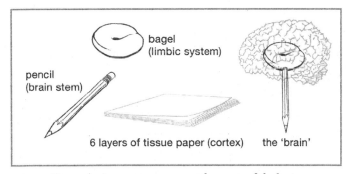

*Figure 4. An easy way to remember parts of the brain.*

I borrowed this idea (and modified it a bit) from Dr. Robert Sylwester, Professor Emeritus at the University of Oregon.

for things like regulating heartbeat, respiration, and other bodily functions that remain unconscious to us. When a person is under stress or is doing strenuous exercise, things like the heart rate and blood pressure (autonomic systems) respond and vary, but for the most part, these basic functions remain steady and do not vary much from moment to moment, nor are they designed to change with each fleeting thought or conversation we have. Some of the later-wired systems *are* designed to be responsive to moment-by-moment changes in thoughts and experiences . . . but not the brain stem.

If a baby is born prematurely, some of these brain stem functions need additional support in the NICU. For example, premature infants are placed in warm incubators to stabilize their body temperature. Their breathing is supported via respirators. Even in full-term infants, some of these systems take a few months to regulate. Any new parent can attest to this: First the baby seems to sleep and waken willy-nilly, then gradually he gets his days and nights straight, and finally, at last, starts to sleep through the night.

- **The bagel**, sitting on top of the pencil, represents the group of structures that, together, constitute the *limbic system* of a brain. The limbic system consists of a grouping of separate yet interconnected structures that process the emotional nature of all incoming information. When functioning well, the limbic parts of the brain allow a person to monitor, detect, and distinguish real threat from imagined threat, and to remember to a greater degree those experiences that are important to us. The most familiar function of the limbic system is probably the "fight or flight" response, which originates in one of the limbic structures called the *amygdala*. This response can be triggered, for example, by seeing something, say a long, skinny object on the ground in the woods. Immediately, the brain's limbic system is involved in processing what to do if that object turns out to be a snake versus a stick. The limbic system sends the proper signals (such as increased heart rate and increased blood to the muscles of the legs) to other brain regions to enable the person to run away quickly. Another structure in the limbic system is the *hippocampus*, which is involved in the storage and retrieval of one's memories. Also, when the amygdala sends out a warning message, the hippocampus responds by remembering and filing away the information for future reference.

The limbic system essentially wires up from birth to age five, which is why it is so important for babies to have safe, secure, and loving environments. When a child has been neglected or abused, these structures (notably the amygdala and hippocampus) are often smaller and do not function properly. Such children frequently become hypervigilant—they constantly monitor their environment for things that might harm them or for ways to satisfy their basic human needs for food, comfort, and companionship. They sacrifice the ability to learn new information because their energies are, naturally, so focused on having these more elemental needs met. I'll discuss this in detail in Chapter 8, "'B' is for Bonding."

- The six layers of **tissue paper** represent the neural tissue in the six layers of the *neocortex* (also just called the *cortex*), the outermost area of the brain. In my classes and presentations, I mold the six sheets into a rough brain shape, as you see in the illustration. In a real brain the cortex is the gray, highly folded outer "bark" of the brain. It makes up the lumpy wrinkles we all picture when we think of a typical brain.

  If one were to flatten out the folded mass, it would be about the size of an extra-large pizza. It's a substantial amount of matter because the cortex is the part of the brain where incoming information is both processed and stored. Notice how these layers of tissue paper are crumpled closely around the bagel. Essential communication occurs between the densely connected cortex and limbic areas. A structure found deep within the limbic system, the *thalamus*, receives most of the information coming into the brain through the senses (except for smell). The thalamus then relays this data for further processing to the proper area of the cortex, such as the visual-processing area (visual cortex), the auditory processing area, the motor area, and so on.

The cortex is important for many reasons. Parents and caregivers can best appreciate it as the area that processes information and stores memory—memory for all the types of things, including what children learn in school, from reading and language skills to history and algebra, from creativity and making music to solving problems and standing quietly in line.

The ability of the cortex to function optimally depends on the healthy formation of the limbic system beneath. The limbic system is the "heart" of the brain. (Or for purposes of our illustration, you could say that the bagel is the staff of life!) Because it is involved in a child's social and emotional development, a healthy limbic system also influences the child's later ability to:

- Pay attention and more easily absorb information
- Retain more of the information she learns
- Be better able to control her own behavior and emotional reactions to others

These are goals every parent has for their child. Not surprisingly, these things also play a critical role in the self-esteem your child develops.

## A Jenny Story: The Power of What Comes First

It wasn't until years after my handicapped daughter Jenny's birth that I finally figured out that it was her "pencil and bagel" (brain stem and limbic system) that had been initially damaged. Her early surgeries with no anesthetic, and constant machinery, buzzers, and too-bright lights in the (now old-fashioned) NICU had assaulted her developing nervous system; as she grew older they were constantly, though subconsciously, remembered. Not in the sort of memory snapshot common to us as adults when we recall a significant event, but as a more pervasive kind of memory. This kind of memory warns her continuously that painful, terrible things can happen at any moment. She's now in her thirties, but even today her behaviors can turn in a moment—from a sweet, chatty person to a tense, hypervigilant, frightened soul, one noticeably hyperventilating and responding with a vestigial startle reflex, ready to scratch or scream.

Luckily for her, and for us (her family), we now know many of the triggers, including sudden changes or loud noises. Year after year, for example, I had dragged her to Fourth of July fireworks, with her Dad and sister, hoping she'd enjoy the all-American tradition to patriotically love "the rockets red glare, the bombs bursting in air." Instead, she fussed and cried and, in an uncontrollable panic, begged to leave. Now I understand that there's no intellectualizing her through it by reassuring her that the noise won't hurt her. She's responding from a place deep, low, and in the center of her brain. We now work to prepare her for the triggers that upset her or we avoid them altogether. These days I happily take her to a mindless, calm "chick flick" on the Fourth and we are both smiling at the end of the night.

# PART TWO

## Attention

# 2

# "A" Is for Attention: Why It Matters

You probably instinctively know that attention is important, even if you haven't thought of it in terms of your baby's brain. Maybe you've heard someone say, "Oh my! He's so alert, so attentive! You have a smart little baby there!" Attention is often unconsciously linked to intelligence.

As it should be! Attention is the very foundation of learning. Most of us recognize that for anyone to consciously learn anything, they must first be paying attention. Babies are born with the ability to be alert, but directing their attention and controlling it is behavior that develops over time. The way your child's attention system develops in the earliest years influences his ability to attend throughout life. It affects his ability to listen when you explain why he can't run out in the street, to watch you demonstrate how a shoelace is tied, to read a book, to sit in a classroom and absorb today's math lesson, to write a Ph.D. dissertation, to function in the workplace. All hinge on an attention system that wires properly in babyhood.

Much of this wiring unfolds naturally. But scientists are learning that environment—how your child spends his days and the experiences he's exposed to—shapes this natural process. Being securely attached to a very few caregivers is critical, for example, because it allows a child's brain to be relaxed and alert, attending to the world around instead of spending all brain energy worrying "who will feed me and respond to my basic survival needs?" (I'll go into this aspect more in Chapter 8, "'B' Is for Bonding.") We also now know that it's possible to help your baby focus and increase his attention span. The main ways you can impact your child's developing attention system are:

- Spending face-to-face time together. Faces have a particular allure and benefits, especially for babies
- Providing varied, age-appropriate play opportunities
- Monitoring the amount and quality of screen exposure (computers, TV)
- Including "down time"—the time and space not to pay attention to anything at all—in every day

The following chapters in this section explore each of these ideas in detail. But you'll feel better about doing these things if you understand *why they matter*.

## HOW ATTENTION WORKS

"Paying attention" isn't just one thing requiring one part of the brain. Attention is a system, just like the digestive system or the respiratory system, involving the coordinated effort of several different parts of the anatomy (in this case, the senses and various structures of the brain). Using scans of the brain and behavioral studies, researchers at the Institute of Cognitive and Decision Sciences at the University of Oregon, led by psychologist Michael Posner, Ph.D., are showing that there are really three components of the attention system.

To pay attention, you must:

- *Alert*: Initially turn toward something that captures your interest.
- *Shift:* Change what you are attending to (you orient to some new thing).

- *Maintain*: Focus mainly on one thing while ignoring competing stimuli, thoughts, and emotions.

The first component, alerting, is what a baby is born with the ability to do. At first, infants are drawn to pay attention to the familiar. For example, in the onslaught of brand-new sensations and experiences, newborns will attend to the already familiar voices of their parents, having grown accustomed to the cadence of these voices over months in utero. Eminent pediatrician T. Berry Brazelton, M.D., shows parents this with a fascinating exercise that anyone can replicate in the hospital or at home. First, a newborn is positioned so that he can see both his dad and a stranger (a hospital staffer, for example), each adult standing slightly off to the opposite side. Then at the same time, both Dad and the stranger start calling the baby's name in a soft, lilting tone, "Hi Jacob, good boy Jacob. . . ." The baby will turn his head toward his father's familiar voice, and may even kick his legs and wave his arms. Dad, of course, will smile and be amazed. Soon after birth, though, babies also begin to pay attention to unfamiliar things in their world.

Alerting, along with shifting (the second component) wires up within the first fourteen months after birth. Before many kids are even confidently walking or talking, the attention system is well on its way to development. That's why *the first year of life* is an ideal time to enhance your baby's ability to alert and shift attention, through your interactions and facial expressions and simple games that use visual tracking and voice inflection.

The third component, sustaining attention on one thing despite potential distractions (maintaining), develops more slowly. Being able to focus for a period of time on one thing while ignoring other things requires what's called an *inhibitory response*. "Inhibit" means to suppress or restrain—to stop an impulse. You have to be able to damp down responses to other incoming stimuli and allocate your attention to the thing at hand. For example, if I am to sit and concentrate on my computer screen, I not only have to marshal all my energy to stay in my seat with my eyes focused on the screen, I also must block other input competing for my awareness. In order to focus on my work, I have to ignore the siren in the background and the fact that my stomach is growling. I also need to be able to delay gratification: If I work for an hour, I will finish the work and then I can relax and have dinner. These inhibitory abilities rely primarily on the functioning of the frontal lobes, which mature more slowly than other parts of the brain. By age two, inhibitory skill development needed for maintaining attention is underway but won't be well developed until about age seven.

The ability to control immediate impulses is probably more important for future success in life than anyone previously realized. A classic, old study, now known as the marshmallow test, illustrates this:

Four-year-olds were led, one at a time, to a room where a marshmallow sat on the table in front of them. The examiner told each child that she had to go down the hall to do something; if the child needed her to come back he or she could press a button. *However*, if the child waited to eat the marshmallow until the examiner returned on her own, she'd give the child an extra marshmallow in addition to the one on the table. She then disappeared for fifteen minutes. Researchers, led by Walter Mischel, Ph.D., (then at Stanford University and now at Columbia University), videotaped each child's reaction and saw that the children reacted in different ways. Some ate the marshmallow immediately. Others were able to refrain. Some kids even developed strategies to distract themselves, like singing, walking around, or closing their eyes.

The fascinating part of the study came fourteen years later, when these same children were followed and re-examined at age eighteen. Lo and behold, those who at age four were able to refrain from eating the marshmallow while the examiner was out of the room were, at eighteen, more likely to be self-confident, popular with peers, able to cope with frustration, and successful in school, scoring an average of 210 points higher on Scholastic Aptitude Tests than their counterparts who ate the marshmallow right away.

The ability to control impulses at a young age (waiting, in order to receive more marshmallows) tends to predict a pattern of future behavior. Inhibitory skills, essential for problem solving and success across life, are gained as the brain matures. Luckily, it looks like these skills can be fostered.

## YOU CAN "EXERCISE" THE ATTENTION SYSTEM

A growing number of neuroscientists are beginning to test the best ways to do this. They're building on the knowledge that the brain develops in a *use-dependent* fashion. This means that the ways a brain is used can influence, to a degree, what competencies and abilities a person eventually develops.

Researchers in Posner's lab tested whether four- and six-year-olds' ability to maintain attention on a task could be boosted through training using specially designed computer games. The games used tasks that required tracking items as they moved across the screen and matching two of the same item from within a larger group, for example. Results, reported in 2005, show that such interventions indeed extended the children's ability to maintain their attention, as measured by electroencephalograms (EEGs), attention and intelligence tests. Posner believes that this kind of research may lead to attention training that not only helps kids with attention problems (attention-deficit hyperactivity disorder or ADHD), but can generally improve education for all kids at the preschool level.

Does this mean you can use computers with your child to achieve similar results? "Don't try this at home," as they say. Computer games seem to have very different effects on the brain in the first two years of life than later. (See chapter 5.) The particular games in this study were created for this experiment, having been adapted from computer exercises originally used to train monkeys for space travel! I will show you better ways to encourage a longer attention span.

## NEW THREATS TO ATTENTION

*"Welcome to the attention economy, in which the new scarcest resource isn't ideas or even talent, but attention itself."*
—Thomas H. Davenport and Thomas C. Beck in
*The Attention Economy.*

We all have more and more things competing for our attention. Take me. I wouldn't call myself especially tech savvy—still no iPod—yet I do have:

- Two cell phones: one in my car mounted for "hands free" use, and one I carry in my purse. (Yes, on occasion I have been on *both* at the same time, at a stoplight.)
- Two different email accounts: my university address and a New Directions Institute address, both accessible to me 24/7, thanks to Web mail.
- Three voicemail numbers that I routinely check in addition to both cell phone message centers.

There's a lot of multi-tasking going on in my life. And I'm someone who already *knows* what the research on divided attention says! It warns us that split attention gives us the illusion that we are accomplishing more, but the quality of our results is actually degraded. Yet it seems that I'm powerless to resist the lure of all these attention monsters.

My reality illustrates two new problems for young children in the twenty-first century:

1. **Having to compete all the harder for caregiver attention.** Imagine you were a baby in my environment. Talk about needing to compete for my attention! Tally up what kinds of gadget-related activities suck away your attention in your own home: TV? Videogames? Surfing the 'Net or IM-ing friends? Checking a Palm Pilot? Listening to an iPod? The truth is that many ordinary, loving parents find themselves living a life that looks a lot like mine. It's harder than ever to separate work and home. For parents who work *at* home, even part-time, this can be especially true: You can be physically present, with your attention far away. Even when we try to have focused "quality time," the lure of *You've got mail* pulls us away. Despite knowing better, we submit.

   **What you can do:** Enforce some no-tech times. When you're playing with your baby, eating, or reading together, turn off the cell and put away the Blackberry. Obviously you can't do this all day, but it's wise to create a few "no—tech zones" in your life. Respond quickly when your child needs you; "in a minute" can quickly come to sound like "never" to a young child.

**2. Inadvertently developing a natural preference for technology.**
Our routine use of phones and electronic gadgets means that these
devices become a part of the child's everyday reality. It also endows
these items with a certain allure. Because they're part of the "givens"
in the child's world, right from the start, the brain's organizing
schemas about that world include these gizmos. A toddler doesn't naturally prefer to spend time in front of a screen over time outdoors at
the playground, nor tapping a plastic keyboard instead of manipulating sand. But when he sees his parents always online, his brain regis-
ters this as a normal activity that he wants to be a part of, too. Kids
learn to a great extent through imitation, so it's not surprising that today's two-year-olds may ask their parents for a computer. It's not that
they understand how it works and truly desire their own iMac as a
learning tool or a toy, even though parents usually interpret such a
request this way. ("Wow! Mikey's so advanced! He wants a computer!") The child simply sees it as a normal and therefore desirable
part of life so that they can do what you do. One of the dangers is that
this natural preference takes away from other kinds of varied experiences that might better hone the developing attention system.

**What you can do.** Today's children pick up an understanding of
technology on their own; you don't need to *teach* a young child how
to use gadgets in order for him to be techno-savvy later in life. There's
nothing necessarily wrong with Katy having a toy cell phone "just like
Mommy's" or a starter computer with a bright baby keyboard "just
like Daddy's." Pretend toys allow your child to follow her interests,
and in playing with these items she explores how to copy what you are
doing. But in general, today's parents have to be especially vigilant
about providing a wide variety of play experiences for a child, in in-
door and outdoor settings, and using natural materials as well as toys
with lights and whistles. For a baby or toddler with a fledgling attention system, a varied, naturally stimulating environment is essential.
The value of learning to match pairs of socks while folding the laundry, which requires him to keep the sock he is searching for in mind
while ignoring the other similar socks and pieces of clothing (and the

conversations you'll have while doing so—"Where's the other fuzzy, blue sock?"), is likely greater than all the hours he could spend in front of the flashing lights on a learning keyboard.

## HEALTHY ATTENTION MAGNETS

To combat the forces of your child having to compete for attention and being immersed in a techno society, you can also use what researchers have long known about what a human will pay attention to and why. Cognitive scientists—who study how we learn—have discovered that there are certain factors known to affect a brain's ability to pay attention at any age. You can use this information to help guide your choices of playthings, activities, and the way you interact with your child.

Here are six factors you can use to initially capture your little one's attention:

1. *Intensity*

The brain takes note of great contrasts, paying more attention to extremes (like a booming voice or a quiet whisper) than to the midrange. For example, if you want to get a child to really listen, it's often more effective to whisper softly. This change of tone from your ordinary speaking voice will gain attention. (Classroom teachers know this well, which is why some of the most mild-mannered instructors are able to wield good class control.)

Attention to contrasts in intensity is true not only for sound, but for vision as well. Young babies will pay closer attention to objects that have clear, deep, or sharp contrasts than to those objects that are pale, blended, or very busy. Research on vision has shown that before six months, high contrast colors like black and white, or red and black and bright yellow, are best to attract and maintain a baby's attention.

**Try it:** An older baby may prefer picture books with bold, simple, clear images (like the Maisy books) to very complex and busy drawings (say, Beatrix Potter's pastel Peter Rabbit paintings). See the effectiveness of using a whisper the next time you talk to your child as you change his diaper—especially if he's at the wiggly stage, the first time you try this he may stay still long enough for you to get the job done!

## 2. *Size*

The brain takes note of very large things and very small things more than things in the middle. It notices the very tall man, the tallest building, the giant elephant. It also notices the smallest speck of lint on the black suit, the tiniest kitten in the litter, the small water spot on the glass table. Kids immediately show us, by their reactions to what they see, that size matters to them and gets noticed.

**Try it:** Provide toys of different sizes, such as stacking blocks or stacking rings. Very large or very small stuffed animals and books also tend to attract a child's attention. A particular favorite of mine are the decorative "nested dolls" where the largest doll opens in half to reveal an identical, but smaller doll. That doll opens to reveal a yet smaller version and so on until you reach the very tiniest one! Note: Be careful to never leave your child alone with this activity as the very small dolls represent a severe choking hazard.

## 3. *Novelty*

Novelty is so important that it rises to the level of one of the basic "operating principles" of the biology of learning in general. We're wired to respond to the new. Brains attend most carefully to new objects, sights, sounds, or people as a survival mechanism. What we typically note as curiosity is, in fact, the need of the brain to make sense of every new experience. On a primal level our brain is making an initial "friend or foe" assessment. *What is this new item? Can it hurt me? Can I eat it? Can it entertain me?* Once the brain assesses that the stimulus is safe and won't cause personal harm, the biological process of *habituation* begins. The neurons actually reduce the number of sensory branches they've sprouted and in a sense "relax" the need to explore that input further. Once the thing has been "categorized," however, attention moves quickly on to the next novel thing. That's a young brain's job, to figure out the importance or meaning of everything. For a newborn, nearly every event is novel, because it's happening for the first time! So eager are young infants to zero in on what's new that by the time they are several months old, they will have already "figured out" their immediate surroundings. They can tell right away when something changes: Mom gets a drastic haircut, dad wears glasses for the first time, furniture in a room is rearranged, a new mobile is hung. Your baby will stare longer than usual at a fresh sight—or in the case of the drastic haircut, may even become distressed until they figure out you're still the same mom!

**Try it:** You don't have to run to the toy store every week to stoke the fires of freshness. You could simply rotate toys, recycle them in different areas of the house, hang different objects from an infant gym, trade basic baby toys with friends, or even move pictures around your house. You can take walks and point out both new and familiar things along the way. Introduce new foods, a few new people—by varying life's experiences you capitalize on a brain's need for novelty and therefore cause more learning to occur. *Voila!* You've provided the next *new thing*.

4. *Incongruity*

"One of these things is not like the other" has a familiar ring to parents who themselves were reared on *Sesame Street*. Even if you only watched occasionally, I'll bet you can hear the music of that ditty playing in your head as you read these words. These lyrics describe the concept of incongruity—it's the thing that does not fit; it does not belong because it is not the same as everything else around it. A kindergarten teacher introducing the letter "P" might first slip it into a row of already-familiar letter Cs and wait for her students to notice it. (It won't take long!)

**Try it:** If you want a baby to notice a new food, for example, put it in the middle of lots of things that match and presto, it will be the first thing investigated! Toddlers find a sock placed on Daddy's head to be uproariously funny because it does not belong there.

5. *Emotion*

Emotional events as well as the feelings that we experience in every-day situations are stored to a greater degree in our brains than is random information. A brain is configured to assess the importance of incoming information and to pay greater attention to emotional content. Emotion drives attention and attention drives memory. This important statement shows that emotions are central to allocating enough attention for learning to take place.

When you are nervous, worried, afraid, depressed, agitated, or upset, it's difficult to focus on learning. *Our emotional state affects our ability to pay attention.* Researchers are beginning to understand that for effective learning to occur, the conditions for learning need to engage a learner's positive emotions and their focus of attention. Conditions for learning are optimal when you are able to be relaxed and yet alert.

**Try it:** You can use this knowledge to your advantage in many ways, from birth. A newborn who is sleepy or hungry is not ready to play (and therefore learn). Playful interactions work best when a baby has been fed and changed, is rested, and enters a quiet, alert state. Or, if you were trying to teach a sixteen-month-old about toothbrushing, you'd make better headway by using her beloved teddy bear as a prop. She has positive associations with the teddy, so demonstrating the use of a brush on him can make this chore easier to accept than if you were showing it as a strange new thing isolated from any strong positive emotions.

6. *Personal Significance*

Each of us pays closer attention to things that are directly related to us and to our sense of well being. Have you ever had the experience of being in a crowded, noisy party, engaged deeply in conversation with someone right in front of you, when suddenly, from across the room, you hear *your* name mentioned in some completely different conversation? You laser in on your name though it seems to have come out of thin air. Because the other people are talking about you, it matters and you pay attention!

Anything with our name associated to it, on it, or about it has a greater importance to us. Kids especially love to see or hear their own name. Hence, the popularity of so many child-oriented products with monograms or names painted, stenciled, or stamped. (And hence the keen disappointment of the child with a rare or uniquely-spelled name who can never find his moniker on those souvenir cups, pencils, and key chains sold in gift shops and museum stores.)

Self-interest is central to our very survival. Otherwise boring information, such as the Department of Motor Vehicles *Rules of the Road*, takes on great importance if you happen to be turning sixteen, precisely because those rules of road now have personal significance if you want to pass your test to get your driver's license.

**Try it:** Your child will be more attentive to a story you're reading if you change the main character to her name. Childcare directors know that a toddler gets excited about putting her coat or papers in her cubby (and therefore learns to do it when asked) because it's her space, with her name on it; some parents use this trick at home, especially in a family with many members.

## Attention Problems: My Perspective on ADHD

If parents think at all about attention, it's usually in the context of the lack of it, or attention-*deficit*. Attention-deficit hyperactivity disorder (ADHD) is characterized by a persistent pattern of inattention and/or hyperactivity/impulsivity. Symptoms tend to worsen in situations that require sustained attention or mental effort, or when the task at hand is monotonous, repetitive, or lacks novelty. Many kids are diagnosed before age seven, with some diagnosed as early as two years old.

ADHD is thought to have a hereditary cause; that is, there is probably a gene that causes a chemical imbalance or a deficiency in certain neurotransmitters, the chemicals that are released by brain cells across the synapse to communicate to other brain cells. Hereditary markers for ADHD have not yet been conclusively identified in the human genome, but researchers do have some candidate genes that they do believe may play a role in the functioning of the attention system. It's believed that the disorder can be partially inherited from a parent carrying a gene for it. If both parents have ADHD, a child is more likely to also show signs of it. In fact, 25 percent of kids who have ADHD also have a first-degree family member who has it.

ADHD is diagnosed in 3 to 7 percent of children in the United States today. So in a classroom of thirty children, you'd expect one or possibly two kids to have ADHD. Yet in many schools there are reports of up to 20 percent of children who show symptoms of ADHD—that's six kids per thirty, and sometimes more. According to the American Psychiatric Association, ADHD is the most commonly diagnosed mental health condition in American children today.

Why are so many kids today thought to have attention-deficit problems? I think two sources explain a large portion of this gap between hereditary cases you could expect and the actual reported cases. Both of these scenarios may be examples of the environment of a child influencing whether a particular genetic tendency gets expressed or not:

1. *The early, unintended training of the attention system—especially for short hits and bits of information, a byproduct of the information age.* This training comes from several sources, including a new trend toward too much television in children younger than two and a half years old. Also TV viewing by adults and older children requires rapid-fire shifting of attention, which is witnessed by the infants and toddlers who live with them. (See also: Chapter 5, "Screen Time.")

2. *Demands on the brains of boys for academic skills they are not cognitively ready for.* ADHD is diagnosed three times more often in boys than in girls. There are gender differences in the sequence of the development of certain brain regions, particularly those used for some school skills. For example, language areas of the brain needed for early reading and the fine motor areas needed for writing follow a different, and usually earlier, trajectory in girls. This makes it easier for a girl

to accommodate to the noticeable acceleration of academics that's now become common in many preschools and kindergartens than it is for a boy, whether he's genetically predisposed to attention difficulties or not.

Importantly, even if 20 percent or more of children are attention-challenged, the majority of children do just fine. But understanding the basics of the attention system and what it really needs can help guide common-sense interactions with your child, while avoiding potential risks.

## DEVELOPING ATTENTION: WHAT YOU CAN DO AT DIFFERENT AGES

Developmental charts are typically organized to give a snapshot of what the *baby* is supposed to be able to do at each age. Seldom are charts organized to show what the *parent* is supposed to be doing! Here's where my bias, developed through my experiences as the mom of Jenny, impacts my work as an educator. As anyone can imagine, one of the challenges of parents of multiply-handicapped children is that when *we* look at those developmental charts, our kids are *never* "on target." In many areas, our kids are not even ON the charts as measured by their abilities. To be able to manage my own life as a parent, I started early on to ask myself the question, "What can *I do* to influence Jenny's ability to ever reach this particular developmental milestone?" Once I changed the focus from what she could not do . . . to what *I could do*, we were in business!

The chart on page 47 and those that follow for Bonding and for Communication (pages 147 and 214) focus on YOU. You'll find suggestions of what *you—and your child's primary caregivers—can do* at each age and stage to promote attentive behaviors in your child. (The age-by-age distinctions may differ from other such charts you've seen. The stages used here are based on common neurological and social changes that mark these time frames for cognitive changes that are described in "About This Book.") The particulars of how to do many of the behaviors listed in this chart will be explained in the five chapters that follow.

## Infant: 0–6 Months

Deliberately attend to infant with frequent face-to-face time, bringing face within ten to twelve inches when speaking, using exaggerated facial expressions and mouth movements.

Make direct eye contact with infant, trying to stimulate and maintain infant's eye contact.

Use rattle or other object for tracking across the midline, re-engaging infant's eye contact continuously on the object.

Point out objects while labeling objects and actions throughout the day.

Speak to infant using parentese to engage infant's auditory attention.

Note times of day when infant is awake and alert. Use those times for deliberate interactions.

Change/rotate toys or bright objects periodically for novelty.

Use objects and toys with high contrast colors (red, yellow, black, and white) and high contrast patterns, such as stripes or checks, to attract infant's attention. Gradually add other strong colors such as blue and green.

Place mobiles and toys ten to twelve inches from infant's face.

Make faces at the infant and watch her imitate (e.g., sticking out your tongue).

## Baby: 6–18 Months

At the beginning of this stage (six–nine months), deliberately attend to baby with frequent face-to-face time, bringing face within ten to twelve inches when speaking, using exaggerated facial expressions and mouth movements.

Make direct eye contact with baby, trying to stimulate and maintain baby's eye contact.

Use rattle or other object for tracking across the midline, re-engaging baby's eye contact continuously on the object.

Point out objects while labeling objects and actions throughout the day.

At the beginning of this stage (six–nine months), sometimes use parentese to engage baby's auditory attention, then transition to child-directed speech in a conversational tone and speed.

Note times of day when baby is awake and alert. Use those times for deliberate interactions.

Change/rotate toys or bright objects periodically for novelty.

Say cue word "watch" when wanting baby to observe the adult action. Make sure baby is focused before beginning the action. This starts the "routine" of a cue for attention.

After gaining baby's attention, use a quiet voice or be silent when modeling (demonstrating) a specific action to encourage baby's attention to that action.

Introduce only one variable (concept) at a time so that baby can concentrate on a single variable while other variables are held constant. For example, sort objects by color only; have all objects be the same size and shape, and only vary by color (such as red, blue, and yellow balls or red, blue, and yellow socks).

Toward the end of the stage (sixteen–eighteen months), introduce *place mat* as a "prop" to encourage baby to focus attention on where the activity will be.

Keep baby out of baby carrier seat when not necessary for safety so baby can follow parents' eye gaze.

## Toddler: 18 Months–3 Years

Frequently bring face down to toddler's eye level when wanting to capture toddler's attention.

Make direct eye contact with toddler, trying to stimulate and maintain toddler's eye contact.

Practice rolling a ball back and forth with toddler to encourage visual tracking and eye-hand coordination.

Point out objects while labeling objects and actions throughout the day.

When introducing new words, enunciate clearly with toddler able to see adult's mouth and facial movements.

Note times of day when toddler is awake and alert. Use those times for deliberate interactions.

Change/rotate toys or bright objects periodically for novelty.

Say cue word "watch" when wanting toddler to observe the adult action. Make sure toddler is focused before beginning the action. This starts the "routine" of a cue for attention.

After gaining toddler's attention, use a quiet voice or be silent when modeling (demonstrating) a specific action to encourage toddler's attention to that action.

After success with one variable (concept), increase to two variables. For example, group all things by color regardless of size or shape (such as red, blue, and yellow balls of different sizes or different objects such as trucks, balls, and socks that are grouped by color).

Use *place mat* "prop" as a deliberate cue for the toddler to settle down and focus attention for activity.

| |
|---|
| Use objects/people in books to focus on details (e.g., "What is Ernie holding? Find the blue bird. Where did the driver go first? Next? Last?"). |
| Play physical movement games that have child cross the midline (e.g., reaching across to put object in bin on opposite side of body—large gross motor skill play.) |
| Play finger play/songs that have a sequence to follow with increased complexity as toddler ages. |
| Play "I Spy" games with rules. |
| Repeat simple rhythmic clapping sequences or use signals to settle child (e.g., "If you can hear me, touch your shoulders; if you can hear me, clap like this."). |
| Use touching and/or massage to calm, settle, and refocus toddler. |
| Play games like statues, red light/green light at the end of this stage to foster inhibitory control. |

# 3

# Face Time:
# You Are Your Baby's First Toy

If your baby could tell you what she wanted to see most, she would say, "Faces!" Everything else pales next to those bright eyes and moving mouths, coming in close to express reassurance, smiles, and love. Many experiments have shown that an infant will pay attention to a human face longer than anything else. In fact, newborns come into the world with a preference for the human face.

A flat picture of a face on a photo or screen isn't the same. It's the changing expressions, and the matching of these moving features with sounds, that infants find so compelling.

Each day as your baby grows, he will enjoy "using" your face as a toy to entertain him and capture his interest. It's comfortingly familiar and wonderful to look at . . . basically *stays enough the same* so as not to be scary . . . but provides a million small differences according to your mood, your words, and your intentions. Best of all, your face is something that *your baby can influence* by his own actions. So sure, rattles and stuffed animals have a place in your baby's life. But your face is actually his first and most important *interactive toy*.

## WHAT THE SCIENCE SAYS: WHY BABIES NEED FACES

*"I spy with my little eye. . . ."*

—*CLASSIC CHILDREN'S GAME*

It's no accident that faces play a central role in how your baby's brain learns to pay attention. Your baby is designed to want to see you "up close and personal"; face-to-face. Right from the start, the visual system is tuned to see most clearly what's 8 to 12 inches away—conveniently, the approximate distance from a baby's eyes to a mother's face when held in her arms to be fed. Scientists have learned a lot about what babies can see that demonstrates why the face is such an object of fascination:

- **Babies like best what they can see best.** A newborn mostly sees sharp contrasts of darks and lights. Because there is greater visual contrast at the edge of something when compared to its background, babies see the edges of an object better than the middle. When your face comes in close to your baby's, what stands out most clearly to him—and is therefore most noticed—are your eyes, your mouth, and perhaps your hairline, all the features that show a distinct difference from the background of your skin.

- **As a baby's vision improves, faces are favored over clearer images.** In the lab of Daphne Maurer, Ph.D., a vision scientist and psychologist at McMaster University in Ontario, Canada, researchers hold up a poster board with two objects on it: a circle that contains random blobs of black, gray, and white arranged so that there is a high contrast between them, and a circle that contains blobs arranged to look like a face, but without high contrast between these blob-features and the background. A six-week-old prefers to look at a circle containing high contrast, but by eight weeks, the baby wants to look at the face even when its contrasts are less sharp.

- **Early experiences in recognizing faces helps a baby recognize people.** Even at ten days old, infants have already intently studied the configuration of your face and learned how it is arranged. Dr. Maurer has also shown, using a poster-board setup similar to the one above, that newborns prefer to look at a circle with three squares on it when the squares are arranged like the eyes and mouth on a face than when the three squares are inverted and therefore look much less like a face. In 2002, she showed that this early visual input helps set up the brain to later recognize people across a room or from a new point of view (such as sideways or while bending) using cues practiced by studying faces in early infancy.

- **In fact, a baby's interest in faces may well be the very foundation of the development of later social skills.** Infants seem to be born ready to detect socially relevant information. Even two- to five-day-old newborns prefer to look at faces that engage them in direct eye contact as opposed to faces where the gaze is averted. As infants continue to develop in the first few months of life, their eyes scan faces in a particular pattern, with repeated and ever-increasing interest in the eyes and mouth areas.

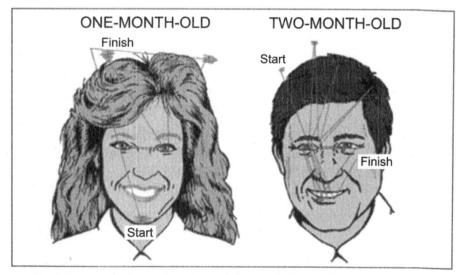

*Figure 5. An infant's scanning patterns shift to emphasize caregiver's eyes and mouth.*

Why would a baby zero in on the eyes and mouth? Because these happen to be the features that convey critical information about:

- *Emotional state:* Is Mom happy? Is my nanny concerned? Is she upset? Relaxed? Researchers show that emotion can be most easily read by changes in the expression of the eyes and mouth. These subtle changes play such a major role in conveying emotion, in fact, that some airport screeners are now being trained to read faces as well as behavior and body language to spot potentially suspicious passengers.
- *The meaning of verbal utterances:* When you croon, "There, there, everything's okay," your baby doesn't yet understand these words. But your pursed lips and calm eyes gazing into his help him understand that you're offering reassurance, and that clearly means something different from when your eyebrows are raised, your eyes are looking away, and your mouth is curved into a smile as you say, "Look at the doggie!"

At the most primal level, one's survival depends on being able to read the expressions on an approaching person's face in order to help determine "friend or foe?" The human baby begins immediately to practice knowing how to tell the difference. So making deliberate eye contact with your baby is important. Your eyes literally capture hers.

## Gender Matters: He Sees, She Sees, Why Girls Especially Like Faces

Although both boy and girl babies seek out and enjoy faces, researchers are discovering some interesting differences between the genders. These differences in visual preferences can be seen even at one day old—before culture can exert any influence.

In one experiment, by Simon Baron-Cohen, Ph.D., professor of developmental psychopathology at Cambridge University, one-day-olds (half of them male, half female) were placed in infant seats. On one side of each baby was a female with her face forward (not mom, just a pleasant-looking woman) while on the other side was a spinning mobile. The girls turned their heads more consistently to the face; the boys preferred the mobile. How can this kind of difference exist when a person hasn't even been on the planet yet for forty-eight hours?

It turns out that there are physical differences in the formation of cells connected to the retina of the eye. Certain structures differ in quantity depending on gender, reports Leonard Sax, M.D., Ph.D., a pediatrician and psychologist who studies gender and learning. Girls have more *p-cells* (parvocellular) that are linked to color-sensitive *cones* in the retina of the eye. These cells, found primarily in the center of the visual processing area, process color and texture of mostly stationary objects. They help answer the question, "What is it?" Interestingly, boys have more *m-cells* (magnocellular) that are wired to *rods* in the retina and record black, white, and shades of gray; they're distributed throughout the retina and process primarily moving objects. M-cells help answer the questions, "Where is it and where is it going?"

Figuring out "what something is" and "where something is" are processed in completely different parts of the brain. We've known this since the 1980s thanks to work involving PET-scan technology by psychologist Martha Farah, Ph.D., who directs the Center for Cognitive Neuroscience at the University of Pennsylvania. But the discovery that girls' visual systems are wired to see more "what" and boys' systems to see more "where" is a very new twist!

This fascinating work doesn't indicate that parents should interact any differently with a male or a female infant. What I find so interesting, however, is how these cell-level gender differences impact performance years later in a preschool setting. Just look at differences in what kids will draw: Boys typically choose six or fewer crayons with a focus on black, gray, silver, and blue, and they love to draw *verbs:* actions, motion—things like car crashes. Girls, on the other hand, will use ten or more crayons of brilliant colors like red, orange, green, and yellow, as well as subtler shades. Girls tend to draw more stationary objects—

*nouns*—depicting things like houses, trees, people, and pets with lots of detail.

Dr. Sax points out that not understanding these biological differences can have unintended consequences. One common example: When well-meaning preschool and early childhood teachers (who are mostly female) inadvertently criticize the boy who they think could "use more colors and put more happy people into his pictures!" By his teacher not understanding the innate interest that little Matthew has in depicting two objects colliding, she can end up making Matthew feel he is lacking in some way. This early feeling of failure becomes important in light of research from Stanford University, where the Dean of the School of Education, Deborah Stipek, Ph.D., finds that children make up their minds about whether they like school or not by the end of their first year's experience. That "take away" message, she reports, remains stable over a lifetime!

Teachers who understand this gender difference might praise both the little girl who has drawn an intricate picture of her family, as well as the boy for the way he used "lots of black circles to show motion in his big car crash." As your baby grows, you too can be sensitive to the differing interests of little boys and little girls, relaxing and enjoying your child just the way he or she is. If you have a girl, she will love your face from the moment she enters the world. If you have a boy, give him even more face-to-face attention to allow your face to become something familiar he will love back.

Let's look at some important reasons for face-to-face connections between any baby and primary caregivers—and some easy ways you can have fun promoting this natural interest.

## THE BRIGHT IDEAS: FACE TIME

### 1. Make Time for Face Time (Put Down the Cell! Close the Laptop!)
Of course most parents can hardly resist gazing into their baby's big eyes. Spending time in face-to-face, eye-to-eye contact with your child should happen normally in routine baby care: Talking to your baby while you

change a diaper, watching her during a feeding, pointing out new things while you take a walk together. I'm not saying that "face time" is a special kind of activity time you need to schedule into your baby's day!

Modern life, however, has a way of creeping into our everyday lives and sabotaging our best intentions. One of the biggest face-time thieves that concerns me is the cell phone. It's small, it's portable, and it can be a lifesaving link to our partner, mom, girlfriends, work—all the necessary or simply welcome diversions from what can be, I admit, *tedious* about being with a baby all day long. Walking around while on a call has become a fact of life. I see moms with phones at their ears at the pediatrician's office, in the car, at the playground, in the stores. Though they're physically with their babies, the critical eye contact just isn't happening.

Obviously mothers need to talk on the phone sometimes, just like anybody else. But we all know people who seem umbilically tethered to their cells (or addictive BlackBerry—aka "crackberry"—handheld computers, laptops, pagers, and so on), spending long periods of time on them all day long. Well, it's a problem for a baby if their parent or caregiver is one of these people.

The amount of "face time" you create with your child matters. Spending time sharing your delight in *just being with your child* is perceived by him as the magical combination of a twinkle in your eye, a smile on your face, and a lilt in your voice, which together speaks volumes about how important little Charlie or Marissa is to you. This natural message system of the combined impact of eyes, smiles, and voice tones are the beginning of the development of an effective attention system in the brain (**Attention**), solid social and emotional health (**Bonding**), *and* the development of language (both receptive, being able to understand words, and expressive, being able to speak words, **Communication**).

### 2. Let "Face Time" Come Naturally

Now that I've hammered about how important spending time enjoying your baby is, I'm going to quickly add that I'm *not* suggesting you should be locking eyes with your baby 24/7. While I want you to be conscious of the reasons that eye contact is useful to your baby, I am not asking you to be "in his face" in an over-the-top way. In fact, what we now know is that mothers may be instinctively programmed away from this notion.

Nursing mothers or bottle-feeding mothers around the world share an unusual practice when it comes to eye contact. Daniel Stern, M.D., at University of Geneva, Switzerland, has determined in his worldwide studies of caregiving practices that the first few minutes of the feeding routine always begin the same way everywhere. The mother purposefully does *not* make any eye contact with her infant! The universal message seems to be: "Let's get down to business. You need nourishment to survive. So EAT." The lack of eye contact is "read" unconsciously by the infant as a clear message to get focused and, as Stern says, "get the important task of receiving critical nourishment done." Around the world, despite the culture, the message is the same. These initial minutes of the feeding cycle are not the time for loving communication. Nutrients and nourishment are essential for survival. This is business! Not socializing time.

*After* this initial focus on getting into the meal, social contact and communication take off. The mid- and final stages of the feeding are prime opportunities for eye-to-eye contact, showing affection, and engagement, that social "dance" of expression and emotion that serves as the basis of bonding and trust between parent and child. The final stage of feeding is often filled with early kinds of play: Hand-holding, massaging, talking, laughing, just "messing around," and feeling satisfied. "Fat and happy" time!

This routine is repeated six to eight times a day during feedings. These findings are great examples of how you can feel confident in letting face time come naturally while you follow the biological rhythm of interaction between caregiver and child.

### 3. Limit the Time Your Baby Is "Strapped In"
Since 1985 every state has passed laws requiring young children to ride in child safety seats when in a moving vehicle. What a terrific, lifesaving

development. Over the years the various models available have been refined and redeveloped to make them safer in the event of an accident, as well as ever more attractive to parents. I absolutely agree that safety is important at all stages of infant/toddler development, but there's a potential dark side to the newly popular infant-seat-travel system that parents aren't aware of because they are focused on safety and ease of use. It's also easy to inadvertently overuse them, perhaps to the detriment of normal development of your child's developing attention system.

Modern "travel systems" convert from infant car seat to infant carrier. The seat can snap into a base in the car or in the stroller. I can see why convertible carriers have become all the rage. They emphasize safety, style, and convenience—no more getting the infant in and out of one carrier, into the car seat, out of the car seat, into a stroller. You can transfer a sleeping baby from your car to your house, and let him sit in safety when he wakes up—all without moving him from his seat.

What's not obvious is how such a system, when *overused* once you and baby are out of the car, deprives the baby of a normal range (scope) of visual input that is critical to the wiring of attention in the first fourteen months especially. These carriers tend to have high sides and place the baby deep within the seat, as a safety feature—limiting her range of vision to what's directly in front of her and making it difficult to orient to sounds that are coming from either side. If she hears a dog bark or the doorbell ring, she might try to turn her head toward the sound, but cannot readily see anything to connect with this sound. Nor can she follow Mom's gaze when she waves with a welcoming smile to a friend approaching from behind the baby's carrier seat. A seven-month-old in mom's hip sling, in comparison, can rotate not only her head, but practically her whole body to see what or who mom is looking at. (*Mom's friend is behind me . . . better turn all the way around to see.*)

Researchers are learning that a child's ability to follow eye gaze and orient to sounds is important for the effective wiring of the attention system and the systems involved in social interaction. When a baby hears a doorbell, turns her head instinctively to follow the sound, but can't see anything, she may signal distress about this frustrating lack of connection by fussing. But after this disconnect occurs over and over and over, she's less likely to keep trying to turn her head to follow along with the situation around her. She "tunes out."

Because they're so convenient and multi-purpose, many babies are spending *lots* of time in travel systems. While there has yet to be a controlled study on the impact of the extensive use of such new devices on the developing brain, I suggest that parents limit the amount of time that babies spend in travel systems to only the time that you need to be concerned for their physical safety (e.g., while in the car). When you have safely arrived at your destination, get your baby out of her seat and give her a chance to use her natural inclination to shift attention and to follow your lead.

Encourage healthy brain wiring by fostering your child's ability to see and interact with the world around her in the fullest way possible. Some ways to vary your baby's perspective:

- Instead of carting your child everywhere in a carrier seat, carry her on your hip, in a side sling, or in a soft front carrier or backpack. Or use all of these things at different times.
- If you must place her somewhere safely in the house (say, while you shower), consider a bouncy seat or swing whose sides don't restrict her range of vision.
- Make sure she spends time on a floor rug or seated in your lap so she can "practice" noticing things and attending to her world.

### 4. "Brain-Feed" Your Baby

If you are breastfeeding, you already know the many benefits of feeding your baby this way, from protection against certain infections to improved nutrient absorption. If your baby is formula fed, you know you can rest assured that your baby, too, is well nourished, given advances in the composition of modern formula. Without entering into the great debates over what a baby should be fed and for how long, I want to hone in on the *act of feeding*—by breast *or* bottle—and how it may influence brain development.

You've probably heard about a positive link between breastfeeding and later testable IQ. Studies have found that breast-fed infants grow up to have an estimated five-point higher IQ than children who were formula-fed.

For a long time, nutritionists have credited the difference to the superior quality of breast milk, specifically, to the special mix of nutrients, vitamins, minerals, enzymes, and immune factors, including components of milk fat such as the fatty acid DHA. In fact, formula manufacturers have spent millions of dollars dissecting the components of breast milk to try to replicate them in formula. They want to assure parents who choose to bottle-feed that their children won't miss the chance for a similar IQ boost.

But what if it weren't just the composition of breast milk that boosted intelligence, but the totality of the feeding experience? Some striking differences between the ways breastfeeding and bottle-feeding are typically done may play a role in the potential wiring of parts of the baby's brain. Specifically, I think some of the IQ differences can be attributed to the nature and quality of the social interactions that happen during a feeding and to factors of positioning while feeding as well. Look at the typical nursing session:

- The baby is latched successfully onto the mother's left breast and suckles for a few minutes of serious "work." Then Mom and her baby lock eyes and mom begins to softly talk or whisper to the baby. At this time, the baby gazes up and to his left.
- Mom may even pick up her infant's tiny left hand and massage it and play with it. The baby's hand may start to pat her breast, or his hand meets her free hand and they play together. Notice that while latched to mom's left breast, the baby explores with his left hand and is being stroked and soothed on the left side of his body.
- Now having finished nursing on the left breast, the baby is switched to the right breast. The social interchange continues.

This time, however, the sensations received, and the exploration he is free to do, happen on his right side, and his eye gaze is up and to his right.

This process is different for most bottle-fed infants in several key ways. In bottle-feeding, most adults have a preferred "side" on which they hold the baby; the bottle is held in the caregiver's dominant hand (usually the right) and the baby cradled in the opposite arm (usually the left). There are limited opportunities to stroke or physically interact with the infant because the caregiver has no free hands! What's more, few parents ever switch sides. For most of us, it feels awkward to hold the baby on the right and use the less-dominant left hand to hold the bottle.

Why might this matter?

The brain's two hemispheres are connected by a band of fibers called the *corpus callosum*. This structure plays an important role in the ease of communication between the hemispheres. A well-formed corpus callosum allows for better integration of the information processed in both the left and right hemispheres. Activities that encourage the natural crossing of the midline of the body help to build the corpus callosum. In fact, if a school-age child is experiencing any of a variety of learning issues, activities that employ crossing the midline are often part of the therapies used by special education teachers everywhere.

In the previous example, this can be seen in the way that:

- the breastfed infant is switching eye gaze, at one breast crossing the midline of his body to have both eyes gaze left, and later crossing the midline of his body to have both eyes gaze right, and,
- the breastfed infant might reach alternating arms and hands across his body when feeding on each side to tug on his mom's necklace or pull off her glasses.

There have yet to be controlled studies that define and measure whether such easy and oft-repeated activities as feeding rituals impact the development of the corpus callosum. While I personally recommend breastfeeding, knowing what I know about early development, my recommendation is that if parents do choose to bottle-feed their infants, they should switch sides! Simple changes matter. (For other play-based ideas of how to encourage smooth coordination connecting the brain's two hemispheres, see Chapter 4 on "Playtime.")

Interestingly, in 2006, Duke University researchers suggested another environmental factor that may possibly account for higher IQ in breast-fed babies aside from the nutritional composition of breast milk: The fact that their mothers tend to have stronger verbal skills—that is, they talk to their babies more often. Like switching sides, this is an example of a simple thing any parent or caregiver can do during feedings. (For more on the link between talking and intelligence, see Chapter 14, "Everyday Talk.")

### 5. Encourage Your Baby's Natural Interest in Mirroring You

People often use the expression, "Monkey see, monkey do" to describe the way young children like to imitate the people around them. Until the 1970s, it was thought that babies didn't develop this ability until between eight and twelve months. Then researchers realized that newborns as young as twelve to twenty-one days old can imitate facial expressions, such as opening their mouths and sticking out their tongues in response to an adult doing the same. (You can try this at home with even a day-old newborn if your baby is in a receptive frame of mind: Bring your face close to his and slowly stick out your tongue. Hold it like that for a moment and wait. Your baby may echo your expression by sticking out his tongue too.) This work, led by Andrew Meltzoff, Ph.D., now co-director of the Institute for Learning and Brain Sciences at the University of Washington, gave birth to a whole body of research into the capabilities of young infants.

Imitation appears to be central to skills as basic as learning how to talk and interact with others appropriately. When we watch someone do something, we "do" it in our heads. Knowing that even babies are able to link the actions they see others perform with the actions that they themselves are performing, demonstrates that they're already capable of social learning.

Thanks to an ice-cream-loving scientist, researchers now believe that they have identified what happens in the brain during imitation. Fifteen years ago, Dr. Giacomo Rizzolatti and colleagues, at the University of Parma in Italy, were conducting tests on a rhesus monkey. They had implanted recording electrodes into its brain to listen to the activity pattern of neurons involved in planning out and executing movements. After a break, one of the researchers entered the lab finishing up an ice cream cone. The monkey's cells they were recording from (which had been silent during the break) started firing—but no test was underway yet. The surprised research team realized that the monkey's brain was activating when it saw the researcher grasp the cone and bring it to his mouth. Soon they were designing and repeating experiments to replicate the experience. Certain cells, it was later realized, fire not only when we perform an action, but when we watch someone else do so.

These special cells are called *mirror neurons*. This breakthrough discovery is helping to shed light on why we yawn when we see someone else yawn, how we learn to talk or kick a ball, and even how emotions such as grief or joy are shared. Work by Marco Iacoboni, M.D., Ph.D., associate professor of psychiatry and biobehavioral sciences in the Brain Mapping Center at the University of California in Los Angeles, has helped to show that there is a network of brain regions in humans with cells that have mirror neuron properties. This network is called the *mirror neuron system*. This system potentially forms the basis for the human capacity to learn by imitation, and for how we understand the actions and intentions of others. While scientists still have a lot to learn about this system, it may be that a child comes to understand what someone is doing when they pick up a cup to take a drink, for example, because the brain regions that are activated while watching the other person reach for the cup overlap with those that are activated when she herself picks up a cup. A 2005 team, including some of the researchers involved with the serendipitous ice-cream-cone-and-monkey discovery of mirror neurons, found that when adults just listened to sentences describing certain actions, the same mirror neurons in their brains were activated as when they performed or watched the actions.

You can see how fundamental these special cells must be to young children who spend so much time just watching! New research in the laboratory of Mirella Dapretto, Ph.D., at UCLA, is demonstrating that the mirror neuron system (in addition to other areas of the brain that process faces such as the visual cortex, the amygdala and the fusiform gyrus) is engaged in children when they observe and imitate emotional facial expressions. In her studies, children are brought into the lab and participate in an fMRI scanning session where, through special goggles, they view people who are expressing different emotions (anger, fear, happiness, sadness, or no emotion). During the scanning session, the children also imitate the expressions they see. The scans measure the amount of blood flowing to regions of the brain as they participate. In addition, the children and their parents fill out questionnaires that explore the children's ability to empathize with and relate to others. When the imaging data are analyzed, it reveals that the greater the amount of activity in mirror neurons within the frontal cortex a child shows, the greater the child's ability to empathize with others.

Dr. Dapretto's research also shows that the mirror neuron system may be disrupted in individuals with autism. She found that autistic children did not activate the same mirror neuron region as the typically developing children did. One of the ways neuroscientists learn about attention and social skill development is through studying people who have problems with these things. Autism, for example, is a brain disorder with hallmark features that include a lack of preferential attention to the face and voice and a lack of the ability to attend to the same stimuli as another person by following his or her eye gaze (*joint attention*).

Children develop different skills at different times, so don't be alarmed if your child is not imitating everything you do or does not seem to be enraptured by your face; however, you should pay general attention to whether and how your child develops these skills. [See Box, pages 67–68 "Red Flag: Avoiding Eye Contact."]

The mirror neuron system develops naturally in healthy infants, as babies automatically engage with their caregivers and the world around them. As parents and caregivers, we can use the fact that they are naturally drawn to the face to teach them about the world and to teach them how to pay attention. Perhaps as part of their ability to understand the actions and intentions of others through the mirror neuron system, babies learn that *paying attention* is one of the things that adult humans do!

Some easy examples of everyday interactions that teach this:

- Play peekaboo. The first times you try this simple interaction the "boo!" comes as a total surprise to your baby. But as he begins to associate the "boo!" with your big smile, he will begin to mirror this smile back to you.
- "Open wide!" When feeding your baby solids, have you ever opened *your* mouth as you lift the spoon to hers? You're trying to elicit a mirror neuron kind of response in her!
- Wave bye-bye. Demonstrating this for a child helps her imitate the physical action and, eventually, learn the "why." At first, your child will wave indiscriminately, copying you without connecting the wave to the fact that there's an appropriate occasion for it. For example, you may wave bye-bye to Grandma and then go in the house; a few moments later while you're talking about Grandma's visit, your baby opens and closes her fist. Quickly, though, a child learns to wave bye-bye when someone is leaving. From simple imitation, she picks up on using this gesture in the right context.
- Sit and read. Even a child under twelve months learns about "reading" through imitation. You don't have to read the actual words of the story; simply pointing to various pictures and talking about the colors or animals on the page does the trick. Soon you will see your child take a book on her own and imitate you, pointing to the pages and making gibberish sounds. Later she may sit with a doll or her teddy bear and "read" to her friend in the same way you read to her.

By toddlerhood, monkey-see, monkey-do behaviors are more noticeable, probably because a child is now capable of recruiting all of his motor capabilities: upright, moving, dexterous, he's better able to imitate the ways he sees adults using their muscles, and we notice this. Toddlerhood is also the phase when language development explodes, so we hear verbal imitations, too. I know one sixteen-month-old who says, "Bad dog, Lily!" every time she sees her dog Lily. That's the phrase she picked up from her parents about the poor dog and it's all she'll say to her now!

### 6. Share the Attention

Something else important happens when caregivers and babies make eye contact. A baby will automatically begin to follow the caregiver's eye gaze when the caregiver suddenly looks away toward someone or something else. Scientists call this *joint attention*. Babies as young as ten months of age already depend on a caregiver's eye gaze and to a caregiver's pointing gestures when learning language. Research in Dr. Meltzoff's lab has just shown that while nine-month-olds will follow adult head turns just as often when the adult has his eyes closed as when they are open, infants at ten and eleven months of age will notice whether the adult's eyes are open or closed and turn their own heads more often when the adult's eyes are open. Perhaps more importantly, the ability to follow eye gaze has been found to be related to future language ability at eighteen months of age. Babies who are better at gaze-following have higher language scores.

Some ways you can foster joint attention:

- *Label objects.* As you begin to teach word labels of objects by pointing to and naming them as you naturally go through your day, first establish eye contact with a child, if even for a fleeting moment, to assure that he is "with you."
- *Point as you read.* When you read picture books together, look at something on the page and point to it. By looking and pointing together, you're conveying to your child, "This is

where I'm looking, and if you look there too, you're going to see something interesting!"

- *Point out sounds to share too.* You can also practice sharing attention through what you hear. For example, say, "What do you think that noise is? Is it a bird? Let's listen. Yes! Can you hear the bird singing?"

## Red Flag: Avoiding Eye Contact

If your child tends to avoid eye contact and does not look at you when you call his name, should you worry? Both are certainly behaviors to watch.

Your pediatrician will likely be talking with you about whether your child is meeting developmental milestones, but you as a parent can watch for signs in three main areas: social skills, communication, and behavior. Of particular concern is autism, a developmental disorder that is diagnosed in about one in 500 children, with some recent estimates reporting numbers as high as one in 150 children. The average age for diagnosis is three years, but doctors believe there are reliable indicators before eighteen months. A list of these, below, comes from First Signs, Inc., a national nonprofit organization dedicated to education about the early warning signs of autism and other developmental disorders. If you have concerns, do not hesitate to discuss them with your pediatrician; make sure to also get a formal audiological assessment to rule out hearing difficulties that may underlie communication deficits.

Let your pediatrician know if you notice your child has:

- No big smiles or other warm, joyful expressions by six months or thereafter
- No back-and-forth sharing of sounds, smiles, or other facial expressions by nine months or thereafter
- No babbling by twelve months
- No back-and-forth gestures, such as pointing, showing, reaching, or waving by twelve months

- No words by sixteen months
- No two-word meaningful phrases (without imitating or repeating) by twenty-four months
- Any loss of speech or babbling or social skills at any age

# 4

# Playtime: The Real Work of Play

- SHOULD I MAKE PLAY MORE EDUCATIONAL?
- HOW MUCH PLAYTIME DO BABIES AND TODDLERS NEED?
- DO THEY NEED LEARNING TOYS?
- WHAT KINDS OF PLAY EXPERIENCES ARE BEST?

You've probably heard the familiar sayings, "Play is a child's work," and "Play is the way children learn." Every parenting magazine you read, every child-care guide you consult, and every early childhood educator you talk to will give this same message. What you may not know is why. *Why is play so important that it would be compared to work,* you might wonder. *Aren't play and work opposites?*

## WHAT THE SCIENCE SAYS: FUN SATISFIES A BIOLOGICAL NEED
*"If it feels good, do it again."*
*—OLD SAYING*

Neuroscience tells us that play *is* critical in helping the brain to work and learn. It's not the play activity itself that causes learning, though. It's the *repetition* that play encourages. Repetitive activity results in patterned neural activity that changes the brain. And the critical link between play and learning—the reason we keep repeating something and therefore learn from it—is *pleasure.*

At the most basic level, humans prefer *pleasure* over pain. We'll go to great lengths to find pleasure. Young babies who receive love and good care don't have to go far: warm milk; a smiling face and a soothing, familiar voice; a soft blanket; rhythmic rocking. As children grow and begin to explore, the mere act of discovery and a developing sense of mastery over one's environment provide pleasure. Notice how delighted your toddler is when he smiles and proudly exclaims, "I did it myself!"

Neuroscientists have successfully located the parts of the brain (known as the *reward pathway*) that become active when a person experiences pleasure. A distinctive cocktail of chemicals is released in the brain. Researchers have shown that, in adults, the same areas of the brain light up on a scan in response to good food, laughter, viewing happy faces, receiving a back rub, winning a wagered bet, feeling accomplished, or thinking about sex, or (for some people) drugs. In children, play of any kind, especially free uninhibited play, activates those same pleasure centers.

What constitutes "play" to someone changes over time. Peekaboo excites a baby and stacking and dumping interests a toddler, while a preschooler might prefer extended fantasy play, dressing up like a ballerina or Spider-Man. For a mother or a father "play" may be a rousing game of tennis or curling up with a book. But the biology of play always stays the same. When something feels good, the accompanying chemical response makes our brain cells want to experience those positive feelings again. (Or as a toddler is fond of saying, "Do it again! Do it again!")

This is true whether we're talking about you eating one more potato chip or your baby creating that thrilling sound again by shaking a rattle. When we do "do it again," connections in the brain receive reinforcement. Over time, those reinforced connections become strong. The brain literally changes in response to the play experiences because they are repeated.

These crucial physical connections in the brain are part of the definition of play that we cannot see. What we *can* see is that play allows children to explore the physical world, to test their own capabilities and limits and, most importantly, to understand themselves in relationships they are building with key people in their widening world. As a child plays, the brain works hard to integrate all incoming information from external and internal sensations into meaningful patterns. As experiences are "played out," repeated, and practiced, a child gains a sense of control over himself and his environment.

When you look closely, you can see this process unfold even from early infancy. It really blooms in an obvious way from around seven to twelve months, when babies begin to make sense of the world through cause-and-effect learning. Endless hours of what-causes-what-to-happen experimenting—pushing, pulling, turning, twisting, and touching things—helps a child to figure out how and why things work. The question of *why* things happen is a critical aspect of learning to survive—and a source of continuous fascination. *What happens when I pull this tablecloth off the dinner table? How far can I walk in mommy's new high heels? Can my brother's frog swim in our toilet? Does this egg break if I drop it from the countertop? What about the spoon? The bib?* A good bit of a baby's day is consumed by exploring "what happens *if* . . ." I think it's nothing short of magical to watch this learning-through-play in action. Learning new things is fun for a young brain! As long as a child feels safe and his basic needs are being met, he's free to have fun exploring and investigating his world.

## A Special Note for Dads

In my workshops, fathers, especially, tend to cast a suspicious eye toward the subject of play as a vehicle for solid learning. Impatient with dress-up and building blocks, they're eager for their children to move on to ABCs, worksheets, lessons, and other "useful stuff." That's what they consider *real* learning.

So I love the moment when I explain that child's free play is critical because it actually causes the brain's energy to be used in a different way—because the pleasure it brings causes repetition, play reinforces healthy wiring. Play suddenly stops being some kind of idle time-waster in their eyes. It's elevated to the status of something vitally important for their child to do. (As it should be!)

## HOW REPETITION POWERS LEARNING

*"Again! Again!"*

—FROM "TELETUBBIES"

Why does it matter that we enjoy something enough to do it over and over? Because learning anything new is hard. Yet it gets easier as you go along. Pleasure is a biological incentive to keep tinkering and persisting.

Here's an exercise I use in workshops to illustrate this:

Imagine a group of thirty people standing in a circle facing one another. Each person is given a glove for his or her right hand, with a bold black number written on the palm of the glove. The gloves have been passed out in random order and, though the group doesn't know it, a few numbers are missing.

The person with the lowest number is given a large rubber kickball and the group is instructed to throw it to one another in numerical order. It quickly becomes apparent that no one knows who has the next number in the sequence. There is momentary confusion as the group starts to organize itself and talk through how to establish some rules. They slowly begin to successfully throw the ball from one number to the next. They have to communicate to get this done. There's lots of helping, shouting, laughing, figuring out what to do when they realize some numbers are missing, correcting . . . and eventually they get to what they discover is the last number.

A leader has timed the effort: one minute, forty-five seconds. Then they are asked to try again. Each person knows better what to expect. Together they remember, but not perfectly, who comes next in the order. A few mistakes are made, but the final time is dramatically cut to one minute, three seconds.

Now, the group does the exercise a third time. This time there are smooth transitions from person to person and a seriousness of purpose—get that ball from here to there, and fast. There is less laughter as the concentration mounts, and when the last person catches the ball, the group erupts with cheers because they know they did well. The stopwatch confirms this: forty-nine seconds.

Although the demonstration has ended, the group will beg to do it again. They are proud. They like the feeling of success. If they did make a fourth try, they would, in fact, probably shave a few more seconds from their time as they perfected their throws and coached the slower members how to pick up the speed. But it would not be as dramatic an improvement as before. Essentially the learning curve has been mastered.

This curve mirrors what scientists have shown to be the learning curve for most things. Effort, effort, less effort, dramatically less effort . . . and mastery. Learning has taken place. That level of achievement reached can be maintained (with occasional refreshers), but additional effort produces relatively few gains unless one is coached and over-practiced.

This process hinges on repetition. Practice improves performance because it makes energy flow more easily each time we repeat and reuse a connection in our brain. With repetition, the pathway of neural connections in areas of the brain that are needed to perform a task gets strengthened. The synapses between brain cells in the pathway are activated with each repetition, and, over time, scientists believe, the level of chemical needed to make that connection is reduced. Repeated use of neural pathways (and resulting neural networks of connections) fire in a sequence, creating a pattern of "what is connected to what." The more you use a firing pattern, the more easily that pattern fires. At the same time, this frees up energy not needed as much in areas of the brain involved in attention, working memory, and cognitive control, allowing for the task to be performed more automatically and efficiently. Practice and repetition, therefore, lead to changes in how energy is allocated in different brain regions and, over a long period of time, to physical changes in the structure of the brain.

That's why the more a person repeats something, the better he learns it. When a child has made a connection through playing and experimenting, and has a chance to repeat that experience, connections are strengthened and future learning takes less effort.

We can clearly see the effects of practice in something physical like when your child struggles, improves, and finally masters being able to tie her shoelaces into a bow. Less obvious, yet nevertheless real, are the brain changes that occur as she practices and finally masters smooth, effortless reading.

The science says, "Practice makes for reduced energy needs and for connections to be made with less effort, thereby saving energy for other learning and refinement." No wonder Grandma shortened the idea to, "Practice makes perfect!"

I'm thrilled to see that schools, doctors, and other groups are now working together to elevate the importance of child play in everyone's minds. Nudged aside by such diverse factors as packed curriculums (even at the preschool level), video games, formal youth sports programs, and other organized activities, play is becoming an endangered part of childhood! The American Academy of Pediatrics now encourages its members to recommend and promote "free child-centered play."

Here's what you can do at home. Don't miss the activity chapters (7, 12, and 17) which, while promoting Attention, Bonding, and Communication, all do so through play!

## THE BRIGHT IDEAS: PLAY TIME

*"If it isn't fun, it isn't play."*
—Dr. Bruce Perry, M.D., Ph.D.

### 1. Just Do It!
Some quick important points about play in general:

- Play should constitute the most of your baby's or toddler's waking hours, aside from feeding.
- There are two kinds of play: directed play (involving an adult) and free play (on his own). Both are important.
- You can feel confident that you're helping to build a better brain when your child is playing. It's not idle time; it's real work on a critical brain-cell level!

### 2. Best First Game: The Crossing-the-Midline Game (0–6 months)
"Tracking" activities—following an object with the eyes—and other experiences that cross the midline of the body help wire the brain

effectively by connecting the two hemispheres of the brain. "Crossing the midline" refers to the ability to move one's eye, hand, arm, or foot from its natural field on one side of the body to the other.

The brain's left and right hemispheres are designed to work together in processing and relaying information back and forth across the brain's midline structure, the *corpus callosum*. For all of us, very normal abilities require the combined processing of both hemispheres facilitated by the corpus callosum. For example, in conversation you must be able to both hear spoken words and understand the meaning of those words (left hemisphere functions) as well as interpret the intonation used by the speaker (a right hemisphere function). To play music, you must be able to both play the notes on a score of music (left hemisphere) and to able to interpret the emotion of the passage (right).

Although the left and the right hemispheres each have very specialized roles, the brain functions as a whole brain; the better the connections between its sides, the more smoothly the whole brain is able to work and, therefore, the better the learning of certain skills. Higher cognitive functions and rapid processing of information later in life depend on a corpus callosum that's developed with many well-myelinated connector fiber tracks.

In fact, this concept is so critical that therapies that help a child "cross the midline" play a major role in treating such later learning problems as dyslexia and other reading difficulties, and in occupational therapies for issues involving balance and coordination.

Once you understand the need for well-connected hemispheres, the more important something like this simple "crossing the midline" game becomes. I guarantee that you will never again play a tracking game without thinking about the corpus callosum! This is the first of many changes you can make when contemplating your role as a playmate for your child. Simple games, like this one, can mean a lot to the brain, especially when done from the start!

*Directions:*
- Hold your baby in your lap on his back.

- With the rattle eight to twelve inches above your baby's head, slowly shake it up and down or from side to side. Each of these rattle movements will make a sound.
- Say, "Shake."
- Slowly move the rattle from side to side.
- Pause to see if the baby's eyes have "locked on" to the rattle.
- When you think he is focused on the rattle, slowly move it from his left side to his right side. Watch to see if the baby becomes disengaged at the "midpoint." *This is not unusual.*
- Shake the rattle a bit to "re-engage" the baby's eye contact, and then continue moving the rattle to the baby's far right.
- Repeat this tracking game. As you do this kind of "crossing the midline," your baby can begin to better connect the two hemispheres of the brain.
- Praise him and have fun!

### 3. Encourage Tummy Time Play (3–6 months)

Babies also need another particular kind of play—or more specifically, play in a certain position. Thirty, twenty, or even ten years ago, moms didn't need to be reminded to put their babies on their bellies. That was the first, most natural way people thought to put their babies down, whether to sleep or to play. But now that babies are routinely put to sleep on their backs to reduce the risk of SIDS (sudden infant death syndrome), they spend less time than ever on their bellies. They're not already in that position when they wake up, and parents sometimes have been so programmed about the dangers of belly-sleeping that they are reluctant to lay their baby down on the floor on the tummy even when awake.

*Your baby needs tummy time*, especially around three to six months. Lying on the belly enables a baby to develop the upper body strength and motor patterns needed for pre-crawling motions. When you crawl, the right hand and left knee move forward together, then the left hand and right knee. This reciprocal motion activates the fibers in the *corpus callosum* that connect the brain's left and right hemispheres. And once again, for your infant, the better developed these fibers are, the better connected the two hemispheres will be, enabling faster communication between the left and right sides of the brain.

There's a related trend of babies essentially skipping crawling and advancing directly to walking. This is often a direct result of not having had time to practice pre-crawling through tummy time. Some parents, programmed by our hurry-up world, see this kind of developmental shortcut as a sign of that the child is advanced. In truth, crawling is a very important developmental stage.

*Please note:* Some little ones, despite their parents' efforts, are just inclined to skip crawling. Don't panic. Continue to play games as he grows that have physical movements that encourage the alternate use of the left and right sides of the body.

Here's a great tummy-time activity for pre-crawlers:

- When your baby is alert and awake, place her on her tummy on a blanket or mat on the floor.
- Position a baby-safe (unbreakable) stand-up mirror upright on the floor in front of your baby's head, using the stand attached to the backside of the mirror. (You can buy these mirrors where toys are sold; my favorite is the Manhattan Toy company's Color Burst Mirror, edged in fabric of many patterns and colors. If you can't find such a mirror, place the baby in front of a well-secured, floor-to-ceiling type wall mirror at ground level.)
- Encourage your baby to lift her head to see herself in the mirror. If you have a mirror with a colorful border, encourage her to look at this too as you talk and describe the bright colors.
- Talk to your baby using very slow, expressive language: "*Look at the preetty baaaby.*" Continue talking while interacting with your infant.

Your baby will enjoy longer and longer periods of "studying" this fascinating object that changes as her reflection moves. You can also

parents search for toys that will stimulate the development of skills that they associate with school learning, such as being able to count to 100 or to repeat the letters of the alphabet. This isn't necessary. Many of the concepts of letter recognition can be most easily learned by reading the letters on cereal boxes and pattern matching with ordinary objects around the house such as socks or different colored Froot Loops cereal. And counting by rote to some large number can wait 'til kindergarten.

The most educational toys are those that have limitless uses or otherwise encourage tinkering and repeated use.

### 5a. Introduce Play-and-Learn Cues, Part 1: The Place Mat
### (first introduced about 12 months to 3 years)

Toddlers can be helped to know *how and where* to pay attention by introducing a tangible cue to begin to form a routine—a routine for paying attention as they play with you.

This cue, a plain place mat, can be used at times when you work with and play with your toddler (directed play). It's not meant for when you want her to play on her own. Here's how to use it:

- **Start with a mat.** Find a solid place mat to serve as an easy surface on which to place interesting objects and playtoys. The mat should be plain, not filled with Disney characters, ABCs, patterns, or even generic flowers. The reason it needs to be plain is that it should not itself be a distraction. I want your child to focus on the activity at hand, not on the detail of a patterned mat. Such distractions defeat the purpose of the mat, which is to show the child *where* and *when* to pay attention. The place mat is a *visible, concrete* cue to the child that you want her to pay attention to the "work" (which is really PLAY) that the two of you are going to do. The mat defines the "work space."

- **Use it regularly.** *Every* time you want to show your child a fascinating object, a toy, or special learning activity that you want her to really pay attention to, get out the mat. Eventually she'll associate it with something incredibly interesting that is coming. And part of that wonderful association is that she knows it involves time with YOU. The magic of the place mat is this positive association between having *your attention* (now shared with her) and the idea that she will soon be introduced to something new and cool to learn!

- **Don't talk up the mat.** When first introducing the place mat as an attention device, don't really mention it. Draw your child's focus to the object you've placed on the mat.

- **Set a positive tone.** As you spread the place mat out in front of your child, remember to show an expression of excitement and anticipation. This signals to the child that you think this fun activity is important—and pleasurable. If pleasure and anticipation become associated with paying attention, your child will have been given a very valuable "gift" that will last a lifetime of learning.

- **Go slowly.** When you begin to present the activity, make your movements deliberate, while also showing anticipation with your facial expressions. Be sure to gain your child's eye contact as you slowly begin to reveal what you are going to do together. If you do this consistently, the child will also then learn, over time, to anticipate the fun and excitement of what she is about to learn.

I now see some very tiny kids in centers where I've taught this tactic who, when they want their adult caregiver's attention, will run and get out a place mat, sit down on the floor with it spread out, and then look up with a smile as if to say, "Hey . . . somebody. I'm ready to play. Come do something interesting with me!" The first time it happened, I was standing with a small group of caregivers, and we all just looked in amazement at each other before quickly scurrying over to oblige this excited little boy! Montessori teachers use this tactic routinely, providing mats for the children to work ("play") on, as well as special trays for transporting materials in a systematized way.

Later, after lots of use, you may find that your child will prefer something that substitutes for a way to "define a work space"—in adult life we call this a desk! This exercise makes even more sense when you realize how difficult it can be for grown-ups to focus on something carefully if there is no defined space on which to do it!

Many of the fun activities in Chapter 7: "Attention-Builders Little Ones Love" begin with use of a place mat to begin the play-interaction time you will share with your child. The use of the place mat deliberately and consistently cues, and eventually teaches, a young child how to pay attention—by directing their attention to the place mat and to the activity you want them to concentrate on.

### 5b. Introduce Play-and Learn-Cues, Part 2: The "Watch" Way (age 18 months and up)

Sometimes the words you say, or don't say, to your child can help gain a focus of attention. Unless the particular activity you are doing together is designed to elicit lots of talk and conversation, one way to direct and guide attention is to use minimal verbal commands, such saying the word, **"Watch."**

In a world that bombards every man, woman, and child with hundreds of "inputs" simultaneously, often the thing that will stand out and be noticed is *silence*. Using an expression of anticipation (eyes wide-open, eyebrows raised), speak softly . . . and slowly, say: "Watch." After you have modeled the activity for the child . . . showing clearly how you are doing it . . . then cue the child slowly and quietly: **"Now, it's your turn!"** or, "Now you try it!"

All of the comments in this chapter so far are geared toward YOUR actions during playtime with your child—actions that I hope can be based on your new basic understanding of the three components of the Attention System of the brain introduced in Chapter 2.

- Playing by tracking, as well as reaching for and then grasping a simple rattle, builds the first (alerting) and second (shifting) types of attention as you encourage your infant to first *find* the rattle (alerting to a stimulus that engages central brain structures) and then follow the rattle as you move it (shifting attention, which engages the motor strip and the parietal lobes). (See "Appendix: Brain Basics" for pictures of brain structures.)

- Place mat use, during each fun one-on-one play activity, helps to direct attention and maintain it. The place mat links directly to both number two (shifting) and number three (maintaining) aspects of attention as you use this cue to direct your child to where he should focus (shift from where he may currently be looking) and then to keep his attention on one thing—the thing you want him to be interacting with.

- Intentional use of limited talk followed by silence also has the impact of directing a child's attention to what to attend to. This way of interacting involves primarily aspect number two (shifting) because it redirects a child from what she may have been looking at or listening to and asks her to watch what you direct her to look at.

In general, by employing these techniques during play, the subtle but intended effect is that your child's attention system will develop naturally through the "work of play!"

## Safe, Safe, Safe!

There are many safety checklists available of how to assure that your environment is safe. It's critical that you heed those warnings—all of them—before your toddler-to-be starts to walk. Once he's mobile, it is too late. If there is an unlocked cabinet somewhere, he will find it.

Reassess overall home safety every time your child approaches a new physical milestone, such as scooting, crawling, cruising, walking, running.

### 6. *Allow Play to Grow With Your Child (12 months to 3 years)*
A young toddler's play and exploration jumps into high gear once he is walking! Once a child is coordinated enough to be mobile, nearly all objects are now reachable, and are therefore part of the expanding

universe of potential targets for his attention. This provides amazing opportunities to learn through experimentation and repetition.

Your child's play at this stage will be a unique blend of those opportunities provided to him and his own trajectory of maturation. Different play opportunities should be available that match his sequence of development because as children grow, the complexity of play grows. You need to be aware of stages of development so that expectations are realistic. Below is a sequence you can easily identify through careful observation:

- **Functional Play (0–3 years)**
  First, a young child learns how the world works and how things function, discovering the principles of physics (things don't roll uphill, how gravity works when she tosses things from her highchair—repeatedly, how much water will actually fit into the container without overflowing onto the floor). The ways kids learn these concepts is by manipulating their environment: stacking and knocking down blocks, digging in the sandbox, playing in water, pushing toys, running and jumping. Older babies and young toddlers also begin to play with books. After being "eaten" and having their bindings loosened through rough treatment, some books become favorites that a child "reads" memorized favorite sections of, imitating her parents reading to her.

- **Pretend Drama (2–6 years)**
  Children learn about social roles through pretend and dramatic play. They learn and prepare for life's dreams through the use of costumes and dress-up clothes (store bought or mom's and dad's castoffs, as well as old sheets and other household objects), and such playthings as puppets, stuffed animals, dolls, and toy dinosaurs. As long as it is child-directed, there are lots of opportunities for adults to play a part, such as acting out stories in different voices or reversing roles ("I'll be the daddy and you be the baby, Dad."). Let your child help in daily chores, which for your child serves as a another kind of play as she

learns a variety of adult roles (setting the table, sweeping, putting a letter in the mailbox). This is an age when kids love to do anything that lets them "try it on for size."

- **Constructive Play (4–6 years)**
  Using objects and materials to build something is a dominant form of play in many preschool and kindergarten classes. These play activities should be child-directed and adult-facilitated (provide the materials and the time). Turn-taking is learned through the collaborative nature of constructing almost anything.

- **Games-and-Rules Play (5 and beyond)**
  This stage of play focuses on social and emotional skills through co-operative play with others. To understand pre-established rules, young children need to have developed memory skills in order to be able to recall and recognize rules/cues, and be able to accept and conform to those rules. Old classic board games like Candy Land provide a good place to start to learn rules and turn-taking.

Above all remember, there's no right or wrong way to play—as long as it's fun.

# 5

# Screen Time: When Baby Meets Modern Life

- So is TV bad or good or somewhere in between?
- What about educational programming?
- What about videos and DVDs made for babies and toddlers?
- Can computer games for young children boost brainpower?

"Watching something" means a lot more than it did when I was raising my daughters thirty years ago, or when you were a child:

An eight-month-old nestles in her daddy's lap in the kitchen watching dancing shapes on a computer screen while she bangs a "starter" keyboard designed for babies.

A fifteen-month-old toddles over to the DVD player in her nursery with one of her favorite "playthings": a Brainy Baby disc about animals.

A twenty-four-month-old parrots back, "Hola!" to the bilingual cartoon girl on *Dora the Explorer*.

At the family computer, a thirty-month-old asks her mom, "Can we go to 'pbskids.org?'"

Back in my mommy days, the big thing was *Sesame Street*. Through this wonderful, then still new, idea of *public educational television*, America's children were going to be ready for school earlier than ever. It was the 1960s' and 1970s' answer to raising smarter children. Today, many parents have similar expectations for the screen media—TV, computers, DVDs, and videos—their children consume, fed by the promises of manufacturers and programmers.

I'm asked more about this topic than any other. The past ten years or so have seen an entire new landscape of "edu-tainment" (education plus entertainment) options for tots, including "lapware" for infants. On cable and broadcast network television, whole channels or blocks of children's programming target the very young. Shows such as *Curious George* and *Blue's Clues* have been conceived to be more learning-oriented than any Saturday morning cartoon of the Bugs Bunny and Yogi Bear era ever was. Babies and toddlers are considered a separate demographic from even preschoolers: BabyFirstTV, a commercial-free, twenty-four-hour channel distributed via satellite, was the first to promote round-the-clock commercial-free viewing for kids six months to three years.

Also on hand 24/7, of course, are the wildly popular videos and DVDs (a.k.a. "learning videos" or "developmental videos") created specifically for infants and toddlers, with aspirational names like *Left Brain, Right Brain; Bilingual Baby; Baby's First Impressions*; and the *Babies Einstein, Bach, Galileo, Beethoven, Monet, Wordsworth*, et. al. Even *Sesame Street* is still bringing the letters A to Z to children—and now to their baby siblings. *Sesame Beginnings* DVDs, according to Sesame Workshop, are "specially designed to help parents and caregivers encourage their child's curiosity and interest in learning during everyday interactions"— for children six months and up.

*There is absolutely no scientific evidence that any of this helps a baby!* Despite this glaring omission:

- In a typical day, 69 percent of children under three years watch television.
- Forty-three percent of kids under two years old watch every day.
- On average, babies six months to three years spent one hour watching TV and an additional forty-seven minutes using computers, videos, and video games each day.
- More than one in four children under age two have a TV in their bedroom.
- In most households, the TV is on for seven hours and forty-four minutes a day.

- One third of children three or under have used a computer.
- Sales of "developmental" videos and DVDs produced for infants and toddlers added up to $1 billion in 2006, according to *The Washington Post*.

Three popular lines of thinking help explain these facts. Unfortunately none has science on its side.

1. *"The first twenty-four months are so critical to the architecture of the brain, why not give them maximum stimulation?"*

   The ironic side effect of recent discoveries about the brain has been the unfounded line of thinking, especially by clever marketers but also some by educators, that since the brain cells are multiplying in these first years, let's stimulate the heck out of them!

   Bombarding a growing brain with screen stimulation doesn't make a very young brain smarter, by any measure we have.

2. *"I'm not sure but why not try everything just in case it helps my child get ahead in school?"*

   I call this the "just in case" approach, which many understandably confused parents adopt.

   Unfortunately, not only is there is no proof that media stimulation has any benefit to a developing brain, but *there is also not a clear understanding of what too much early media exposure may be inadvertently doing.* The fear is that the same kinds of exposure that might be beneficial, or at least harmless, in a school-age child is actually *causing* negative things to happen in an infant or toddler's brain—and we may not realize those consequences until years later.

3. *"Hey, I watch it and I'm okay."*

   The most compelling new research tells us that how screen media influences adults, for better and for worse—and even how it influences kindergarten children—is different from its impact on the developing brain of a baby or toddler.

*Sesame Street* did not, we now know, bridge the knowledge gap and skills gap for many children of low income in America as was hoped. Nor, I'm afraid, can the new generation of "smart media" live up to its claims. Let's sort out the science from the popular wisdom and see how you can be both realistic and yet smart about screen time and your child.

## WHAT THE SCIENCE SAYS: PROCEED WITH CAUTION

*"All television is educational. The question is what we are learning from it."*
—FORMER FCC COMMISSIONER NICHOLAS JOHNSON

One summer day in 1999, a startling headline rippled across the country: *No TV under age two.* The American Academy of Pediatrics (AAP), the professional organization for the nation's pediatricians, had announced that it was officially urging parents to avoid television for children under two years old.

This was disconcerting news to the millions of moms who thought of TV as a safe, reliable babysitter—or at least, an innocuous activity for a younger sibling to join in on. Even if your young toddler didn't spend hours watching *Barney* and *Nick Jr.* every day, how were you supposed to take a shower and wash your hair without the safety net of a beloved kiddie program? Even the most diligent mom needs the chance to take a shower, after all! And what about having the set on in your house in the background? *No TV?* Why would a group of pediatricians say such an outrageous thing?

Interestingly, it's the first half of the edict that got all the media attention and stuck in everybody's consciousness: *No TV.* The fresher, really important part of the message, however, is the second part: *under age two.*

Screen time seems to have different effects at different ages, and in the first months of life the stakes are especially high.

## HOW TV CAN ALTER BRAIN STRUCTURE

*"I believe television is going to be the test of the modern world, and that in this new opportunity to see beyond the range of our vision we shall discover either a new and unbearable disturbance of the general peace or a saving radiance in the sky. We shall stand or fall by television."*

—E. B. WHITE

Most Americans—adults and children alike—watch way too much television. But an adult, even the worst couch potato, can watch television all day long, and it doesn't really change his or her brain *structure* one bit. When very young children watch too much television, however, it can impact the very structure of their brains.

This is important. Every parent/caregiver needs to understand this distinction.

You'll remember that the very structure and functioning of each person's brain depends on how one uses it. Also, the brain "wires up" in a predictable sequence. By definition, *timing matters* when you're talking about a sequence. What impacts something in one part of a sequence may create a very different effect in some other part of that sequence.

The back of the brain, which processes vision, wires rapidly. Moving forward, this wiring continues until the frontal lobes (where one processes more complex thought, focuses attention, and where the brain holds current information) come fully online, even into adulthood. The frontal lobes house what's called *working memory*. Working memory is the part of your memory system that holds current information needed to help you to accomplish a task. A familiar example would be the need to keep a new telephone number you've just looked up in the phone book active in your mind long enough to take out your cell phone to dial it. If you don't repeat the number to yourself in the interim, chances are you'll forget it and have to find it again.

Over time, as the frontal lobes grow and develop, the brain is better able to hold onto needed information for these short periods of time. The brain also develops the ability to consider multiple aspects of a situation simultaneously. As a person develops, he or she can remember and *hold onto* more pieces of information and keep them all in mind at the same time.

A baby's or toddler's brain is not yet able to do this. Receiving the short hits of entertaining messages on a typical TV program for example, a young child is not able to see things the same way as an adult's brain. It gets used to, and wires up for, short attention span use. It literally forms differently.

Consider this scenario: You, as an adult, watch your favorite TV sitcom. The show introduces the characters and sets up the funny story. Then . . . a commercial. Another commercial. Another. And another. Amazingly . . . another. Then the sitcom picks up where it left off, and you re-engage in the funny story. That is what an adult sees and experiences.

Now here's what an infant or toddler brain sees: The show introduces the characters and sets up the funny story. Then . . . *another story* comes on. Then another story, and another, and another. Infants and toddlers don't distinguish a commercial from the regular show. The frontal lobes of the young brain are not yet well enough developed to carry the memory of the original story over the intervening time period of the many commercials. By the time the sitcom resumes, the very young brain sees it as still one more *new* story. A young child's working memory is more limited in its capacity *to hold* the storyline over the many intervening commercials.

That child's brain is wired to scan and shift, rather than to pay attention—this pattern, once established can inhibit later learning ability. Some scientists believe that excessive early TV viewing may help explain the rise in ADHD cases. Teachers today are also seeing children who are increasingly attuned to distractions in their school environment—the hum of the air conditioner, a squirrel seen out the window, a classmate's whispers—and are less able to stay on task—even if they aren't yet carrying around an ADHD diagnosis.

Dimitri Christakis, M.D., co-director of The Child Health Institute at the University of Washington, has looked specifically at one- to three-year-olds and found a disturbing correlation between the sheer amount of television they watch and later problems with being able to pay attention. For every hour of TV viewed per day before age three, his 2004 study reports, a child is 10 percent more likely to show ADHD symptoms at age seven (as reported by the parents according to a standard assessment index). This study did not show a direct cause-and-effect relationship between TV time and ADHD. We still don't have all the answers as to single or aggregated causes showing why ADHD rates are rising in these children. But the study does warn us of a potential association.

Until more well-controlled studies are conducted, we can't know exactly the long-term effects of all screen time on brain function. One difficulty to doing these kinds of tightly controlled studies is that researchers ethically can't randomly assign kids to a high-TV-dose group given that we're worried that large amounts of TV watching can be harmful to a young brain. We're often limited to using family reports of how much TV young kids already watch.

Another challenge is that not all types of electronic media may be alike and have the same impact. Most studies to date also do not distinguish among different types of programming. It may be possible that a leisurely learning video or a *Wiggles* episode affects the brain differently than the more frenetic *Sesame Street* or afternoon soap operas made for adults. Christakis and his collaborator Zimmerman next plan to study the differences between those who watch TV as they normally do and those who watch none at all.

## Downsides for All Ages

Although research has been conducted on television and learning for decades, most of that was done on preschoolers and, more often, on older children. Not infants. Nevertheless, from this body of research, we've learned that excessive television viewing is linked to:

- *Weight problems.* Kids who watch the most TV or who have a TV in their rooms are most likely to be overweight or obese, numerous studies have shown. A 2003 study by The Henry J. Kaiser Family Foundation reported that kids under six spent as much time with media as they did playing outside. The more time children of any age spent with media, the less time they have available for more active pursuits.

- *Fears.* Kids ages two to seven are unable to distinguish fantasy from reality well and are more likely to be frightened or upset by violent or scary things they see on TV.
- *Aggression.* Children who watch violent action-adventure programs have been found to have more behavior problems in schools than those who watched more pro-social programs.

## WHAT TV *DOESN'T* DO

*"Video for infants and toddlers is a great uncontrolled experiment on the nation's under-two set."*
—Donald Shifrin, M.D., chairman of AAP Committee on Communications

What about all the educational claims of screen media? Certainly some positive effects of television and computer exposure have been found. A very close look at this research, however, tells us that there's a distinct difference in the likelihood of a positive versus negative impact on a child that happens at about age two and a half years of age. For example, there are studies that show that watching educational TV can help an older child improve his vocabulary and score higher on standardized measures of problem solving and flexible thinking. A major study published in 2001 tracked 570 children from preschool to adolescence and found that those who had watched *educational* TV programs before school age had higher grades and read more books in high school. Another study found that four- and five-year-olds who used developmentally appropriate software had improved intelligence test scores. But here's the key thing: Most of this work looked at *older* children.

*Babies and toddlers are different.*

New studies have shown that children learn better from live people than from people on a screen. Among other factors, it may be that the *shared eye gazing* that takes place in live interaction helps the brain process information differently. Researcher Patricia Kuhl, Ph.D., a professor of speech and hearing sciences and co-director of the Institute for Learning and Brain Sciences at the University of Washington, set out to examine whether just reading storybooks in Chinese to nine-month-old infants of English-speaking families would allow these babies to generalize this experience and therefore be able to tell the difference between similar-sounding sound units (phonemes) in that Chinese language. This ability to tell the difference between phonemes in foreign languages is something that usually declines between six and twelve months of age as infants become attuned to the sounds that are in their native language at the expense of attunement to the sounds of foreign languages. The most interesting part of the design of this 2005 study was that the infants were either read stories *by a person* or watched *a video recording of someone reading* the stories. One of most important findings of the study showed that the babies only learned from live exposure to the sounds—not from the recorded (video) exposure.

These results suggest that learning is enhanced by social interaction, perhaps because story reading with a live person provides the opportunity for the speaker's eye gaze to fall on objects in the book, which the infant then follows with his or her own eye gaze. The researchers speculate that this *joint attention* to an object that is being named may help to draw more attention to the sounds identified with that object, further enhancing learning.

So the next time you think of popping in an educational video to teach your child about the sounds of the alphabet or her numbers (however captivating the images on the screen might be), just remember that she might learn better from you. Even interactive screen time is still *much less active* than "live"!

Despite recent efforts to make computer time more interactive, let's face it, those interactions do not come remotely close to *real* experiences. Hitting a baseball target on a computer screen does nothing for the full-body feedback loop between the muscles in your arm, combined with the twist of your body and the puff of air released from your lungs as you strain to throw a *real* baseball to the batter! Additionally, even the loveliest developmental video is still merely a one-dimensional representation of an object. A toddler watching a simple video showing a common object like a flower, no matter how professionally lit and photographed the moving screen image might be, experiences nothing like the full sensations he can have as he touches a real flower. It is entirely different to feel both its soft velvety petals and its stronger yet still bendable stem, to pick the flower and pull the pieces apart in his hands, to smell its fragrance. Likewise, a moving picture of children playing in a sprinkler isn't remotely like the feeling of cool water droplets on your own skin as your bare feet touch the prickly wet grass. An adult is more likely to gain enrichment from a video because we already understand what an object up on the screen *is*. If it's your first experience with a flower or a sprinkler, however, you don't really know it. Multi-sensory experiences teach far more than the most expensive flat screen can deliver.

We also know that when kids are occupied with passive watching, they themselves are far less active. By definition, if they spend *more* time with characters on TV, they have *less* time to grow close to and connect to the people and "characters" in the next room . . . their parents and siblings!

Even though there are still many unanswered questions, it's safest to err on the side of moderation. I can't help wondering, what happens when, ten years down the line, we discover that all those hours and hours of brainy videos for babies and toddlers have actually *mis*wired the brain? I think a child is too precious to experiment on!

Let's look at the best ways to help you help your child to grow up in an electronic world.

## THE BRIGHT IDEAS: SCREEN TIME

### 1. Start Slow!

Just because something exists doesn't mean it's necessary. A full set of learning videos is no more essential to a nursery than a live zoo animal. If your child receives a learning video for his birthday, you don't have to play it for him right away. Save it for a day when you need ten minutes to take a critical call or handle an emergency. You certainly don't need to go out and buy *any* media created especially for babies and toddlers. Your child is not going to "miss out" on anything or "fall behind" peers academically in the slightest because he didn't have any screen time before age two or three.

Just because your child seems to like something doesn't mean it's necessary, either. Parents often see their young infant glued to the screen and deduce that the child loves it. It's just as likely that they look because they have no choice—their brain is wired to attend to novel, moving objects; they have to look! Quick, colorful images shifting rapidly are difficult for a brain to resist because they activate the brain's orienting response. This is a *biological imperative*; it's part of the human survival mechanism. We're physiologically drawn to the fluctuating brightness contrasts and to the movement of images across the screen. Just because people *will* attend to this kind of input, does not mean, however, that one *should* constantly bombard an infant with such visual stimuli!

Let's recap the good reasons to hold back on exposure to media—including TV, videos/DVDs, and computer games—in the early years:

- *There is no scientific evidence yet as to whether the mesmerized young baby who is sitting in front of a "Baby Whatever" video is either benefiting—or harming—the attention centers of her brain.*
- Meanwhile we do have proof of more effective ways to engage, shift, and hold a young child's attention: talking in an engaging way, playing in easy interactive ways, pointing to and labeling things in the environment. Each of these activities does have research to verify its effectiveness for encouraging learning.
- Automatically turning to media as a babysitter or plaything sends the message that the screen is a desirable thing; it's best to keep TV as a neutral thing in the background of your child's life for as long as possible.
- Time spent in front of a screen is time a baby or toddler isn't doing something else more valuable.

## Should You Ban Screen Time Altogether?

Sometimes I meet parents—a modern minority—who want to insulate their children from screen time completely and for as long as possible. I understand their intentions, and I'd certainly say that a baby or toddler can survive quite nicely without any screen time at all. That said, it's hard to completely ignore the media in modern life. Technology and the resulting changes in our society are here to stay. Families that think they can protect their children forever from the effects of the electronic media are probably naive. It is better to understand how to manage the possible effects and try to establish reasonable guidelines for electronic media use.

### 2. Watch the Clock

Although the AAP recommends a total ban on TV for children under two, I do believe that every mom in America has surely earned the right to pop in a video for ten minutes to have a nice shower, wash her hair, and even blow it dry in a stylish way. I certainly don't believe that glimpsing at a TV screen just now and then is going to damage any child's brain. (Besides, we're happier people and better parents when we look and feel fresh—and that has huge implications for your child's brain!)

Especially when your child is still a baby or young toddler, though, try to keep all viewing—including of videos especially designed for babies and toddlers—to a bare minimum. They just aren't necessary.

For children older than two, the AAP recommendation is no more than two hours total per day of any combination of high-quality, educational screen time.

### 3. Provide Substitutes

"*What you say will speak to your kids. What you do will scream to them.*"
—OLD SAYING

TV or video is often our handy first-resort activity when we need to occupy a child, especially when we need to get something done around the house. Try to make screen time a last resort instead. Before popping a DVD into the player or turning on a kids' show, give your child a chance to be a child.

For example:

- For an infant: Lay your baby on her belly on a floor mat with an assortment of toys or in an activity gym.
- For an older baby: Let him play in your cupboards with pots and pans.
- For a young toddler: Let him pull out all the shoes from Mom and Dad's closet, fit blocks into containers, follow you around as you go through your day.
- For older toddlers: Color, build forts out of blankets, play with dolls and puzzles.

Not only do these kinds of activities hold a child's attention, they're guaranteed not to harm the brain.

### 4. *Think About* Where *Your Child Watches*

The very best place for a child to ever watch TV is sitting right next to you. That way, you can help relate what's on the screen to things in the real world. You can talk about what you see, too: "Why do you think the grandpa was sad?" or "What do you like about that character?"

Side-by-side viewing isn't always practical, of course. The next best option is to limit TV viewing to shared areas like the family room. Common spaces promote the possibility of discussion.

Where your child should *not* watch:

- **Not in your child's room.** Solitary viewing pulls time from family social interactions. Most significant though is the fact that with a TV in his room, you have no control over what your child watches or how long he watches.
- **Not in the car.** Don't give in to the temptation to use the newest car "enhancement," the rolling DVD monitor system. Enough is enough. Save your money. No TV in the car.

- **Not while otherwise playing in your living room.** Turn off the set while your child is playing. Don't get in the habit of keeping a TV on all day for your own entertainment or for "background company." Researchers distinguish between two kinds of TV viewing: *foreground television* (the kind your child sits down to watch, usually children's programming) and *background television* (when the TV is on but a child is not paying much attention to it). For children under age two, most TV watching in the past used to be the background kind—they didn't pay too much attention to it. It's been the explosion of baby- and toddler-specific videos and programs that have caused the increase in foreground TV watching in this age group.

### 5. *Think About What's On*

When you need a slightly longer period of time to yourself, sure, a TV program or video can undoubtedly provide a helpful break. But be conscious about what you choose. There are no government standards regulating the educational quality of children's TV or other media. Many advertisers and programming staff make educational claims that are completely unfounded. To recap:

**Not good:** Most programming for adults and commercial TV. Quick hits with lots of interruptions from commercials and scene changes are a risk to the developing attention span. Appropriate content is a potential problem with most commercial TV too, with much of network programming containing an overabundance of acts of violence.

A particular kind of show to skip: The *evening* news. The nightly news is filled with terrifying images, warnings about impending disasters in near or far lands. Young children have no idea that Iraq is far away from their house. They develop unnecessary apprehension about the number and magnitude of bad things and bad people in their world. Keep their world small, safe, and predictable. If you're only two years old, there's plenty of time to learn about the rough realities of life.

**Better:** Programming designed for children, especially if it is commercial-free. Many PBS children's shows have been modified to conform to higher standards. Beware of cartoon programs made for older children, however, that model aggressive behavior that young toddlers will imitate.

**Best:** Take a short break to sit and watch real educational TV, such as a documentary that may be of interest to you and your child together. While this doesn't give you a chance to do other work yourself, it can give you a few moments to relax and cuddle with your child. If you want to join in on the educational value of this time together, you can emphasize the new words and ideas discussed. If you just want to relax, do so. Your child's education will not suffer!

Use TV to weave what the AAP calls "a web of learning" for your child. Look for library books related to the characters or subjects in the programs you see. Talk about them even when the TV is off. Think of activities you can do at home that mimic or complement those seen on TV, such as taking a nature walk, finger painting, or building a particular scene or your own imaginary world out of blocks.

### 6. Use Computer Games in Moderation—If at All

*"I have a houseful of colorful plastic toys, stuffed animals, and peekaboo storybooks—but there's one toy my year-old daughter is absolutely convinced is the most fun: my PC. Why else would I spend hours every day playing with it?"*
—JULIE MORAN ALTERIO IN *THE JOURNAL NEWS* (N.Y.)

It's natural for your child to be curious about computers—and to even profess she wants one. After all, any gizmo or machine that occupies such a large amount of an adult's time will inspire interest in a young child. (That's why they find the TV remote to be initially just as enticing as the TV itself.) However, everything in moderation . . . young children should not be spending large amounts of time on computers before they attend preschool. Just by being with you (or any loved one who is an experienced computer user), children will pick up computer usage "out of the air" . . . the same way they learn almost everything else in life. When they need to know, their own powerful computer in their head quickly adapts in order to know "how it goes" with a computer on the desk. There will be plenty of time.

Having read the preceding pages, you might assume that I'm an anti-technology reactionary. I am not. In fact, it's been my life's recent work to bring critical new technical information about how brains actually develop (learned through *sophisticated technology*) to families like yours! I believe it's critical to invent new and better ways to learn information and I get excited to find out, for instance, about new machines that allow us to "see" inside the brain to help us better understand our own minds. My own daughter Kristin's specialization in her Ph.D. program in neuroscience is brain imaging technology!

Some studies have shown advantages in familiarizing kids with technology. It can give them practice in problem solving and logic and in learning about rules (such as in computer strategy games and puzzles). Many technologies, including video games, can also increase fine motor skills and coordination skills (eye-hand coordination and reflexes) in older children. Computer games for a variety of ages can teach matching, shifting attention, new words, and math skills.

All this is valuable, but certainly not *necessary* for the first three years of life. There's no evidence that computer-game play at younger ages puts a child at an advantage, and as with the research on television, excessive use may produce a disadvantage.

Just use common sense and remember that human interaction has a higher place in your child's early learning! Many of these same skills can be easily taught by you, and you will be able to cherish watching your child learn.

Also keep in mind that your child will not fall behind if he is not computer literate by the time he reaches school. Competent brains that develop effectively—in a healthy sequence of the combined unfolding of biological power and of nurturing environments—are *ready to learn anything*, when the time comes. Rushing seldom produces anything but added stress.

## A Jenny Story: Mister Rogers, Brain Scientist

I eventually came to realize that Fred ("Mister") Rogers was a genius. Without a single brain scan to inform his practice, Mister Rogers understood what young children need in order to develop a capable brain.

When I was a new mom, my friends were all talking about how much their little ones loved *Sesame Street*. I knew I'd have to take advantage of every waking minute if I was going to help Jenny overcome her slow, slow start; she was starting so far behind. Maybe I could sit with her and, with the help of *Sesame Street*, work at getting her to learn the lessons laid out so clearly in Technicolor. *The shows are so clever*, I remember thinking. *Lots of action-packed skits, songs, jokes.* I saw my friends' kids shout out letters in chorus with puppets as they went flying across the screen.

Jenny would not—and then I began to realize, *could not*—watch television. Day after day I would try to interest her. She would fuss, squirm, and finally cry. I began to realize that she couldn't really "see" this show because it moved so fast . . . everything was constantly changing on the screen. Novelty, novelty, novelty. Fast moving. Disjointed. It was all too much for Jenny.

One day we happened to catch Mister Rogers come cheerfully through the door of his television house. He did some very regular things like changing his sweater and shoes, talking so deliberately and directly into the camera, his face close, voice calm. He was talking to me. *To me.* And, most importantly, to Jenny. I'll never forget that very first time when she finally "watched," or at least appeared to pay attention to this gentle voice. That day began a new daily ritual in our house. Mister Rogers would come and give me the only reprieve in an otherwise endlessly stressful, effortful, minute-by-minute caretaking day of Jenny.

What did Fred Rogers do that is so helpful to the developing brain? He did a number of things often missing from recent videos and computer products and from so much of the supposed educational TV:

- He keeps the *immediate* environment of the young child small. Picture his house: it only has a tiny, simply furnished living room and kitchen. A fish tank is the most prominent feature, along with a kitchen table where he would draw or do simple experiments. Occasionally, we get a glimpse of a small front porch where he greets a neighbor briefly.
- He keeps the focus small. The show's main environment is small, but he builds from there by bringing in one "big" idea each day. He introduces the new item or idea slowly, naturally, and calmly, but with enthusiasm and optimism in his voice. He exudes confidence that you (the child) are going to just love what he will show you today.
- He looks right at you. He makes eye contact. He talks directly to you in a gentle, simple way, confident that you can understand him. He's the master of the critical concept of "face time" explained in Chapter 3.
- He tells you that love is important. He shows you that *you* are important
- He shows you that you are unique. He models each person's uniqueness by introducing you to the deep humanity of a baker, a mailman, a concert cellist, a man in a wheelchair.
- He sings to you.
- He takes you on brief, simple trips to learn about everyday places and people. You go to a local factory where they make dolls. To a music store down the street. To the dentist.
- He models the concept of predicable routines. At the start of every show, he changes from a jacket into a cardigan, and into more comfortable shoes. Predictable routines have the power to calm a frazzled child, to reassure a worried soul, to free the brain to focus on new and interesting things . . . because a child's brain knows it is safe. Mister Rogers is safe.

The iconic *Neighborhood* program ran from 1967 to 2001, making it PBS's longest-running program, still seen in reruns. But its "style" as listed above can be your guide for future appropriate programming to benefit your child.

Now that the show is no longer available in the Phoenix market, Jenny has found a few alternatives that she just loves—on the Food Network. Both Emeril Lagasse and Rachael Ray can keep Jenny's attention for a full half hour. Recently I stopped to analyze why she liked these particular shows: They share many of the same characteristics I listed above. Check it out for yourself . . . the programming matches almost perfectly.

# 6

# Downtime: Doing Nothing Is Important Too

- Isn't all of childhood a "teachable moment"?
- How can I make the optimal use of my child's waking hours?
- What can I do when my child complains of boredom?

Which is the "good" parent? The one who attentively strives to fill her baby's day with new sights, sounds, and stimulation, or the one hanging out on the floor blowing raspberries on her baby's belly? Both, actually.

Knowing how important the early years are to brain development, it's logical to think that we should take full advantage of this window of opportunity by providing a young mind with interesting experiences. Too often, though, this worthy goal is stretched too far. Ever wonder why manufacturers add lights, toys, sounds to every bit of baby gear, from potty chairs to strollers? The whole edu-tainment industry feeds the modern idea that *every moment must be utilized*. Our fast-paced society does not value unproductive time. We grown-ups send email and check the headlines while carrying on a live conversation with a person right in the room. We talk on the phone and eat breakfast while we drive and we exercise while we watch the news and plan tomorrow's agenda. Multitasking is good and super-multitasking is better! We feel an imperative not to be idle—and this mindset is often transferred to the way we view our children's lives, even when they're lying in the crib or sitting on the potty.

Between our do-more culture and the mistaken belief that there's no time to waste developmentally, otherwise sane moms and dads have come to feel it's part of their parental responsibility to fill their child's day with productive activity every hour and every minute.

Good news: You don't have to "make every second count." Or even every hour! "More is more" doesn't always apply to nurturing a developing mind. Sometimes more can be *too much*.

## WHAT THE SCIENCE SAYS: DOWNTIME FUELS LEARNING

*"Yet it is in our idleness, in our dreams, that the submerged truth sometimes comes to the top."*
—Virginia Woolf

Brains actually need downtime just as they need experiences that allow them to wire up. Being idle allows the circuitry to develop, to let the brain take what it already knows and think, reflect, and change.

Did you ever cram for a test? Studying fourteen hours in a row through the night often helps you remember enough to regurgitate the information the next day for the exam. Four days or four weeks later, though, you probably don't retain much of what you "learned." On the other hand, if you study the test material in a slower way over several days instead of cramming, you're likely to do better on the test and also retain the information weeks later. What accounts for this difference? Cognitive scientists know that when we cram, the information doesn't get consolidated effectively in our long-term memory; the brain simply can't store that much information reliably in a short period.

Similarly, your baby needs breaks in order to allow his brain to process the incoming flood of new data. A two-year-old, for example, is learning language at such a terrific rate that sleep and idle time allow him to store the new words efficiently. It's not unlike the feeling adults experience at the end of a vacation. You're rested and rejuvenated, better able to tackle the pile of work on your desk or the demands in your life. You probably feel this way even after getting a break by hiring a babysitter for the evening or having your partner put your baby to bed while you take a walk. Breaks help. Having the opportunity to be idle is an important way to recharge for the hard work of everyday doing—and learning.

*Memory consolidation* is an extended sorting-out process through which memories become more permanent. The activity mainly takes place in the *hippocampus,* which acts like a filing system that governs where memories are stored—visual memories in one place, auditory ones in another, how things smell in a different place. A memory isn't instantly stored forever. The hippocampus also functions as a kind of holding tank where a memory is "put" until it can be permanently stored. Storage occurs through repeated interactions between the hippocampus and the cortical areas of the brain where memories are eventually housed. Much is still unknown about the process, such as exactly how memories get recalled when we remember something.

Basically, memory consolidation is critical to learning, and downtime is critical to memory consolidation.

A related issue is that the brain can pay attention to only a certain amount of information at any given time; downtime is occasionally needed to allocate energy for the integration of information rather than for perception. That's because the brain is an energy-conserving organ. When more energy is being used for one function, there is less energy available for other functions. To get a sense of how your own brain conserves energy, quickly read the next sentence and count the number of "Fs" in the following passage (again, go quickly):

FINISHED FILES ARE THE
RESULT OF YEARS OF SCIENTIFIC
STUDY COMBINED WITH THE
EXPERIENCE OF YEARS

How many did you find? Three? Four? Five?

There are six "Fs". Surprised? If you are like most people trying this, you probably noticed fewer. Your brain automatically focuses on the important "Fs", and ignores, for example, the ones in the common word *of*. It's not that you couldn't see these, but that your brain did not register them as important enough to notice! The brain simplifies nonessential and routine occurrences in order to save energy to use for learning important things to stay alive. Your brain therefore puts as many routine things on autopilot as possible.

Think back to when you first learned to drive a car. Every aspect of that process took a lot of effort. Just backing out of your driveway was an ordeal. First, you had to check the rearview mirror, adjust the mirror, think about putting the key in and turning the car on . . . then recheck the mirror, put the car in reverse gear . . . then triple-check the mirror . . . and so on. Now, you likely hop in the car, back out, drive to work, and seldom even remember exactly how you got there! You have achieved a state of *automaticity* for driving a car.

Your baby's brain has not yet achieved such automaticity for many processes because she is having so many experiences for the first time as she learns about the world. Downtime helps your baby's brain conserve energy to reflect on and remember newly learned information.

Sensory data floods into the brain very quickly, but making sense of the data takes time. A huge part of learning anything is not only the loading of new information into the visual, auditory, and other parts of the brain, but integrating existing information in useful new ways, says biologist James Zull, Ph.D., of Case Western Reserve University. More neurons in the brain are involved in the process of integration than in sensation. Reflection takes time. Thinking takes time.

Children who are given all of the wonderful experiences that I am recommending throughout this book will need some downtime to process and think about what they are learning.

## DOWNTIME FEEDS CREATIVITY

Being creative doesn't come from receiving more input; it comes from taking input already in our unique brain and tweaking it and then giving output in some other form: acting it out, painting it, doing it, or writing about it.

To do this also requires time and idleness. In fact, you should be glad when your child complains, "Mommy, I'm bored."

One morning while driving to school when I was a fifth-grade teacher, I heard on the car radio that the British actor George Sanders had committed suicide. I had always been fond of this distinguished gentleman, so I was saddened by the news. But when the announcer read his suicide note, I was amazed: "I am leaving because I am bored. I feel I have lived long enough." I couldn't get his words out of my head. This man had taken his life, by his own account, because he was bored!

In my classroom I had a long-established routine of writing a quote on the chalkboard each day to prompt the children to think about and respond to, either verbally or in writing. I wanted to use Sanders's farewell, though I wasn't sure it would be appropriate: *Dare I tell them this information about a suicide? Was this a topic for an eleven-year-old to even think about?*

I did, and it wound up as one of my favorite teaching days. We began talking about whose responsibility it is if you are bored. Every child in my class reported feeling bored fairly often—but they absolutely knew it was a condition they could control. They talked at length about how they got out of that mood. In fact, we wound up in a beautiful conversation about how much fun they have deciding what to do in order to not feel bored. They talked about building things, making up games and plays, drawing, and finding friends with whom to hang out. I knew in that moment that wonderful things come from deciding how to create adventure and pleasure all on your own. And I now believe these feelings of joy, accomplishment, and creativity can be gained at any age.

Creativity is something that neuroscience is just beginning to study. Nancy Andreasen, M.D., Ph.D., a professor of psychiatry at the University of Iowa College of Medicine, suggests that creativity arises largely from the association cortex (portions of the frontal, parietal, and temporal lobes that integrate sensory information). She's done PET scans of people's brains during free-association tasks. One can see where the brain is active during a creative exercise, but we still do not know how to develop the brain to elicit those responses. She believes, though, that creativity involves making totally new links between objects or concepts, bringing a fresh perspective to *existing* information.

Her suggestions for children include many of the things suggested in this book: less television exposure, more music, more outdoor activity.

*Barney.* This "service" is promoted as a way to keep children quiet and entertained while Mom goes about the business of grocery shopping.

But I say, *Why?* TVs in shopping carts is more than another troubling example of modern kids being "plugged in" continuously rather than enjoying real-world experiences—it's actually depriving them of the downtime their brains need. Being pushed in a cart or stroller is usually, for a child, veg-out time. His mom is not totally focused on him; she's running through her shopping list, selecting items, more making idle chatter with her child than initiating meaningful conversation: "I need some coffee. Coffee, coffee, where are you? Oh, they don't have my brand today. I wonder why." This frees the child to look at colors and shapes going by, watch people, or pay attention to nothing in particular. His brain can spend its time consolidating prior stimuli because it doesn't need to concentrate especially hard on what's in front of it. If the child is strapped into a cart with a TV set inches in front of him, however, he's *forced to pay attention.* He can't *not* watch. His brain is not allowed to turn "off" the active mode.

This is another important argument against VCR/DVD player units in cars, too.

*If you use child care:* Kids in group care don't necessarily get the chance to follow their natural rhythms. The emphasis is on a group, rather than individual pace or plan. So the children tend to all nap at the same time, eat at the same time, play at the same time, and so on. As a result, a child may wind up overstimulated on a given day with insufficient chance for downtime.

The problem can be compounded when parent and child are reunited. Not having been together all day, and having only limited time in the evening, Mom and Dad naturally want to make the most of it. The last thing you may think is best is to just let your child "veg." As one mom explained to me, "By the time I pick my daughter up, get her home, and feed her, it's almost seven p.m. That's my only time to teach her!" But if your child has already had a full day without a break for hanging out, the last thing she needs now is more stimulation.

Better: Cuddle on the sofa with a storybook. (Not a "Can you point to the red circle?" kind of book.) Take a walk carrying your child in a front carrier or backpack, or push her in a stroller. Give a piggyback ride. Sing songs. Hang out.

### 2. Watch for Signs of Overload

Babies and toddlers send us signals when they've had enough. Learn to follow the cues that your child gives. If your child gets "fussy" while doing something *you think* he needs to learn . . . stop. Come back at it another time. He's probably telling you that he needs a break or rest.

Signs of overstimulation in a baby:

- Looking away
- Refusing to follow your eye gaze (no joint attention)
- Becoming wriggly or restless
- Whining
- Crying

Signs of overstimulation in a toddler:

- Inability to focus on the task at hand
- Aggressive behaviors
- Hyperactivity—running from one activity to the next in a frenetic fashion
- Increased defiance
- Crankiness or resistance at bedtime
- Difficulty falling asleep, even when you know he's tired

### 3. Deprogram Your Day

Formal programs for infants and toddlers—kindermovement, kinder-music, kinderplay, kinderyoga—are increasingly popular. Are they a good idea? Sure, they can be a fun way to spend time with your child. Just don't enroll in classes for the higher claims they make. More guidelines:

*Red flag*: If it takes longer to fight through traffic jams to get to the fun baby yoga together-time class than the class itself lasts, it's probably not a wise choice. Instead, use the time you'd have spent driving to and from class and in the class to do something relaxing, freeing, and fun with your child at home.

*Red flag:* If your child resists and needs a lot of cajoling to get to a class, it's probably not worth the effort. Sign him up because the activity seems to match his natural interests and enthusiasms, not because it sounds enriching or his friends are all doing it. And drop it if he doesn't like it or resists going. Prodding makes it a chore for both of you, not fun.

*Red flag:* If the class intrudes on nap time, avoid it. Sleep is more important.

Parents often build their own enrichment programs by making field trips to museums, parks, and zoos or by setting up projects and learning materials at home with the goal of exposing their child to computer art, jungle animals, music, the history of American indigenous peoples, you name it. Again, any of these things can pass the time with your little one in an entertaining way. They can even provide some teaching moments. But you shouldn't feel like you have to package big learning moments into every day or even every week.

### 4. *Respect Sleep Needs*

Downtime can't be penciled in on a planner. It needs to occur naturally throughout the day, following your child's natural rhythms. A baby or toddler needs stimulation when she is awake and alert, and she needs relaxation, rest, and sleep when she has had enough.

It's no coincidence that a well-rested child whose day follows a routine is happier and better behaved. Scientists are now beginning to understand the biology of sleep. Getting enough sleep is essential for the brain to recharge its energy stores. Even if your child simply rests during nap time, this is a wonderful opportunity for him to relax, review what has happened during the day, and to calm himself.

Sleep—you can think of it as "extreme downtime"—is also known to improve memory and learning and boost problem-solving skills in adults. Increasingly, researchers believe that sleep plays a major role in early learning. In one experiment by Rebecca Gomez, Ph.D., and colleagues at the University of Arizona, fifteen-month-olds were exposed for fifteen minutes to an artificial language involving certain kinds of word strings. One group napped during the interval between first being familiarized with the words and being tested later. The control group did not nap. The groups were tested to see whether they had learned 1) the specific items in the language and/or 2) some abstract rules about how the language was set up. Although both groups learned some individual words, the nappers showed better ability at abstraction. That is, they had extracted a more *general pattern* from the specifics and were able to generalize their knowledge to similar cases. The implication is that perhaps sleep is needed to allow the brain to abstract the specifics of what has been learned and to then be able to apply that to more general instances. This is a crucial form of learning; important for learning of all kinds of skills, particularly about rules and language.

General tips:

- Try not to skip naps.
- Follow a routine for nap time and bedtime so these things happen at about the same time every day according to your child's rhythms.
- If nap time is a constant fight . . . pick your battles, and settle for resting (and maybe together, to give you a rest too).

The degree to which brains of all ages *need* downtime and relaxation in order to function well is just beginning to be understood. But it's clearly a central part of the puzzle that is the human brain. Give your child the gifts of time to dream, time to imagine, time to store memories, time to reflect on what he thinks about his own experiences, time to do not much at all except TO BE. A terrific side benefit of this kind of freedom is that it's *free*.

# 7

# Attention-Builders Little Ones Love

**Why we do an Attention activity . . .**
Attention activities provide practice for caregivers in how to encourage a child to carefully observe the world. Children can be taught to see the similarities and differences in objects and to focus their attention.

**Children with good visual discrimination and focus of attention learn better.**

Here are some activities that are fun for you and your baby and may help promote the development of a healthy attention system. I want to stress that these activities are for fun and are not predictive of any problem if your child does not seem interested when you play them. If this happens, come back and try them at a later time. Have fun!

Following each activity, there are short sections that give you additional information to understand *why* certain kinds of activities have been shown to be helpful in developing a young brain:

- The *Brain Link* tells you how the activity can influence your child's brain now.
- The *School Link* tells you the potential impact on later school readiness.
- *Variations* are related kinds of activities that serve a similar function.

*Note:* Because the visual system comes online so rapidly in the first six months, you will notice that many of my suggestions have to do with stimulating vision. Visual games play a key role very early in development and continue to be important later when your child enters a pre-reading stage. Visual refinement remains important because the visual system needs to be wired in an integrative way with the auditory system (sounds) in order for processes such as typical reading to take place.

## ATTENTION-BUILDERS FOR INFANTS (0 TO 6 MONTHS)

Be sure to use a very exaggeratedly slow, expressive kind of talk (known as "parentese") when you play to help capture your young baby's attention. To learn more about parentese, see page 227.

*Looking and Listening to a Book (most effective to start at 3 to 6 months)*
*It's never too early to start reading to a baby. But your aim here is not to "teach" your baby how to read, or count. In a more fundamental way, you'll be developing a habit of showing your child how to carefully observe the world. Your baby's attention to how much pleasure you find in books is one of the greatest benefits at this early age.*

> *Directions:*
> - Choose a board book with very simple, bright, and colorful photographs, such as one that introduces colors. I like to use a book of simple, clear photos called *Colors* (Howard Shooter, DK Publishing). Hold your baby in your lap with his back against your chest so he can see the beautiful bright colors as you turn the pages.
> - Name the colors. Label each object. Go slowly.
> - Point out details and how each object is used. For example, "This beautiful bluuue butterfly can flyyy away." Or, "Let's count the blue crayons: one . . . two . . . three . . . four."

*Brain Link:* Because bright colors capture your infant's attention, the part of the brain that wires up to be able to pay attention, to orient attention, and to maintain attention is being "exercised." This activity also stimulates the auditory connectors and parts of the brain that process and store language in the critical frontal and left temporal regions.

*School Link:* Develops a child's visual discrimination abilities; children who have good visual discrimination learn better. Also develops concepts including vocabulary that are prerequisites for learning.

### Face Games
*Directions:*
- For infants, begin by capturing your baby's eyes and very slowly form your mouth in a circle and say, "O-o-ooh. Can you say o-o-ooh?" Wait to see if your baby begins to form his mouth to say it.
- A few weeks later, say, "This is my happy face. Can you make a happy face?"
- Wait for your baby to respond or try to imitate you. Keep modeling this as you speak encouragingly.
- Your baby may study you carefully and then try to do the same. When this happens, delight in her accomplishment! Use slow, expressive language: "I seeee a haaaapppy baaaaby!"

*Brain Link:* Stimulates visual, auditory, and motor skills. The newly discovered mirror neuron system in the brain is known to activate automatically when children see others' expressions. This may lead to imitation behaviors that help children to learn.

*Variations:*
- Stick out your tongue and see if your baby does the same. Make other expressions, such as surprise (eyebrows lifted, mouth open) or mad (knitted brows).
- Hold your baby in front of a mirror so he can explore his own features. Say, "Seee the baaaby. I seee a happy baby!"

### Puppet Play
*Directions:*
- Place your baby in your lap where he feels secure, or place him in a bouncy seat facing you.

- Hold a simple puppet, such as an animal puppet, about eight to fifteen inches above or in front of the baby's face. Ideally, look for a puppet with high contrasts and colors such as black, white, and red (though by six months, your baby can see a full spectrum of colors). One of my favorites is by Carrington Brain Research (see www.babybrainbox.com).
- Wiggle the puppet to attract the baby's attention.
- Speak in parentese: "Hellloooo! I'mmm a puppet. My naaaame is [child's name]."
- Slowly move the puppet's head from side to side. Watch to see if your baby's eyes are following the puppet's movement.
- If your baby wants to grasp the puppet, allow him to do so. Physical contact with the puppet may increase his interest in the activity.
- Enjoy talking to your baby through the friendly puppet.

*Brain Link:* Stimulation of your baby's visual perception is enhanced with high-definition moving objects. This play stimulates cognitive, motor, and emotional connections in the brain.

*School Link:* In addition to promoting the development of an increased attention span, this activity boosts confidence, self-esteem, and language skills.

*Variations:*
- Expensive puppets aren't necessary. Make puppets out of paper bags, using colored markers to trace or draw the heads of animals or people from your child's books and attach them to the bag.
- Enlarge a photo of a family member or pet and glue it to a paper bag or a sock, to make a familiar friendly puppet.
- Animate familiar toy dolls or stuffed animals; though you can't make the mouths move, you can make them dance while talking, or make them kiss and hug your child.

### Peekaboo with Laundry
*Directions:*
- Take a basket of clean laundry to a place where you can safely put your baby down.
- As you fold a kitchen towel or burp cloth, cover your face momentarily. As you take it away, use very slow expressive baby talk to say, "Peeeekaboo, I seee youuuu!" "
- Smile and laugh as you repeat this several times with each item before you fold it.

*Brain Link:* Peekaboo begins to teach your child that just because he can't see something temporarily doesn't mean it's gone forever. This concept is called *object permanence.* It's a critical factor for brain changes in the early months. Knowing something exists when out of sight is the beginning stage of mental representation, a first step in many functions requiring memory.

*Variations:*
- Gently and very briefly cover your baby's eyes with the cloth.
- Or when you are dressing your baby, play peekaboo with his clothes. Say, "Where did [child's name] go? Where is my beautiful baby?" Uncover your eyes and smile: "Peekaboo! I found you [child's name]. You are such a beautiful baby!" Repeat several times.

## ATTENTION-BUILDERS FOR BABIES (6 TO 18 MONTHS)
### The Reaching-Out-and-Grasping Game
*This is a game that you can use as your baby gets older. By about six months of age, it's common to see infants become very attentive to objects that are within their reach.*

*Directions:*
- Hold your baby in your lap on her back.
- With a rattle 8 to 12 inches above your baby's head, slowly shake the rattle up and down or from side to side. Each of

these rattle movements will make a sound. When baby reaches for the rattle, put it in her grasp.

- As baby moves the rattle, say: "Shake."
- Talk to your baby using very slow, expressive language: "Loook at the priiitty raaattle." [Look at the pretty rattle.] Continue talking while interacting with your baby. If your baby cannot maintain a grasp, continue to move the rattle in interesting ways while talking to her. Let her try again to maintain her grasp for longer periods of time.

*Brain Link:* This game stimulates normal visual development and encourages connections in the motor strip as the baby reaches out for colorful items.

*School Link:* Promotes visual interest in the environment, the development of motor skills used later in grasping a crayon or pencil, and self-awareness.

### The Cheerios Book

You can find a whole series of these familiar-food-based board books in stores. (See "Best First Books," page 255). They're great interactive tools that help a child focus. Be sure to do this activity with a book and the corresponding food on hand.

*Directions:*

- Sit next to your child at a table or high chair. Spread a place mat* (see note at end of chapter) on the table and place an interactive book on top of it. Try using one of my favorites, *The Cheerios Animal Play Book* (Lee Wade, Little Simon), for this example. Take out a few Cheerios.
- On each page you'll see pictures with Cheerios and some empty circles. Place one of the Cheerios in each empty circle. Describe the picture to your child. Show her how to place the Cheerios on the book.

- If your child shows frustration when trying to place the Cheerios in the openings, guide her. If frustration builds, wait until your child is older to continue—remember, this is supposed to be fun!

*Brain Link:* Activates the sensory-motor strip and the connections to the frontal lobes that are known to activate when a person has to pay close attention to a task.

*School Link:* Exercises small muscle groups needed later for holding a pencil. Also develops vocabulary words and concepts needed later for reading.

*Variation:*
- On paper, draw your own pictures and objects that can have Cheerios added to represent small circular "parts." Examples: wheels on a bus, eyes, flower centers.

### Scoop and Fill

Babies never seem to tire of scooping and filling substances into containers. It's useful practice for self-feeding, too.

*Directions:*
- Spread a place mat on a table or the floor and sit beside your child. Place a divided dish, a spoon, and some cereal with large pieces (such as Cheerios) on the mat.
- Without talking, pour some cereal into one side of the divided dish.
- Say "Watch."
- Model picking up the spoon and scooping some cereal into the empty part of the dish.
- Then say, "Now it's your turn."
- As the child scoops the cereal, some may spill. Be patient about this and praise her accomplishment of getting most of the cereal from one side of the dish to the other.

*Brain Link:* Stimulates parts of the brain that process spatial reasoning (volume and quantity) in the sensory-motor strip and parietal lobe.

*School Link:* Scooping is a good tactile and eye-hand coordination skill. It develops spatial reasoning critical for math and science and develops hand-wrist coordination required to hold a pencil.

*Variations:*
- Provide opportunities for your child to fill buckets and other containers with sand or dirt.
- Allow your child to help in the kitchen by scooping foods that are fun to eat, such as peas or cooked corn.

### Hide and Find
*Directions:*
- While playing with your child on the floor, take one of her favorite toys and show it to her.
- Tell her to "Watch" [see page 82] while you hide it in your pocket or put it behind your back.
- Say, "Where did your toy go?" See if she will crawl to reach for it or point to its hiding spot.
- After playing, give her back her toy. Be sure to praise her for her attention and efforts.

*Brain Link:* Encourages crawling, which stimulates the shifting aspect of attention. This game also helps build self-confidence as the child discovers he has control over his movements and teaches object permanence.

### Bath Time Bliss
*Directions:*
- Make bath time fun with bubbles and toys.
- Be sure to talk a lot about what you are doing as you bathe and play with your child in the tub.
- You can also sing: "Rub a dub dub, [your child's name] is in the tub, yeah!"

*Brain Link:* This type of activity stimulates the part of the brain that processes spatial reasoning (such as volume, quantity, size, and shape).

*Variations:*
- Provide an older baby with a large pot of water, plastic cups, or other unbreakable kitchen items.
- Let him pour, splash, and play in the water. Be sure to label what he's doing.

*Note:* Never leave a child unattended around even a small container of water.

## ATTENTION-BUILDERS FOR TODDLERS (18 TO 36 MONTHS)
*Nifty Nesting*
   *Directions:*
- Spread out a place mat. Collect several different size plastic bowls, Tupperware containers, or measuring cups that nest inside one another.
- Say, "Watch." Demonstrate placing three or four of them inside one another, from largest to smallest. Then reverse, taking them apart, smallest one first.
- Say, "Now it's your turn. You do it."
- Wait. If there is a long delay or confusion, assist your child by guiding his choices. Add more and more to the stack to be nested as long as your child is having success.

*Brain Link:* Through repeated exposure to varying sizes (depths and widths) of otherwise similar objects, your child begins to create an understanding of volume. This concept is difficult to grasp, so children need frequent opportunities to "test" their new understandings. Be patient.

*School Link:* Sorting, sequencing, and classifying objects help children develop concept and problem-solving skills necessary for later reasoning in math (spatial awareness and problem solving) and improves patience.

*Variations:*
- Ask your child to sort the silverware in the dishwasher: forks, teaspoons, tablespoons (remove knives first).
- Encourage your child to find two or more balls around the house and ask him to pick up the bigger ball, and then the smaller ball.
- Find other objects you can arrange from biggest to smallest. Teach new descriptive vocabulary words as you play: big, bigger, biggest; small, smaller, smallest.
- Ask your child to sort the items by a different characteristic, such as color.

*Note:* When learning to compare objects, young children need to be able to focus exclusively on one aspect (attribute) at a time. So if you are focusing on the relative sizes of the objects, be sure they are all identical except for size, such as three spoons that are all silver but have different sizes. Or choose four balls that are identical in size, but of differing colors.

### Matching Size and Shape
*Directions:*
- Show your child three objects that are alike in size or style but with one that is slightly different from the other two, such as a pair of shoes and one that's different, or two little spoons and one big spoon.
- Describe how two of the objects are the same and how one is different.
- Hold up one of the matching pair. Say, "Find the one just like this one."
- Praise and encourage his efforts. If he's having trouble, guide him to the correct match as you describe how they are the same.

*Brain Link:* Matching activities help children learn how to discriminate, categorize, and group objects. These activities also develop concepts: same, different, size, shape, and color.

*School Link:* Promotes visual interest in the environment that later can be used to discriminate small differences in things like letters needed for reading and numbers in math.

*Variations:*
- Play the same game with three similar household objects in which two are the same color and one is a different color (such as blocks, socks, cups).

**Grocery Store Hunt**
*This scavenger hunt game keeps your child entertained at the store while boosting attention skills.*

*Directions:*
- When you come to a familiar aisle, such as the cereal aisle, play the "I Spy" game with your little helper.
- Say something like, "I spy a box that is orange, has a bee on the front, and starts with the letter C."
- Allow her to look for the clues you are giving. You can also give hints such as, "You're getting closer" or "You're almost there, just two more steps."

*Brain Link*: Stimulates the attention centers of the brain by encouraging a "search" behavior that takes what a child remembers about the object and matches it to what is available.

*School Link:* Begins an awareness of print that occurs in real-life contexts (called *environmental print*) and encourages the recognition of letters and symbols that represent pre-reading skills.

**Shape or Color Hunt**
*Directions:*
- Lie on your backs and "explore with your eyes."
- Play "I Spy" with shapes or colors. For example, point to the ceiling and say, "This ceiling is a square. Show me the square ceiling." Point into the air and trace "the square."

- Point to things with a similar shape: picture frames, doorways, and so on. You can also do this with colors.

*Brain Link:* Stimulates the visual processing areas of the brain that are used for fine discrimination of shape. Allows the child practice in "pattern matching" of shapes.

*School Link:* Focuses on the attributes of objects in the environment. Visual discrimination encouraged by searching for a "match" of a characteristic is a part of many cognitive tasks.

---

* The purpose of the place mat is to show the child *where* and *when* to pay attention. The place mat is a visible, concrete cue that you want your child to pay attention to the work (which is really *play*) that you are doing together. Consistently using the place mat eventually teaches a young child how to direct his attention. Show excitement and anticipation as you spread out the place mat. By doing this consistently, pleasure and anticipation become associated with paying attention. See also page 80.

# PART THREE

## Bonding

# 8

# "B" Is for Bonding: Why It Matters

Your baby cries. You glance at the glowing numbers on your clock in the dark. Three fifteen. You groan—and then stumble over to the cradle to lift up your squalling bundle. "There, there, sweetie," you croon as you cuddle him against your chest and prepare to feed him. "Don't worry, Mommy's here." You both settle into a big rocker, where you stroke his hair and hold him close. You can feel his body relax as he settles into the feeding.

When you respond to your baby in a prompt and loving way, you're doing far more for his brainpower than if you had bought him the fanciest new learning toy or read him the entire encyclopedia.

Your baby depends biologically on your responsiveness. But he's counting on more than the food and warmth you provide. Because he can't yet control his own feelings very well, your baby needs you to help him stay emotionally in balance. Though he was born with the capability for joy, sadness, fear, and many other feelings, he needs help regulating these emotional states so that they don't overwhelm his system. By calming him in times of distress and preventing him from becoming over-stimulated or overly afraid, you literally shape the construction of all other systems of his brain and influence the way his brain adapts to future situations.

Parents and caregivers have long known that warm, responsive early care helps infants and toddlers thrive. Now scientists are beginning to understand the biological mechanisms that explain why. It turns out that attachment, or bonding, is perhaps the most critical factor in future development. The quality of your child's first relationships has broader and longer-lasting effects than any other factor in your control.

## WHAT THE SCIENCE SAYS: BRAINS NEED HUGS

*"Somebody's got to be crazy about that kid. That's number one.*
*First, last, and always."*

—URIE BRONFENBRENNER, PH.D., DEVELOPMENTAL PSYCHOLOGIST

Your baby was born ready to connect. A minutes-old newborn often enters a state of quiet alertness, eyes wide open and face turned wonderingly toward the people who eagerly surround her. Dr. T. Berry Brazelton describes the newborn as "designed to capture new parents." Remember how a day-old newborn will show a preference for her parents' voices over others by turning toward them? This miraculous ability increases the feeling of connectedness between parents and baby at the beginning of their lifelong relationship of love.

An emotionally and physically healthy mother is drawn to her infant just as her infant is drawn to her. She feels a physical longing to smell, cuddle, rock, coo, gaze at, and be with her child. In turn, the baby responds with snuggling, sucking, clinging, and, later, with babbling and smiling. The mother's behaviors bring pleasure, soothing, and nourishment to the infant, and the infant's behaviors bring pleasure and satisfaction to the mother. It's during these shared, positive experiences that emotional attachment begins to develop.

This biologically propelled love song—a pattern of emotional communication between child and caregiver—creates bonding, or attachment. It's this bond between a baby and mother that drives infant development.

It works like this:

When a caregiver responds to the baby's practical and emotional needs in a consistent way, the baby starts to form a sense of trust. The limbic system, deep within the baby's brain, begins to develop. This system is responsible for a human's ability to form healthy emotional relationships. The limbic system also includes the structures that alert other brain systems to fearful or harmful situations. It is important for adult caregivers to soothe away sadness, discomfort, fear, and other upsetting emotions—signs of threats to the brain's drive for survival—and provide the baby with a safe "home base." This enables the baby to divert his focus away from the business of survival; he doesn't have to constantly monitor the environment to check whether he is in or out of harm's way. Instead, his energy is fully available to move on, wiring the rest of his brain in a normal, healthy manner.

Hour after hour, day after day, the little repeated interactions between baby and parent become encoded in the brain. Through consistent care, a child learns to expect love and responsiveness from the main adult presences in his life who provide them. As a result, he feels securely attached to them and has a generally positive view of life so far!

What sounds simply warm and fuzzy creates demonstrable changes in the brain and nervous system. Emotion affects attention (the ability to focus and attend), and attention, in turn, affects learning. How secure a baby feels therefore influences all the development that follows, including:

- Intellectual potential (and how well a child does in school)
- Language development
- How feelings are regulated (self-control)
- The development of empathy, trust, and motivation
- How a conscience, identity, self-confidence and self-esteem are acquired
- The ability to cope with stress and bounce back from setbacks
- The ability to make and sustain future relationships, including friendships and future love relationships.

All this starts with something as simple as a hug!

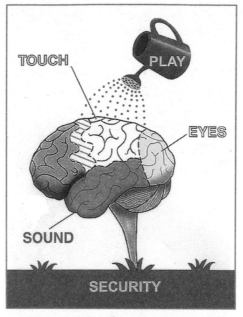

*Figure 6. What the growing brain needs.*

The growing brain is influenced by input from touch, sound, vision, and a generous sprinkling of play—just the way that rain, oxygen, and TLC nourish a plant. But without deep roots in nutrient-rich soil the plant could not thrive. Security (represented by the grass) is the base medium for growing a healthy brain. You can have sun all day long and water a plant like crazy, but without any soil for the seed to grow in, the results would be very compromised.

## MYTHS ABOUT BONDING

The very word "bonding" sometimes causes parents confusion and unnecessary distress. So before I explain how hugging and cuddling pave the way for your child's success in third grade or at Harvard, let me clarify a few common misconceptions.

### MYTH #1: THAT BONDING IS A MAGICAL EVENT THAT HAPPENS WITHIN THE FIRST MINUTES OF BIRTH

Parents often worry that, if there was a separation at birth (for example, if the baby was in the neonatal intensive care unit, the mom was out of sorts after a C-section, or the dad was in the military halfway around the world), then they've missed a one-time opportunity.

Bonding is not an instantaneous event that occurs only at delivery. It's true that many parents do report falling in love with their babies from the first moments they experience this new life in their arms. Ambivalence is not an uncommon reaction, however, especially if the birth was traumatic or the parents don't feel prepared for the parenting journey ahead.

Bonding refers to the *ongoing relationship* of attachment between child and caregiver. Attachment grows out of thousands of interactions between a child and her primary caregivers. It builds across time.

MYTH #2: THAT BONDING CAN ONLY TAKE PLACE
BETWEEN MOTHER AND BABY, OR BETWEEN PARENT AND BABY
There are good reasons that the mother-child bond is often described as ideal: It began long before birth, after all, while the two shared blood, nutrients, and hormones as the baby grew inside the mom. She could feel her baby move within her and her baby could hear his mother's heartbeat and voice. Right from birth, her breast milk is custom-tailored to meet her baby's changing nutritional needs, at times on a minute-by-minute basis. The suckling baby's body then releases a hormone that eventually signals satiety and sleep in the baby; meanwhile the suckling causes the mother to produce prolactin, which has a tranquilizing effect on her. Pediatrician William Sears, M.D., quips, "It's as if the mommy puts the baby to sleep and the baby puts the mommy to sleep."

Of course most fathers and adoptive parents fall deeply in love with their children as well, and vice-versa. And with so many mothers of infants working, loving attachment relationships often involve other caregivers. Attachment can occur between babies and any of the individuals primarily responsible for them.

For proper brain development, what's essential is that the child knows there's at least one person he can rely on for consistent, predictable, and loving care. It doesn't have to be Mom or Dad, but there has to be *at least one person*. And it should be the same person every day, particularly during infancy.

For a baby, the immediate environment is all about relationships. The key people in her life are her gateway to everything. Typically a baby only establishes a handful of attachments. The window of opportunity for optimal attachment and bonding is from birth (actually from before birth) through the first three years of life, and the earliest attachments are typically formed within the first seven months of life.

## THIS IS YOUR BABY'S BRAIN ON STRESS

*"What you teach from birth to three is what will matter most to me."*

The opposite of security, to a baby, is stress. Stress can be anything from being picked up by someone unfamiliar (which is not in itself a damaging experience for a baby) to outright abuse and neglect. Every human being experiences some degree of stress; it's pretty much an unavoidable part of life. The duration and intensity of one's stressful experiences are what make the difference between healthy development and damaging trauma.

In response to any kind of stress, chemicals are released in the brain that influence neural activity and steer the way that the body responds. The initial *stress response* affects both immediate behavior and, in a baby, can also affect long-term brain functioning.

Consider a crying baby. Her diaper is dirty and she's uncomfortable. As her discomfort grows—and she can't do anything about it herself—she grows more distressed. Aroused, her sympathetic nervous system kicks in: her heart rate, blood pressure, and breathing increase. She begins to cry. As she does, her brain responds to the stress by releasing *adrenaline* to mobilize her energy stores and alter her blood flow in order to attend to the stressor. A brain hormone called *cortisol* is also produced and released into the system. It's the brain's way of mobilizing resources to face the stressor—ideally for a brief period.

Now the baby's father picks her up, changes her diaper, and soothes her. The baby settles and, cuddled in his warm embrace, starts to examine a fabric rattle he has handed her. The stress hormones recede. Now oxytocin and vasopressin, hormonal substances that work as chemical messengers in the brain, increase. Animal studies have shown that levels of these substances rise in response to socially pleasant sensory experiences, such as touches and smells.

But what if he didn't pick her up right away? Her stress response would persist a bit longer. She's out of emotional balance, overwhelmed by her feelings and crying harder. Her brain is in survival mode. Cortisol spikes and reduces her functioning to a primal level, unable to focus on anything other than sending out distress signals and looking for a response. Long-term negative effects are unlikely in this example, though, because she's learned from her previous contacts with her parents that when she is dirty and hungry, someone will come. And sure enough, in a few minutes when her father hangs up the phone, he comes to reassure her. Although she is very agitated, she eventually settles as her stress response fades. Infrequent occasional release of stress hormones, as in this example, can have beneficial effects that actually protect the brain from trauma.

Next imagine that nobody came to pick up the crying baby. And that a pattern of delayed or indifferent response happened day after day after day. When brain chemistry is kept on "high alert" for long sustained periods, cortisol levels remain persistently elevated—long after the initial stressor ends. During the time that large amounts of cortisol are released, the brain is not as capable of learning or retaining new information effectively.

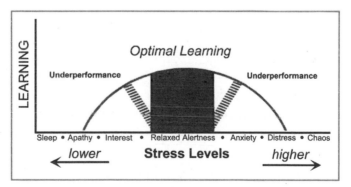

*Figure 7. Gauge of impact of stress on learning performance.*
Your child's brain is maximally capable of learning when your child is alert and yet relaxed.

High amounts of cortisol in the brain wreak all kinds of havoc. It can literally turn on or turn off certain genes that affect the way the brain reacts to future stress. Among the genes affected are the ones that regulate the number of receptors for cortisol in the brain (known as the *glucocorticoid receptor gene*) and the gene that regulates myelin, the "insulation" substance that enables more efficient transmission of signals between the brain cells (the *myelin basic protein gene*). Elevated levels of stress hormones can suppress immune system function and hormones related to growth, too.

High levels of cortisol also cause structural brain damage. Recent research shows that neglect, abuse, and prolonged stress are associated with significant reductions in the volume of the hippocampus (the part of the brain involved in memory and learning), the amygdala (the part of the brain involved in emotion processing), and the corpus callosum (the fiber pathway that connects the two sides of the brain). A baby experiencing prolonged, intense stress may also withdraw: Eventually he stops crying because he feels hopeless that crying will bring a response. He shuts down. Yet his stress hormones such as cortisol will remain high.

The human stress response is complex, with reactions that range from hyper-arousal (the "fight or flight" response) to dissociation (the "freeze and surrender" response) when fighting or fleeing is not possible. A baby cannot fight or flee. And when the brain activates the systems associated with alarm or dissociation, use-dependent changes in the brain systems involved in producing the stress response result. It's these cumulative changes that can affect emotional and cognitive abilities in a growing child.

If a child's brain doesn't learn to respond normally to ordinary stress, he will be less likely to focus on learning other things. Instead, the stressed child is kept on hair-trigger alert constantly. Eventually, if the situation is prolonged, the slightest stress can cause hyperactivity, anxiety, and impulsive behavior. The brain is preoccupied with its own safety. For example, if a "trigger alert" child is accidentally bumped in a school line, that child may overreact and strike out at the child who accidentally bumped him. His life experiences have *taught him* that his best option is to fight back. Instead of viewing this child as "dysfunctional," consider that his brain has actually adapted nicely to *his* world and is doing the required response in order to escape threat. In reality, it was only a mindless bump, but his brain has learned very well to respond immediately and with aggression.

The point of this series of examples isn't to say that a baby should never cry! Crying is an important way that babies communicate with their parents. The stress has to be *significant and prolonged* to produce the kind of effects that show up in a hypervigilant school-aged child. But you can see how important ordinary, responsive, loving care is in the context of how the brain is shaped.

## LESS STRESS: EVERYDAY EXAMPLES

You don't need to do anything the slightest bit extraordinary in order to give your baby the benefits of less stress. Bonding is not so much a matter of providing "extras" as of eliminating unwanted extras in the form of stress and anxiety, and instead allowing time for close contact and connection. Consider the following two scenarios in a typical pediatrician's waiting room:

Mom "A" walks in carrying her six-month-old in a car seat. She puts the seat down to sign in. While waiting, she dangles a toy in front of her baby and gently rocks the seat with her foot, while continuing a cell-phone conversation she'd begun in the car. When the nurse calls mom and baby in, she carries the seat into the exam room, then removes and undresses her baby, who begins to fuss and cry. As the baby is placed on the hard examining table for her shot, cries turn to screams. Afterward, the mom picks her up, comforts her, dresses her, places her back in the car seat, and dials Dad on her phone to give him an update while she checks out and leaves.

Now, Mom "B" walks in, also carrying her baby in a car seat. She sets it down, then takes her baby out and holds her on her hip as she signs in. While waiting, they play peekaboo with the baby's blankie, then the mom picks up a magazine. "Oh oh," she says as the baby tries to grab it. "Let's look at the pictures. Look, a baby like you!" In the examining room, the mom undresses her baby and asks if she can hold her

care that her brain is necessarily going to be severely disadvantaged. To quote a phrase from the manuscript published at the conclusion of one of the earliest conferences on early brain development research in 1997, *Rethinking the Brain*, RISK IS NOT DESTINY. Many kids who spend *fewer* than two years in an orphanage are mentally healthy, according to a 2005 University of Minnesota study tracking 2,300 children adopted from other countries in the 1990s; warehouse-style institutions, also once common in parts of the former Soviet Union, are not as typical today and were never the case everywhere. Generally, however, the younger the child is when adopted and the less time that child spends overall in institutional care, the more likely the odds of a successful outcome. Clearly, *timing matters*, and the sooner one intervenes with excellent care, the better the result. Simple interventions work, as we see from very young children who are in excellent foster care. They tend not to show such poor outcomes because they are more likely to benefit from being held and responded to consistently by an attentive primary caregiver.

I think it is important to state directly that I am not telling you to avoid all or any specific adoption of an orphaned child. Rather, it is just critical to know the roots of the challenges that may lie ahead. Be prepared to be active in your pursuit of effective therapies for such children.

## What Behaviors Do Secure Children Demonstrate as They Grow?

*0 to 6 months:* An infant's developing **attachment** to his primary caregiver causes him to smile and make eye contact that expands from a few seconds to a few minutes. During this period, a baby is fascinated by his parent's face and makes happy noises to attract and hold his parent's attention.

*7 to 9 months:* A baby usually begins to experience **stranger anxiety**. While this may seem like a contradiction, stranger anxiety confirms the strength of a baby's attachment to the parent. It's this attachment that defines everyone else as a "stranger." Babies demonstrate stranger anxiety by becoming upset when someone new approaches, usually clinging closer to the parent for reassurance and perhaps even crying. Without a strong attachment to a primary caregiver, there are no strangers; everyone is of equal emotional importance or unimportance.

*9 to 15 months:* Most children experience **separation anxiety**, which emerges from the baby's growing awareness that she is a separate person from her parent. Like stranger anxiety, it's a testament to the strength of the child's attachment to her primary caregivers. A range of behavioral reactions may be seen. Some children cry in protest and cling to the parent; others temporarily withdraw from the world until the parent returns; still others protest by becoming angry and aggressive. While these behaviors may seem troublesome at the moment, they are proof that the work of attachment has proceeded normally to this point.

During this same period, toddlers begin their voyages of discovery. It's a time of joyfully discovering the world and refining motor skills. A toddler will repeatedly go to the edge of her comfort zone and return to "check in" with her parent before venturing out farther.

Other signs of healthy attachment include showing pleasure in accomplishments, accepting comfort from others, and beginning self-comforting skills with the aid of objects, such as the well-known security blanket.

*15 to 24 months:* Exploration of the world increases the toddler's awareness of being separate from his mother. At this time, attempts by the toddler to balance a growing need for independence with a continuing need for attachment causes him to **shadow and dart**. Shadowing refers to a child's behavior of following the parent practically everywhere, while darting refers to the child's rapid movements both toward and away from the parent.

*24 to 36 months:* The final building blocks of attachment are put in place as children realize **self-constancy** and **object constancy**. Self-constancy is the child's experience that she is the same person across different emotional states and situations. Object constancy is the child's experience of others as predictable and available. Much of object constancy comes from a child's mental images of others. Both self- and object constancy serve to quell separation anxiety, as well as strengthen a child's ability to delay gratification and accept discipline.

## POSTPARTUM DEPRESSION AND BONDING

Even though as human beings we're genetically programmed for bonding and attachment, it's not a guaranteed, automatic experience. It's more accurate to say that a child is born with the *potential* for attachment—but it's the nature, quantity, pattern, and intensity of early life experiences that make it happen.

Unfortunately, not all mothers are emotionally healthy, and they, therefore, are unwilling or unable to respond to their babies consistently. Other moms who have been very healthy may, after giving birth, display unusual moods and behavior. An example of this is when a mother has postpartum depression. Geraldine Dawson, Ph.D., professor of psychology at University of Washington, has shown that infants of depressed mothers are more withdrawn and less active, have shorter attention spans, and have reduced activity in frontal brain regions known to be involved in regulation of emotions when compared with infants of nondepressed mothers. Depression results in a "disconnect" from the anticipated mother-child bond. Because an infant's brain begins to wire up in *relationship to other brains*, there is a resulting lessening of normal brain activation in the child.

The good news is that, when mothers' depression was treated or went into remission before the babies reached six months of age, the babies did not show lasting behavioral or cognitive impairments. If you as a parent or caregiver are experiencing depression, don't hesitate to ask for help. Researchers are not yet entirely sure why some mothers get depressed and others don't, but it's not your fault and you can help your child by getting early treatment for your depression.

## REALITY CHECK! COMMON-SENSE RESPONSIVE CARE
*"All things in moderation."*

If you're starting to feel anxious that you should be holding your baby more and responding to her before she can utter a peep, I want you to set this book down and take a long, deep breath before picking it back up again. The simple fact that you're reading this kind of information indicates that you're probably the kind of parent who cares deeply about your child and are *naturally* providing the attentive love that's necessary to build secure attachments. Most parents who love their babies, hold them, and respond promptly and consistently to their needs have secure children who grow up to ready for school and beyond.

You can have a bad day! You can wake up a cranky mom after a sleepless night, let your baby wail in her bouncy seat while you grab a quick shower—and it won't hurt your baby one bit. Daily life is full of bumps and snags, and it probably does your baby good to learn to roll with a few of them. What's damaging to a developing brain is a *pattern* of negligent experiences, day after day. It all comes back to repetition.

If the overall tenor of your interactions with your baby is loving and responsive, featuring lots of touch and comforting routines, you are giving her exactly the nourishment she needs.

## DEVELOPING BONDING: WHAT *YOU* CAN DO AT DIFFERENT AGES

Because young children differ in when they reach developmental milestones, I strongly recommend that instead of focusing on what a child does or does not do (that is largely out of your control), that you focus on what YOU, as the caregiver, can actually do to promote bonding with your child. The particulars of how to do many of the behaviors listed in this chart will be explained in the four chapters that follow.

| Infants: 0–6 Months |
| --- |
| Deliberately hold the infant often vs. having infant in an infant carrier seat. Kiss, hug, and hold infant routinely throughout the day. |
| Encourage skin-to-skin contact. Massage infant on a regular, daily basis (e.g., bath time, bedtime, etc.). |
| Hold infant during feeding vs. propping a bottle. |
| Respond quickly and predictably to infant's cries (i.e., come routinely within a few minutes and begin comforting crying infant verbally in a reassuring tone on the way to picking him up). |
| Try to interpret the meaning of various types of cries (e.g., hunger, change of diaper, tired, boredom/need for stimulation). |

Establish consistent routines for feeding, bathing, and sleeping.

Deliberately introduce infant to a variety of new "feels" (i.e., new textures, temperatures, etc.) while verbally labeling for infant.

Provide a variety of objects to feel and explore with hands, mouth, and feet while verbally labeling for infant.

Act sooner rather than later in making changes that will improve the quality of care provided for the infant with an emphasis on consistency of the same caregiver (do not delay until a more convenient moment in time that may be months, not weeks, away, such as when summer comes, after the holiday period, etc.). This sense of urgency relates to the recognition that there is a limited period of time during early childhood for maximum response (windows of opportunity).

## Babies: 6–18 Months

Deliberately hold the baby often vs. having baby in a baby carrier seat. Kiss, hug, and hold baby routinely throughout the day.

Encourage skin-to-skin contact. Massage baby on a regular, daily basis (e.g., bath time, bedtime, etc.).

At the beginning of the stage (6 to 9 months), hold baby during feeding vs. propping a bottle.

Respond quickly and predictably to baby's cries (i.e., come routinely within a few minutes and begin comforting crying baby verbally in a reassuring tone on the way to picking him up).

Try to interpret the meaning of various types of cries (e.g., hunger, change of diaper, tired, boredom/need for stimulation).

Develop predictable routines for bedtime, mealtime, getting dressed in the morning, etc. so that the baby can anticipate what happens when and knows what to expect.

Introduce baby to a variety of new "feels" (i.e., new textures, temperatures, etc.) while verbally labeling for baby.

Provide a variety of objects to feel and explore with hands, mouth, and feet while verbally labeling for baby.

Slow activity level down periodically—less rushing, calmer atmosphere.

Respond predictably when faced with recurring action by baby.

Develop physical cues (e.g., bringing baby's arms in close to baby's body as in cocooning) that can signal the baby and help to calm him/her.

Label feelings, emotions and experiences as baby's behaviors change (e.g., "Are you feeling *tired* and sleepy now?" "You seem so *proud* of yourself." "That is hard to do; it's OK to feel *frustrated*.").

Deliberately act positively with the baby showing both love and concern (e.g., smile, hug, make direct eye contact, praise, and show pleasure and thankfulness).

Deliberately look for child care that ensures low child/caregiver ratios of: one caregiver to no more than three infants (and total maximum group size limited to nine); one caregiver to five or fewer toddlers.

## Toddlers: 18 Months–3 Years

At special times during the day, take the time to hold and hug the toddler.

Encourage skin-to-skin contact. Massage toddler on a regular, daily basis (e.g., bath time, bedtime, etc.).

Extend touch routines like massage to engage in games like "drawing" on one another's backs.

Consistently reassure toddler when having failures, setting limits, and clear expectations.

Differentiate between a serious cry for help vs. a small "ouch."

Maintain routines established in earlier stages for bedtime, mealtime, getting dressed in the morning, etc. so that the toddler can anticipate what happens when and knows what to expect.

Clearly state and even make lists of routines throughout the day while explaining why they are important.

Encourage toddler to explore a wide range of objects and experiences (while ensuring toddler's basic safety needs).

Resist temptation to over-schedule toddler's time and slow activity level down periodically — less rushing, calmer atmosphere.

Review and model expectations on a regular basis as needed for reminder and reinforcement; respond predictably when faced with recurring action by toddler.

Develop physical cues (e.g., bringing toddler's arms in close to toddler's body as in cocooning) that can signal the toddler and help to calm him/her.

Label feelings, emotions, and experiences as toddler's behaviors change (e.g., "Are you feeling *tired* and sleepy now?" "You seem so *proud* of yourself." "That is hard to do; it's OK to feel *frustrated*.").

Deliberately act positively with the toddler showing both love and concern (e.g., smile, hug, make direct eye contact, praise, and show pleasure and thankfulness).

Make rewards for favorable behavior from toddler less external (e.g., sweet foods or toys) and more internal (e.g., more story time and backrubs).

Begin to label, describe, and model some favorite rituals (religious, cultural, or family).

Establish habit of lap reading together. Turn TV off, especially during times together.

Deliberately look for child care that ensures low child/caregiver ratios of: one caregiver to no more than three infants (and total maximum group size limited to nine); one caregiver to five or fewer toddlers; one caregiver to ten three-year-olds (total maximum group size limited to twenty).

# 9

# Responsive Care: Tuning In to One Another

- Will too much holding spoil a baby?
- How do I know what my baby really needs?
- Should I pick up my baby every time he cries?
- How do I best respond to a toddler's needs?
- How else can I encourage a "secure brain"?

It's a cliché so true I wish it were printed in five-inch-high letters on every newborn's hospital discharge papers: *You cannot spoil a young baby.*

You can't. Not by holding your baby too long, not by picking her up too often, not by nursing her when she seems to want it, not by going to her aid when she cries.

In fact, these activities set the stage for a *brighter* baby.

## WHAT THE SCIENCE SAYS: FORM POSITIVE LINKS

A newborn is simply too biologically immature to be spoiled. The reason goes back to the order in which the brain develops. The brain regions of the frontal lobes that allow a person to deliberately control and manipulate others are housed in the cortex (the wrinkled "tissue paper" part of the brain) and won't be fully functional until later in life. This means it's physically impossible for a young infant to strategize and plan how to manipulate parents through crying—which is what some grandmas erroneously believe when they warn that new parents are going to encourage manipulation by responding too swiftly. In order to learn that kind of higher-order thinking, more elemental brain structures need to develop first—and, ironically, it is partly the experience of repeated, attentive care that can help to optimally develop these early structures to then allow future higher-order skills!

The brain constantly searches for pattern and meaning. It creates meaning by forming *associations* between things that either occur together or happen closely in time one right after another. In fact, this type of learning (called associative learning) continues all through life and represents a large amount of what each of us "knows." Back in 1903, a researcher named Ivan Pavlov demonstrated that animals of many types could associate the arrival of food with an event. In Pavlov's now classic experiment, he would pair the ringing of a bell with giving a dog food right afterward. The dog soon learned to anticipate getting food (by salivating) just from hearing the bell ring by itself, even when no food was given. The sound of the bell and the receipt of food had become linked.

Your child's brain forms basic associations from birth. For example, he quickly learns to make a connection between discomfort (hunger; the cold wetness of a dirty diaper; loud, sudden noises) and the relief he experiences when some caring adult quickly responds to a cry and solves the problem. He builds into his brain *a pattern* that predicts, "When I am hungry, someone will feed me." Or, "When I am cold, someone will warm me." Or, "When I am distressed, someone will comfort me." Searching for patterns among experiences helps the brain organize the flood of incoming sensations. The goal: To better predict *what will happen next*. Being able to make such predictions—including predicting whom you can count on and whom you can't—is key to survival. Basic trust boils down to the brain determining, "This person behaves in a pattern, and I recognize that pattern. Because I know the pattern, I can have some control and know what is likely to happen to me."

Rather than spoiling your baby, your quick, responsive care actually diminishes crying because the infant learns to detect a pattern of caring response. Reacting to your baby swiftly, lovingly, and consistently therefore produces a positive connection of response to a real need, not spoiling.

Now, can you spoil a two-year-old? You bet! There are physiological differences between the brains of an infant and a toddler. As your baby grows, the frontal lobes are increasingly functional and have had plenty of experiences that allow your baby to put together more complex associations, including the ability to figure out how to manipulate a situation in order to get what he wants.

## A Jenny Story: Making Brain Links

When my daughter Jenny was still very young and had been home from the intensive care nursery for a maybe five months, I began to notice an odd behavior that I later realized was an example of association. Because her Daddy read his newspaper at his office each day, we did not receive a daily paper at home. We had decided that each Saturday night, despite the difficulty of finding an appropriate caregiver for Jenny, we would try to do so, and go to dinner and a movie as a routine to refresh ourselves. One of us would pick up a weekend paper and usually by 4:00 p.m. or so on Saturday afternoon, we'd bring in the newspaper and search for the movie of the week.

Soon every time Jenny saw a newspaper, it seemed she'd kick up a real fuss! I began to experiment. Yes, sure enough, she had formed a direct association between the sight of the newspaper and the fact that we would be leaving her, if only for a short time. Talk about the silver lining of a tantrum: It was through moments of discovery such as this that I realized, despite the grim predictions of the doctors that Jenny would be severely retarded and would not be able to think or function, that I *knew* . . . she was in fact a bright, very smart little girl.

### GOOD BONDING IS GOOD DISCIPLINE

Keeping on an even keel—what scientists call *regulation*—gives a baby a solid framework for future development. Your baby can't yet regulate himself; that is, he has no internal regulation, which is why he relies on you to do it for him externally. Parents provide external regulation both through responsive care and a structured environment. What do I mean by structure? It has several ingredients, including:

- **Routine actions.** Regular eating and sleeping times, places, and approaches are an important part of teaching self-regulation. When you provide support and structure, brain and body systems learn to recognize these smooth, predictable patterns and adjust accordingly with calm, secure assurance. A child who gets accustomed to the "feeling" of such smooth patterns comes to prefer this feeling. Over time, this helps your baby better learn to regulate himself. This is actually the beginning of discipline, which is the process of teaching self-control, or self-regulation.

- **Reasonable limits.** By reasonable, I mean age-appropriate. Every one-year-old reaches for the TV remote "one more time" after you say, "No," because this is how the brain is driven to learn, by repeated testing. (*The last time I did this, Mom said no. What will happen this time? What if I touch only one button this time?*) Every two-year-old has tantrums, partly because they developmentally want more things than they are physically capable of. Knowing what's "normal behavior" for a child at a given age helps you to guide behavior in constructive ways. Instead of punishing a toddler who can't resist an intriguing object, you need to move it out of reach or move the toddler out of the situation.

  Knowing that there are reasonable limits and age-appropriate expectations eventually builds in *internal* controls that feel good to a child because they are familiar. In fact, because the brain prefers familiarity, children who grow up with rules and limits tend to prefer that kind of environment when they reach school age, and so they are better behaved. Kids who live in chaos learn to prefer chaos—they need it because it feels familiar to their brain, and may try to re-create chaos in the classroom.

- **Consistency.** Toddler discipline guidebooks are full of ways you can set reasonable limits: Set up an environment that minimizes the need to forever say, "No" and "Don't." Hold fast to your word when you must intervene and try to stay consistent. Pick your battles. Be sure your requests and rules are reasonable and understandable by your toddler. Above all, my main advice about discipline from a brain perspective is that you *do* set limits—gently, gradually, age-appropriately, and *consistently*—because knowing boundaries reinforces feelings of security.

- **Child involvement.** One way to do this is to guide choices within those limits. "Do you want to wear your red PJs or your blue ones?" "You can take one stuffed animal to day care." Your external controls can lead to naturally evolving internal controls in your child's brain.

## THE BRIGHT IDEAS: RESPONSIVE CARE

*"Parents who fall in love with their children have children who fall in love with them."*

— BARBARA BOWMAN, PH.D., ERIKSON INSTITUTE

### 1. Tune In: Your Baby Has a Lot to Say

Getting to know your baby is partly of guesswork and trying different things over time, but mostly it comes from tuning in. This simply means being attentive and observant, and learning to read your baby's nonverbal cues. Even though he cannot speak, he's telling you things all the time. Your baby uses body language, expression, and vocal tone, to communicate. In fact, the majority of all human communication is nonverbal, even among adults. A newborn can't yet understand your words, and yet his brain is picking up reams of subtle information from you—in the way you lift your eyebrows or turn your lips upward when you smile, how firmly your arms are holding him, in the tilt of your head or the pitch of your voice.

Both of you are using this "conversation" to adjust your reactions to one another. Child development specialist Daniel Siegel, M.D., associate clinical professor of psychiatry at UCLA, calls these interactions the "dance of attunement"—the dance of tuning in. As in a waltz or a tango, each person learns to adjust his moves to the other. A wonderful 1998 Siegel video presentation shows this: A mother and her four-month-old infant are shown on a split screen; the viewer can simultaneously see close-ups of both faces. On one half of the screen, the mother sings "Twinkle, Twinkle Little Star" in an animated, engaging way with her eyes wide open, excitement in her voice and bits of broad smiles breaking through between phrases. As she lovingly sings, her baby's response on the other half of the screen shows the child is mirroring the exact emotion and level of arousal to match that of her mother. When Mom smiles, the baby lights up and she returns the smile in both her face and her eyes! Next, the mother is instructed to stop singing and flatly stare without expression at her child. The happy scene immediately changes. The infant becomes clearly distressed. She attempts to reconnect to her mom, but can't. She starts to squirm and her behaviors become disorganized. She starts to move in her infant seat and darts her head and eyes from side to side searching for relief. Finally, at the moment that her mother reconnects again and resumes her prior connected, loving engagement, the infant also reconnects and is attentive and content once again.

The amount and type of each party's response creates a *circle of communication* in which the child or the adult matches the emotional connection equally. With repeated experiences, as a child and an adult learn to control and direct their emotional responses, a "dance" that goes both ways is set up and the love relationship grows. As a parent, you can use careful observation to help you tune into your baby's state and maximize the use of calm times for bonding. Here are just some of the nonverbal cues you can read in your baby and use to guide your interactions:

- Turns head away: "I'm tired of playing now, leave me alone."
- Smacks lips: "I'm getting hungry." (Tip: It's best to feed your baby when she shows these early signals of hunger; by the time she's bawling, she's overly agitated and more difficult to calm.)
- Coos: "I hear you talking and I'm talking back. Say something else, Mom!"
- A shift from relaxed "latched-on" eye contact to a look of concern and an overflow of body movements: "I'm feeling

anxious and concerned; something is happening . . . what's going on?"
- Freeze mode (awake but not moving arms and legs at all—eyes shifting): "I'm really afraid and confused."

### 2. Understand Your Baby's Temperament

No two babies are alike. Some are more difficult to soothe than others. One baby will seem serious and watchful much of the time, another more sociable. Although your baby's behavior is in part shaped by his experiences, it's also shaped by the temperament he was born with.

Temperament is the set of inborn, quite stable traits that your child displays. These traits are thought to be "hard-wired" into the brain. They are apparent almost from birth, and tend to stay with a person all through life. How a person's temperament interacts with their upbringing is what creates a unique personality.

It's useful to think about temperament in raising your child for several reasons:

- Simply knowing that your child *has* a unique temperament, right from birth, helps you avoid guilt or blame when your baby doesn't behave exactly as you would like.
- Understanding your child's individual temperament allows you to adjust your interactions with him accordingly and parent more effectively.
- Recognizing that you, too, were born with a unique temperament can also color your parenting. Some parents "fit" with their child more easily than others for this reason.

Temperament is usually generalized into three categories, first identified by husband-and-wife psychologists Alexander Thomas and Stella Chess based on a longitudinal study begun in the 1950s. They are:

- Easy
- Difficult (also called Intense, Active, Spirited, Uninhibited, or Low-reactive)

- Slow-to-Warm-up (also called Cautious, Slow-to-Adapt, Inhibited, or High-reactive).

It's interesting, isn't it, that everyone understands what's meant by what an "easy" child is—rarely are other labels used for this type—but that we use so many different terms to describe the more challenging ones! Happily, the majority of kids, about 40 percent, are easy. The next largest group is made up of children who don't fit neatly into any of the three categories. As anyone who has wandered into a classroom full of toddlers can see, there are more than three different types of children.

Nine different traits are believed to shape temperament. Each trait is associated with a spectrum of behaviors. This means that a child isn't all one extreme or another but typically somewhere in the middle. Your baby may show a high degree of some traits but low degrees of others. I'm not a big fan of charts or lists of this type because most parents don't find the charts particularly useful in terms of helping them to know *what they can do* based on the information they've just learned in the chart. But I include a summary mainly to show you how variable temperament can be—in order to help you understand and appreciate the unique child you've got.

The nine traits are:

- Activity level: The child's usual speed. Is your baby squirmy and always in motion, or watchful and quiet?
- Distractibility: The degree of concentration and attentiveness displayed when other stimuli interrupt an activity. Do other sights and sounds cause your baby to break her sucking during a feeding or not? Is she difficult to soothe when routine is broken or not?
- Intensity: The energy level of responses. Does your baby show both pleasure and upset in a loud dramatic way, or does she have a calmer, more quiet presence when either happy or sad?
- Regularity: How predictable biological functions like sleep needs and appetite are. Does your baby show hunger and sleepiness at predictable times or are these erratic?

- Sensory threshold: How sensitive the child is to stimulation (from touch, sounds, taste, room temperature). Does he startle easily or not? Is he a fussy eater or an indifferent one? Does he complain of clothing being hot or scratchy, or not?
- Approach/Withdrawal: The child's response to new situations or people. Is your child slow-to-warm-up or hesitant, or tend to be outgoing?
- Adaptability: How easily the child makes transitions. Does he balk at change and have difficulty adapting to something new, or is he more go-with-the-flow?
- Persistence: How long a child sticks with something in the face of obstacles. Does challenge sideline him easily or does he doggedly persist?
- Mood: The way a child generally reacts. Does he tend to be somber and negative, or happy-go-lucky? Is his proverbial glass "half empty" or "half full"?

It's easy to get overly concerned about this list of academic descriptions and wonder, "What can I do to ease my child's life —especially if I don't happen to have a child that falls into the *easy* category?" For me, the most important thing to know is that the brain is built to adapt, to change and to eventually learn more and more effective ways of getting along in the world. For example, many children labeled as "shy" can learn skills that help them to interact easily with others because they have parents and teachers who show them *how* to do that . . . and who guide and shape these abilities. Jerome Kagan, Ph.D., professor of psychology at Harvard University, studied initial traits in four-month-old infants and has done follow-up assessments over many years with these same children. His research has found that many of the infant's initial personality traits still applied years later, although the traits were not necessarily reflected in their outward behaviors. The underlying initial responses that combined to categorize little Suzie as having a shy temperament may still exist years later, but many of the "Suzies" of the world now successfully hold jobs such as management executives. Most people who know what

Suzie does for a living would assume her to be outgoing, and when you see her perform, she can indeed appear to be outgoing because she has learned to be successful in what she does. Nature (her genetics and her temperament) and nurture (her supportive experiences and her love relationships) have combined to help Suzie be whatever she wants to be.

### 3. Provide Everyday Baby Stress-Reducers

There are many simple things you can do to ease your baby's way through the day. Some suggestions:

- Pick up your baby promptly when she cries.
- Tell your baby or toddler often that you love her. This is a stress-reducer your child will never outgrow!
- Show your love with your expressions as well as your voice. Smile when you interact with your young child.
- Speak to your baby in calm, soothing tones. Refrain from arguing or yelling in front of your baby.
- Sing to your baby. (It doesn't matter if you can't hold a tune or don't really know all the words.)
- Bring your baby's arms back in and across the body if child is startled or frightened in a hugging and cocooning fashion.
- Encourage a comfort object. You can't really predict what your baby will grow attached to. But you can try to encourage things along by carrying a piece of cloth or a safe stuffed toy when you pick up your baby, feed her, or put her to sleep. She may grow to connect it with your scent and begin to prefer it when learning to self-soothe and self-regulate as a young toddler. Comfort toys and blankies are also called transitional objects because they help your child make a transition from being with you to being without you.

### 4. Build Your Child's Day Around Routines

Routines help us accomplish the activities of everyday living. They also establish the consistency that your baby's pattern-seeking brain craves.

It's this consistency—doing the same things at roughly the same time, order, and way every day—that provides the sense of security the brain needs to develop appropriately. Studies have shown that children who are the most secure and well behaved come from households where there are consistent daily routines.

A silver lining of routines with toddlers is that they usually prevent power struggles. Let's observe two households, each with two boys ages two and four. It's 7:30 p.m. and their mothers are getting their sons ready for bed.

At the Kenny household, the children have finished their bath, part of the bedtime routine they follow every night. Mrs. Kenny, who devotes this time exclusively to the boys, is supervising their teeth brushing. "Let's see those teeth, gentlemen," she says, reinforcing their efforts. "All right! Good job!" By 7:35 she asks the children to each pick out one book. Within minutes the children are listening to the stories and talking about them with her as they snuggle in bed. At 8:00 they kiss both parents goodnight. By 8:15 both boys are sound asleep.

At 7:30 at the Keller household, meanwhile, Mom (who is on the phone with her sister) is telling her children to go get ready for bed. The youngest immediately shouts, "No!" and the oldest starts negotiating for one more TV show. Mom again announces, more loudly, "It's bedtime!" The two-year-old is now crying and the four-year-old shows no sign of hearing her as he clicks the remote looking for his favorite station. By 8:00, Mrs. Keller has one angry two-year-old who has just finished his bath (which she gave him while also on her cell phone) and a four-year-old who has just finished watching his show and is now steering his toy cars around his bedroom floor. By 8:15, she's asking her sister to hold on a minute while she asks her sons to brush their teeth. At 8:30, when she clicks off her phone, the children—who have not yet brushed their teeth—are both playing with the little cars. The older boy still isn't in his pajamas. As she asks them to hop into bed, her phone rings again. Fifteen minutes later she's back in their room to find both boys fighting over the cars.

Children actually like routines! Routines set orderly limits on the day that feed security because they let a young child know what is coming next. Your baby or toddler can't tell time; he depends on you to move the day along. Having a routine is a concrete, reliable way to help him understand the sequence of events for the day. By knowing what to expect, he is less likely to protest and more likely to incorporate desired behaviors into his own routines as he becomes more independent.

Some sample routines for your home:

**At bedtime:** Getting children of any age into bed and asleep can be a challenge, especially when you're exhausted, too. Rather than to seek the latest craze out there of some magical "sleeping system," try the well-tested and very effective routine of a concise, consistent bedtime and a good-night story. You can also make a snack or last feeding, a bath, and listening to soothing music part of the routine. In general, keep it simple and do it the same way each night, at the same time. If it's so long and complex that you have to write it down for a babysitter, you're probably trying too hard.

Starting a bedtime-story tradition doesn't have to be intimidating or expensive. Your local library has hundreds of selections, and you don't need to spend more than fifteen minutes reading to reap the benefits. Bedtime stories often become cherished favorites that you read again and again, or even recite from memory or make up. The familiarity of the same story is itself soothing and calming, as your child enjoys knowing what is to come. As this occurs, be sure not to try to skip sections in an effort to hurry the process along one night. You will find your toddler's suddenly un-sleepy head pop up in defiance: "That's not how it goes!" No shortcuts with favorites.

**After day care:** All too often, the reunion starts with a happy hug and a kiss—and then the eager parent immediately launches into questions to learn about the child's day. "So, what did you do today?"or "What did you learn?" or "Who did you play with?" To your child, it feels a lot more like a drill than the warm greeting intended. I learned from a friend about a wonderful routine that's much more effective in eliciting a great deal of information, once your child begins to be verbal. She had one of those colorful, printed flat children's rugs with a town and roads and little buildings pictured on it. After giving her son T.J. a few minutes to decompress and get a snack, she would have him join her on the rug and they would debrief his day. He was barely verbal when she started this routine. At first, she did most of the talking. She would take a little toy car and describe, as she pushed the tiny toy along the drawn road, how Mommy drove him to school, and then stopped at the drug store before going to work at her office. Using her day as a model, she would talk through what she did at work, how she was feeling, what she was worried about and so on. She would continue the saga by talking about picking him up, how happy she was to see him again and about how much she loved him. Day after day the routine continued with each day encouraging him to participate more and more as he was learning to communicate. *Because it was routine*, it was not threatening, it was not a performance test, it was not done hurriedly. It was two-way communication. And it was brief.

## A Jenny Story: Routines Can Comfort for Years!

When we finally brought Jenny home from the hospital, weighing all of four pounds at six months of age, no one was talking about the prospect of enhanced development through classical music for infants. (See Chapter 16, "Everyday Music.") Totally by accident on one of her fitful nights, I put on one of the only three tapes I owned that were not rock 'n roll: Vivaldi's "Four Seasons," Pachelbel's "Canon in D," and Handel's "Water Music."

After a few minutes, *I fell sound asleep.* I have no idea how long Jenny lay awake and fussing, but when I awoke, she too was sleeping. I was so pleased and relieved that I tried to repeat the scene the next night. And the next.

It kept working—and so my first effective routine was born. I finally widened our music repertoire, but I found that those first selections worked most reliably. With the kind of iron-clad consistency that probably only the family with a special-needs child can imagine, we followed that bedtime-music routine in the Stamm household nightly. For years! When Kristin was born five years later, with those same melodies floating through the evening air of their shared bedroom, they seemed to soothe her within a few weeks, too.

By the time Kristin was two and Jenny, seven, I'd begun asking them to make the evening's selection. Kristin, already very verbal, would call out vigorously, "Let's have Handel" or whatever was her fancy. One night I accidentally put in the wrong tape. Suddenly a small voice called out, "No . . . that's not Handel. We want Handel." The moment remains frozen in time for me. Jenny knew her classical music! Years later, when she was twenty-five and living in a group-home setting, we were riding along in the car and Vivaldi's "Four Seasons" came on the radio. Jenny grabbed my arm and exclaimed, "Mommy . . . listen . . . it's my song!" Our old evening classical music routine had a lasting tangible magic.

## WHAT ARE YOUR ROUTINES?

Every family has its own rhythms and individual nuances. Consider what routines your family is currently using in order to accomplish each of the following:

|  | What the child does | What the parent does |
|---|---|---|
| Waking up | | |
| Mealtimes | | |
| Bath time | | |
| Bedtime | | |
| Going to school | | |

### 5. *Take Inventory of Your Family Rituals*

A ritual is another kind of rhythmic activity that adds predictability to family life. A ritual is different from routine in that it is often a ceremonial or special-occasion observance rather than an everyday thing. It's also more likely to be deliberately planned and occurs less frequently, and often has a cultural or religious link.

Also called family traditions, your rituals provide security by strengthening family identity and unity. They become a dependable feature of childhood. Rituals and traditions in your families of origin often provide inspiration; be sure to compare notes with your partner about the kinds of rituals you both were raised with.

The following survey can help you reflect on your existing traditions. This can be a good starting point for thinking about the role rituals play in your home now and where you might like to make changes.

Rate each statement for how well it describes your family's rituals and traditions.

1 = Statement **never** reflects my family.　　2 = Statement is **usually true** of my family.

3 = Statement is **always true** of my family.　　NA = Statement **does not apply** to my family.

| | | | | |
|---|---|---|---|---|
| Mealtimes are full of good conversation. | 1 | 2 | 3 | NA |
| We often share enjoyable family activities at home. | 1 | 2 | 3 | NA |
| We have rich holiday rituals. For example: | | | | |
| Christmas or Hanukkah | 1 | 2 | 3 | NA |
| Valentine's Day | 1 | 2 | 3 | NA |
| St. Patrick's Day | 1 | 2 | 3 | NA |
| Easter or Passover | 1 | 2 | 3 | NA |
| Cinco de Mayo | 1 | 2 | 3 | NA |
| Mother's Day | 1 | 2 | 3 | NA |
| Memorial Day | 1 | 2 | 3 | NA |
| Father's Day | 1 | 2 | 3 | NA |
| Fourth of July | 1 | 2 | 3 | NA |
| Labor Day | 1 | 2 | 3 | NA |

| | | | | |
|---|---|---|---|---|
| Halloween or Día de los Muertos | I | 2 | 3 | NA |
| Veterans Day | I | 2 | 3 | NA |
| Thanksgiving | I | 2 | 3 | NA |
| Others: | I | 2 | 3 | NA |
| We share enjoyable family vacations. | I | 2 | 3 | NA |
| We celebrate birthdays well. | I | 2 | 3 | NA |

Portion of the S.T.E.P.S. curriculum reprinted with permission from New Directions Institute for Infant Brain Development.

Review your ratings. On the statements you rated a three, what are the rituals—the special activities that make this tradition so rewarding?

If you rated a one on some statements, what do you believe is missing? Do you want to change this tradition? How could your family begin to make this occasion more meaningful?

### 6. Invent Some New Rituals

Often parents come up to me after talks and say, "Gee, my child is five and we don't really have any rituals." Sometimes these parents didn't grow up with family rituals themselves and therefore aren't sure what to do with their own children. Or their families are scattered across the country and their childhood rituals are hard to sustain without the power of a group behind them. If you don't have, or don't especially like, your own childhood traditions, it's important to make some up! A ritual is simply a special way of doing things that's anticipated and cherished by the members of your family. If you start when your child is a baby, she may not have much idea about what's happening, but over time she will catch on and come to look forward to these.

Although the inventory above centers on major holidays and events, you can have special rituals around events at any time of the year. A ritual can be something as simple as making chocolate-chip pancakes every Sunday morning, or as elaborate as spending summer vacation in a particular location and doing the same things there each year.

Here are some terrific ideas families have shared with me in workshops:

- *"The cool red plate."* Designate a special plate—one that looks different from your everyday dinnerware—to serve a family member who has done something noteworthy or has had something special happen to them on a particular day (such as having a birthday, learning to ride a bike without training wheels, or losing a first tooth).
- *"Barefoot in the park."* On the first warm spring day, the family makes a point of doffing the shoes to walk barefoot on the grass at a local arboretum.
- *"New Christmas PJs."* If you celebrate Christmas, on Christmas Eve, everyone opens one present of this year's brand-new pajamas. (Not only does this build the excitement for Christmas Day, but also everyone looks nice in the morning photos!) This routine can happen on any special day for families of other religions.
- *"Dessert-first day."* Every few months, out of the blue, designate this special occasion and serve the meal backward!
- *"Yearly photo series."* Find twenty-one small frames that are all alike and fill one each year with a current photo of a child on his birthday. Photos can be displayed once a year and hung on a wall or a branch.
- *"Halloween room."* Create a special doorway by hanging colored paper streamers to form an entrance that you have to peek through to enter the special space (which can be any space, such as the laundry room or a hall). Keep the lights low and eat your dinner by candlelight cross-legged on the floor in your now-exciting room!
- *"New Year's wishes."* On January 1, everyone states a wish for the coming year, which is written on a piece of paper and sealed up to be revisited next year.

# 10

# Hands-on Care: Introducing Vitamin "T"

- SHOULD I DO INFANT MASSAGE?
- DO TODDLERS NEED MASSAGE?
- WHAT DOES TOUCH HAVE TO DO WITH INTELLIGENCE?

Whenever I ask a mom to name the five senses, she typically starts with "seeing" and "hearing." Touch almost always gets mentioned last. But I'll bet this overlooked sense would top the list if your baby were answering the question.

By just nine weeks after conception, five tiny fingers can be counted on each hand. The toes develop a few weeks later. Ultrasound reveals images of babies in utero toying with the umbilical cord and sucking their thumbs. In fact, the tongue is initially more sensitive and better able to detect textures than the fingers. So when a fetus sucks his thumb, he's taking his first step toward using his sense of touch to explore his world. The umbilical cord, too, provides an early sensory opportunity, with its long, grooved and bending surface that can be explored and grasped by tiny fingers. And from the first trimester, your fetus can feel the warm embrace of amniotic fluid.

Little wonder, then, that by birth, babies are well on their way to learning about the world through touch. The sensory input a child gains from reaching out to the environment with his fingers, toes, and mouth, as well as the input he receives through being held and nuzzled, help to shape the way he learns to love, move, think, and learn.

The importance of physical contact has been known for a long time. Many years of studies by behavioral scientists have shown that social touch helps the young of almost all species of mammals to bond and thrive. The most famous experiments were done decades ago by psychologist Harry Harlow, Ph.D., with infant macaque monkeys. Among the many poignant variations was a study in which a monkey was put in a cage with a wire "dummy mother" that offered warmth from a light bulb and food from a nipple. Also in the cage was a second surrogate, this one covered in snuggly foam and terry cloth. The baby monkeys spent most of their time cuddling the softer surrogate, indicating that a need for touch was as primal as a need for food. Sometimes dads, because they cannot participate in breastfeeding rituals that naturally allow multiple opportunities for daily touch, typically don't feel like they can do much for their newborns. The results of the Harlow studies show how crucial it can be for fathers to nurture and hold their young babies.

In humans, too, we sometimes see "failure to thrive" in babies who, despite being fed, are deprived of basic nurturance. Although it's a fortunately rare and extreme scenario, it used to happen more commonly when premature infants were isolated in incubators and surrounded by tubes and machinery. Although they received oxygen and nutrition, they sometimes suffered because they were not held and stroked.

## WHAT THE SCIENCE SAYS: HOW TOUCH HELPS BABIES

*"Man cannot live by milk alone."*
—PSYCHOLOGIST HARRY HARLOW, Ph.D.

What's new is that we now understand the "inside story" of why touch—so ordinary an action we tend to take it for granted—is so critical to your child's brain. To a baby, touch is a physical requirement that she needs to both receive and to use every single day, "as critical a nutrient as a vitamin," says Bruce Perry, M.D., Ph.D., a child psychiatrist who is a leading expert on brain development and childhood trauma.

Take the simple act of caressing your baby's arm. Receptors on the baby's skin send signals to the brain, forming new connections between the brain cells. Remember the brain is an organ that grows itself—the way it grows is shaped by the input from what the baby experiences.

Touch tells the brain, "You are a wanted organism!" This stimulates the development of both physical and emotional systems.

Touch is also how a baby knows love. Long before she can understand the spoken word, the language of touch tells her she is wanted and safe. Studies have found that simply being near a child or offering verbal reassurances doesn't provide the same degree of calming as bringing her physically close and cuddling her. It's hands-on touch that helps trigger the relaxation response, a state of deep rest that changes the physical and emotional response to stress. (It's the opposite of the "fight or flight" response.) When a child is relaxed, muscle tension diminishes, heart rate and blood pressure lower, and breathing is deeper and more relaxed. Touch has also been shown to stimulate the immune system and the digestive system.

Massage is a kind of purposeful touch that provides still more benefits—and many of these you can see happening before your very eyes. Research has shown that massaging an infant fifteen minutes a day can help a baby:

- Reduce colic and/or crying
- Sleep more easily
- Gain weight better
- Make better eye contact
- Ease pain associated with teething and constipation
- Reduce the stress responses to painful procedures (such as getting a shot)

For some infants, touch can even make a life-or-death difference. Pioneering research by Tiffany Field, Ph.D., a psychologist who directs the Touch Research Institute at the University of Miami School of Medicine, found that when tiny premature newborns were massaged three times a day for ten days, they averaged a 47 percent greater weight gain, and gained this weight faster, than a control group of preemies who did not receive touch therapy. Infants who received regular massage while in the hospital also were more active, alert, and developmentally mature, and they left the hospital an average of six days sooner. (Like my daughter Jenny, Field's own daughter was born prematurely and, interestingly, became one of her mother's tiny subjects.) Since these studies were begun in the 1980s, infant massage has become a standard part of care in many neonatal intensive care units. If your baby was born prematurely you may have experienced another touch-based hospital therapy, "kangaroo care." This involves laying your preemie skin-to-skin on your chest while holding or gently touching her.

## A Jenny Story: Never Too Late!

I often tell parents I work with to be aware of the tendency of self-recrimination about the things they *did not do* with their child. I know it's important to let it go because guilt immobilizes us all. It can prevent us from moving on or from benefiting from things we learn subsequently that we now *can do*. Massage was just such an example in my life.

The power of touch through massage is one of the things I wish I'd known when my Jenny was a baby. If Tiffany Field's work had only been done a decade earlier, maybe Jenny would have grown faster, gained weight more easily, and developed more movement. *Maybe. If Only. What if?*

I finally let go of the "if only" and decided to see if massage would help Jenny even at her older age, by then twelve or thirteen. The director of the massage program at an exercise club we belonged to, a very nice lady named Jean, said that she'd be happy to try to help. At first Jenny was frightened of this new experience. I stayed with her in the dimly lit room holding her hand and softly humming familiar tunes to her in low, repeating sequences. Over the weeks, as she grew more comfortable, I then withdrew one support at a time until I could finally sit silently nearby and, eventually, leave the room entirely while Jean worked with Jenny. Jenny, who was almost *never* quiet, learned to lie silently and accept Jean's experienced touch. To this day, Jenny gets a weekly massage. The always-tensed muscles of her cerebral-palsied body get relief, and the benefits last for hours. Just recently we added earphones and yes, you guessed it, classical music for her to listen to while relaxing. She loves it all. What's not to love? I told you Jenny was smart!

## SENSORY INTEGRATION

Everything your baby comes into contact with delivers sensory information: *soft scrunchy* blanket, *firm smooth* rattle, *warm pliable* breast. Babies and toddlers busily practice full-body touching, touch with fingers, hands, feet, mouths. In fact, there's a brain-based reason that young babies seem to stick everything right into their mouths. Along the sensory-motor strip in the brain, the mouth- and tongue-processing cells take up lots of space. Relative to one's thigh or forearm, the mouth and tongue occupy more territory! So babies get lots of primary sensory information by checking things out with their mouths and tongues.

Actively using the hands and mouth is critical in yet another way. Information doesn't enter the brain as one isolated sense at a time. Sensory data pours in simultaneously through hearing, seeing, smelling, tasting, as well as through the nerve endings all over our bodies, not just those in our fingertips. Movement, coordination, body awareness, and balance further add to sensory awareness of our surroundings. The way we organize and respond to this lively influx of information is known as *sensory integration.*

All of a child's future skills—tying a shoe, being able to use a pencil easily, swinging on a swing—are complex processes that rely on a strong foundation of the brain's ability to incorporate sensory input. Here's why. Every second, two million bits of sensory information enter the central nervous system. The central nervous system, which consists of the brain and spinal cord, is the main processing center for the whole nervous system and therefore controls much of how our body works. In response, the brain:

- Alerts: attends to new stimuli and/or important stimuli.
- Selects: filters out essential from nonessential input.
- Organizes: groups information into meaningful perception or patterns
- Protects: withdraws from a situation if a stimulus is too overwhelming.

This is done on an automatic level so we don't have to think about it. But it represents a tremendous amount of simultaneous neural activity. Sensory integration is like the brain's super-secretary, directing all the information the brain receives. When the system is well-organized, input from the environment is processed to produce a behavioral response that's appropriate to the situation. For example, you are outside in the yard and the wind begins to suddenly kick up. You see the branches on the trees begin to sway; you hear the rustling of the leaves; you feel bits of sand and dirt from a nearby rock pile hitting your arms and face and you immediately cover your eyes and turn your head to shield your eyes and mouth to avoid the debris. Your brain is effectively able to automatically integrate multiple input and respond appropriately.

The concept of sensory integration was popularized by A. Jean Ayres, Ph.D., an occupational therapist and clinical psychologist who was a pioneer in the field of learning disabilities. Observing that in some children, a foundation of good sensory processing does not develop as smoothly as it should, she theorized that a neural disorder was to blame. Sensory input received by the nervous system was being inefficiently organized—communication between the body and the brain was being tangled up. Her ideas, which have been borne out and further refined by experts across many fields, including neuropsychology and neurology, point to the importance of a baby and toddler being able to bring together many different senses at the same time.

Compare the experiences of two twelve-month-olds:

Caitlin is watching a DVD of animals especially made for babies. It's one of her favorites. "Dog" in fact, is one of her first words. As she watches, her brain processes the flickering images of the dog's face, body, and tail on the screen.

Craig is playing with his neighbor's new pup. He, too, sees the dog's wriggling body and wagging tail. As the puppy licks his face, he also takes in its unfamiliar smell, the feel of the tongue (wet, warm, rough), the different textures of the fur and the paw pads against his legs, the sound of the pet's panting and excited whimpers. At the same time, he's also absorbing the reaction of his mother nearby—probably either laughing or freaking out, depending on what kind of mom she is!

Craig's brain is collecting data from his eyes, ears, nose, hands, feet, and mouth all at once. He's also processing the behavior of both the dog and his mother as they change slightly from minute to minute. But Caitlin's brain is receiving visual information only. Even if you have the best photographer in the world, there's a huge difference between a flat screen image of an object and the real thing. Take a water bottle, for example. A child can quickly learn to identify the words "water bottle" with a picture of one. But only by actually holding the water bottle can you get the broader sensory input that tells you: The bottle is heavy; it squishes slightly in your hand; it makes a crinkly sound when poked in and then pops back out afterward. And that's even before you open it up and feel what's inside.

This may seem like a small deal, but it's huge to the brain. *The brain has to get used to experiencing across multiple modalities simultaneously in order to thrive.* And the more exposures a child has to this kind of "multi-sensory" learning, the better a workout his brain is receiving.

You'd think you could just take it for granted that a child will receive this kind of multi-sensory stimulation in the course of an ordinary day. But I'm afraid that our technology-heavy, highly programmed, germ-phobic culture is depriving babies and toddlers of these once-inevitable opportunities.

Without proper sensory integration, however, the information entering the brain does not get sorted into the proper "file drawers" of the brain and can't be easily coordinated or accessed. This can lead to developmental lags or behavioral, emotional, and learning problems. Sensory integration disorder (also called sensory integration dysfunction, or SID) is a constellation of problems that can result when sensory integration does not develop as it should. Signs include being overly sensitive or under-reactive to touch, movement, sights, or sounds; being easily distracted; social and or emotional problems such as impulsivity and a lack of self control; difficulty making transitions; an inability to calm one's self; speech, language, or motor-skill delays; delays in academic achievement.

That's a broad list and includes behaviors that, on their own, should not cause alarm. (For example, many toddlers are sensitive to "scratchy" clothing tags, for example, and impulsivity is also developmentally based; all fifteen-month-olds can be impulsive.) But SID is not something that should be self-diagnosed. SID is often found in the following groups, according to The Ayres Clinic in Torrance, California, which was founded by the late Dr. Ayres:

- Children who were born prematurely (and may have lacked sensory nourishment early in life);
- Children with autism (who tend to seek out unusual amounts of certain types of sensations while being very hypersensitive to others);
- Children with learning disabilities (an increasing percentage of all school-aged children have such disabilities, though a majority have normal intelligence);
- Those who experienced stress-related disorders in childhood.

When SID is suspected, a qualified occupational or physical therapist can perform an evaluation that includes standardized tests and structured observations to various tasks involving sensory stimulation, posture, balance, coordination, and eye movements. Therapy consists of activities that challenge and exercise the brain to create organized responses and is often successful.

## THE BRIGHT IDEAS: TOUCH
Here are some practical suggestions that can contribute to healthy attachment and good sensory integration throughout the day.

### 1. Hold Your Baby Often
What could be more simple or more pleasant? Most parents, of course, want to hold their babies. Babies who are picked up, cuddled, rocked, and carried tend to be calm. "Baby wearing"—carrying your baby against your chest in a soft, specially designed carrier or sling—frees your hands for other things, even around the house.

As your baby grows, being held continues to be an important way to communicate your affection and provide comfort and support. Toddlers increasingly need separation from their parents to crawl or walk away and explore the room or play. But they will usually still check back often with a parent or caregiver for a reassuring hug!

That's not to say you should carry your baby 24/7—or that doing so would be a good idea even if you had the time and inclination. Your baby needs your touch, but, as discussed in Chapter 6, "Downtime," he also needs time when he's not bombarded by sensory input. To develop motor skills, babies need the physical freedom to stretch muscles and practice moving them around, too.

### 2. Show Some Skin

Especially when your baby is new, spend some time holding him clad only in a diaper against your bare chest. Moms and dads alike can do this. Hearing your heartbeat and feeling the warmth of your skin is one of the best kinds of touch there is.

Holding a newborn skin-to-skin immediately after birth has been found to help regulate body temperature and heart rate, and cause the newborn to cry less. Breastfeeding is a great natural form of skin-to-skin contact. Newborns are actually born with the instinct to "crawl" (actually scootch) up their mother's body to her breast, if given the opportunity—an amazing thing to see!

### 3. Learn Infant Massage

Massage is a wonderful way to give your baby loving touch. A kind of skin-to-skin contact, it's easy and fun to do, and takes only a few minutes a day. Many parents, especially new fathers, find it rewarding to be able to help their babies in this "hands-on" way.

Massaging an infant or toddler does *not* involve the deep-tissue work of an adult massage, however. Rather it is a surface massage done with your choice of baby oil or lotion. It's important to pay attention to the degree of pressure you use: not too rough, in order to be safe, but also not too light. A very light, feathery touch has been found to occasionally overstimulate or irritate a baby. Use one finger or just a part of your hand. You can practice on a baby doll at first if you're unsure.

While massaging your baby, remember to talk to him. Name the parts of the body as you work on or near them: "Here is your smooth forehead. Here is your nose. This is your mouth—I see you smiling at me!"

**When and how to start:** Great times for massage include just before or after a bath, after a diaper change, or in the mornings during your child's calm, alert time. Don't wait until your baby is already cranky or fussy. (If you massage right after a bath, make sure your baby is completely dried off to avoid a chill.)

Be sure to choose a draft-free location. Lay your baby on a towel or receiving blanket. Undress her (except for the diaper, if you like). Begin by "asking" if she is ready to begin her nice massage. Again, this kind of "labeling" of actions as well as the recommended labeling of objects is the start of language development also.

**How long:** For a newborn, limit your massage to the legs, feet, arms, hands, shoulders, and back. The first times you try it, limit the massage to three to five minutes. After a month, you can massage up to ten minutes, and after two months, ten to fifteen minutes. Note the responsiveness of your child to determine the right amount of massage enjoyed.

**How to do it:** Here are some suggestions to guide your movements provided by Lucy Emerson Sullivan, R.N., Ph.D., at the University of Utah. There's no absolute right or wrong sequence for how you should move your hands, however.

*Leg massage:* Elevate your baby's right leg with your left hand. Wrap your right hand around the baby's thigh and slowly stroke toward his foot. Repeat several times, then switch legs.

*Foot massage:* Press the bottom of the foot from the heel to the toe, using your thumbs. Knead each toe. Make circles around the ankles.

*Arm and hand massage:* Use similar strokes as in the leg and foot massages. Holding one of the baby's wrists with one hand, use your other hand to gently squeeze along the length of the arm, starting at the shoulder. When you reach the wrist, switch hands. Repeat several times.

Use your thumb to unfurl your baby's hand if it's clenched. Roll each finger between your forefinger and thumb. Stroke the top of the hand. Make tiny circles around the wrist with your thumb and fingertips.

*Face and head massage:* Using your thumbs, very gently stroke from the center of the forehead out to the temples, around the eyes. With your fingertips, make small circles along the jaw. With the pads of your fingertips (on both hands) make small circles all over the head. Caution: Avoid the soft spot (fontanel) completely.

*Back and shoulder massage:* Gently lay your baby on his stomach. Beginning at the shoulders, use your fingertips to gently stroke the back. Make circles down the back.

### 4. Set Up a "Do Touch" World

As your baby grows, he'll be naturally compelled to explore his surroundings. And since touch is a major way a young child does this, you can count on everything within reach being grabbed, pulled, handled, or put into the mouth. This is not "misbehavior;" it's a good and necessary part of the learning process. Every encounter sets off new links in the brain: Is it hot? Cold? Hard? Soft? Heavy? Easy to pick up? Does it move or stay still? Can I carry it? How does it feel in my mouth? How does it taste? Like a scientist making careful evaluations, the brain is storing away every factoid for later retrieval.

Although after about age one it's possible to begin retraining a child not to touch off-limits items (the TV remote, a flower vase), creating a touch-friendly environment is much more effective.

Children need to be active, curious, engaged learners. They need to know that curiosity is valued. If they hear "no!" over and over, they learn the opposite lesson, that inquisitiveness is something negative.

- Put away the "don't touch!" items in your home or relocate them to higher places out of reach.

- Every two to three months after your child begins to crawl, re-assess your home from your child's vantage point. Remove anything that's dangerous to your baby or precious to you.
- While you don't have to go crazy with child safety devices, parents often find a few items such as drawer latches or toilet locks useful and light-socket plugs a must. Experiment and see what you're comfortable with in your home.
- Don't lock every cupboard. Making household items such as pots and pans or Tupperware accessible gives a baby important safe exploration opportunities—and can keep him busy while you are working in your kitchen.
- Turn down your hot water heater to 120 degrees Fahrenheit to prevent burns.

## Attractive Dangers . . . And What to Do About Them

Balance your child's itch to explore with a need for safety. Here are some common dangers that are easy to remove.

| Danger | Remedy |
|---|---|
| Dangling tablecloths | Remove or switch to placemats temporarily |
| Loose extension cords | Tape up along the wall |
| Exposed outlets | Install plastic plugs or replace the cover plates with childproof ones |
| Accessible cupboards | Install childproof locks; relocate dangerous items such as cleaning solutions, knives, and plastic bags to high cabinets. |
| Staircases | Install safety gates at the base and top of stairs |
| Hard fireplace hearth | Cover temporarily with foam rubber |
| Sharp-edged furniture | Cover with quilts, throws, pillows or corner protectors |

### 5. Provide "Equal-Opportunity" Sensory Explorations

Here are some fun, easy ways to give your child a multi-sensory experience:

**Texture touching (all ages).** As you go through daily routines such as washing laundry or dishes, allow your baby to feel the contrasting surfaces: bumpy towels, smooth sheets, cold or hot water, slithery soap, rough sponge. Label each different experience with words: "Ooh! This is cold water! . . . Ahh, now it's getting warm!" Children learn to make associations between the word label and the sensation felt.

**Touch Books (infant, baby):** Choose board books that feature different textures [such as the classic, *Pat the Bunny* (Dorothy Kunhardt, Golden Books)]; the children's section of your local bookstore will be full of them. Describe the pictures: "Feel how soft the teddy bear is." Cloth or nontoxic board books are best at this age so your baby can really explore them by touch (and mouth). I also like the soft book by Carrington Brain Research, *Baby Brain Box Touch and Learn.*

**Make a "Touch Book" (toddler):** Choose four words that describe textures (e.g., smooth, rough, bumpy, soft, hard, furry, squishy). Write one word on each of four different sheets of construction paper. Allow your child to decorate a cover: "_____'s Touch Book." Then go on a hunt through your home to find objects that match the words you've chosen. ("Smooth" might be a plastic baggie or a piece of fabric, for example.) Let your child glue the object to the page. After it's dry, punch holes in the pages and make a book. You can add more pages later.

**Water experiments (baby, toddler).** Water can be a wonderful way to engage your toddler's senses. These activities provide tactile, visual, and auditory stimulation. A child can see, feel, and hear the water as it streams or sprays. In the bath, a shallow play pool, or a backyard bucket, provide a variety of water tools, such as a measuring cup with spout, two plain measuring cups, small toy cups, small metal or plastic pitcher, funnel, baster, paper towel, tray. *Always supervise your child around water.*

**Terrific Toast (toddler):** Take a piece of bread and place it on a cookie sheet. Fill a few small cups with about one half inch of milk.

Then add a few drops of food coloring to the milk. Make as many different colors as you like. Use a clean sterilized eyedropper to model for your child how to fill it with the colored milk. Say the names of the colors as you discuss and do the activity. Allow your child to take the milk-filled dropper and drop dots of color onto the bread. Put the "painted bread" into the toaster and enjoy eating your terrific toast together.

**Rainbow Pudding (baby, toddler):** Make vanilla pudding (an instant package is easiest) and spoon the set pudding into several small bowls. Add a few drops of food coloring to each. Place the different colors on your child's high chair tray and allow him to finger paint and eat his tasty creation.

**Sensational Squirt Bottles:** Add one and one half cups of water to several squirt bottles. Add eight drops of food coloring to each. Take a piece of paper outdoors on the sidewalk (anchor with small rocks if it's windy) and encourage your child to squirt designs.

**Kool-Aid Play Dough:** Use this easy dough recipe that I got from a teacher friend of mine. Use a cookie sheet lined with wax paper. Start by giving your child a small handful of dough and allowing him to experiment. Later show him how to roll balls, make snakes, and form letters or shapes.

*Kool-Aid Play Dough Recipe*
    1 package of unsweetened Kool-Aid
    1 cup of salt
    1 tablespoon cream of tartar
    3 cups of flour
    2 cups of boiling water
    3 tablespoons salad oil

Add wet ingredients to dry ingredients. Mix well. Knead until smooth and soft. You can store the dough in a zip-lock bag and place in the refrigerator after use to prevent it from drying out.

# 11

## Child Care: How to Make a Brain-Based Choice

- WHAT KIND OF CHILD CARE WILL HELP MY CHILD MOST?
- WHAT SHOULD I LOOK FOR?
- HOW CAN I EVALUATE A CURRICULUM?
- DO CAREGIVER RATIOS AND ACCREDITATIONS REALLY MATTER?

If you've looked for someone to care for your baby, you know how vexing this process can be. More than half of all new mothers return to work within four months of giving birth to their first child in the United States, and 70 percent of mothers of children under age six are in the labor force.

Despite these large numbers, child care in this country is still catch-as-catch-can. Options range from superb to not many notches above the deficient Romanian orphanages described in Chapter 8. Not only is the quality of child care lagging far behind the need for it, but the general perception of just what constitutes "good care" is also behind the times. High-quality child care today should be *brain care*. This chapter offers you a fresh, realistic way to examine your choices and find a situation that truly benefits your child.

### WHAT THE SCIENCE SAYS: THE FIRST YEAR IS UNIQUE

Choosing a child-care environment for an infant requires some special considerations because of what's happening developmentally in the brain—both the sheer amount of neural activity and the critical systems that wire first, particularly in the emotional centers and parts of the attention system.

No evidence suggests that child care before school—and certainly not in the first two years—should be more like school in order to build a better brain. This is an important point because in the past generation care patterns have shifted away from the use of care by relatives (grandparents, aunts, uncles) toward a greater use of center-based arrangements. As more parents investigate center care, it becomes especially important to be able to evaluate it critically, from a brain perspective, rather than just relying on and believing in the marketing materials.

One element that's tricky to come by in center-based care is nevertheless even more important than the usual things parents are told to look for in their search, such as safety, cleanliness, and a bright space full of the latest child-development bells and whistles. That's a predictable, loving caregiver.

The science is not saying that person must only be the mother. But there needs to be at least one nurturing, responsive adult with whom your child can bond. While an ideal attachment relationship is the parent-child, that's not a realistic expectation all day long today given the numbers of working parents. A very young child can also thrive in a setting with someone other than the mother or father, provided he is cared for by the same individual(s) in a loving, consistent, and responsive manner. It's the predictable actions of a very small core of adults (parents and a caregiver) that assures a child he is safe in an otherwise roaring flood of incoming sensory data. Shifts of different child-care workers on different days or at different times, or a quick-changing parade of nannies won't meet this criterion.

My bias is toward individual care when possible for the first six to twelve months, such as that provided by an energetic and nurturing grandmother, relative, nanny, or babysitter. Today's parents often have the perception that a school-like facility must be a "smarter" choice than the granny down the street, but this is not always the case. You have to look more closely. To be sure, it is possible to have one-on-one responsiveness that also exists in well-run centers or in family day-care centers, although it is harder to come by.

One of the biggest barriers to good care is that caregivers themselves— even the directors of large, sophisticated centers—don't necessarily understand the biology of *why* they must have a strong sense of interpersonal connection to the children under their care. Loving, decent (and often trained) care providers still often view themselves as babysitters in the passive sense: feeding, putting to sleep, watching over, period. Don't get me wrong. Most of the women (and they are mostly women) working in early child care today love children. But no one has ever explained to them the critical importance of building attachment, much less how to interact with each child to promote healthy brain development.

I'm very excited that the New Directions Institute is currently involved in a large-scale project unlike any I'm aware of in the country. We're working with an entrepreneur who operates a large chain of child-care centers in Arizona under the name Tutor Time Child Care-Learning Centers, to train all staff in the latest science-based principles of child care. With forty schools, they are currently the largest provider of child care in Arizona, and are responsible for infants, toddlers, and preschool children ages six weeks and up. Additionally, NDI is consulting on programs for a new child-care concept—Children's Learning Aventure. These child-care centers will employ the latest training programs, curriculum, and state-of-the-art facilities. We will help with the training of all staff in these new facilities. I'm eager to see the effects of this kind of unprecedented level of added training in a complete system—this is the kind of new perspective that can really reshape child care as we know it.

Here are some suggestions for choosing care for infants, babies, and toddlers. Use the following brain-development-based suggestions to guide your day-care choices.

## THE BRIGHT IDEAS: CHILD CARE
### 1. *Choose Infant Day Care the Bright Way*
The usual child-care checklists will only take you so far. Some factors are more important than others. Some general considerations for the unique child-care needs of a baby:

What's More Important:

- *Who the actual caregiver is.* One main person should be responsible for your child, not a team. Too many faces requires your baby to continually detach and reattach, which is emotionally distressing.

A wonderful new concept is "looping," in which one caregiver stays with your child throughout his time at the center, with the teacher moving "up" as her group of children get older, rather than the children having to adjust to a new room and new faces simply because they turn six, nine, or twelve months old and must "graduate" to the next room. This is a great example of brain-based, child-based care, rather than the more traditional practice of basing care on a K-12 school model, which should be irrelevant when we're talking about infant child care.

- *Child to caregiver ratios.* Attentive care requires time. According to the American Academy of Pediatrics, staff/child ratios should be 1:3 between six and fifteen months. The National Association for the Education of Young Children (NAEYC), an accrediting group, specifies 1:3 when the group size is six children or fewer, or 1:4 when the group size is seven or eight children, from birth to fifteen months.

- *Staff turnover:* Although it's notoriously high in the low-paying child-care industry, minimal turnover is an ideal goal, again so your child does not have to adjust to new faces and the resulting variable patterns of care. Find out how long caregivers who might work with your child have been on the job. A facility that offers annual contracts is a plus.

- *Staff schedules:* They should be regular and consistent, with the same person looking after your child for the same hours every day—not one person in the morning and another after lunch, or one on Monday-Wednesday-Friday and another on Tuesday-Thursday.

- *General environment:* Is it safe, bright, colorful, and inviting? Would you want to spend hours there?

- *Staffers touching children:* Look for hugging, caressing, holding, rocking.

- *Staffers talking to children.* Just because a baby can't talk doesn't mean he shouldn't be talked to. Babies need to hear language directed to them often throughout all parts of the day.

- *Openness.* Is there an open-door policy so you can drop by whenever you wish? (This is a must for infant care.) Is the care provider open to hearing new information about brain development? Does she want to be a teammate in caring for your child? Does she accept new toys and other truly stimulating materials (such as mirrors or rhyming books, not electronic "learning" toys) you may provide?

What's Less Important:

- *The physical building:* It doesn't matter much whether your baby is in a spiffy new building or a fifty-year-old home, as long as it is safe.
- *How new or fancy the toys are:* Simple, classic toys are just as good as fancy new ones (and in some cases, better). What's more important is that they be plentiful, age-appropriate, and in good repair. *Red flag:* A TV set, especially one on in the background continually. There is no upside to TV for a baby, and plenty of potential negatives.
- *Computers.* A baby doesn't need them. A toddler doesn't need them.
- *Advanced degrees.* A degree in early childhood education is wonderful to have, but may be less important for a caregiver than a basic, solid understanding of brain development and a genuine affection for babies. A college degree is a good sign that the caregiver values education. It is an exciting goal to have caregivers working toward degrees in education.
- *Schedules for the children.* Especially young babies have very individualized sleeping and eating schedules. Group programming doesn't apply.
- *A strong academic program.* Not only is this inappropriate for a baby, but it should not be considered a draw for you as your child gets older; toddlers don't need formal, highly structured, academic instruction, either. A play-based curriculum is sufficient and preferred over a paper-and-pencil, skill-based program.

Other Factors:

- *Proximity to work or home.* You may feel less stressed having your baby near your workplace. A child-care situation that's right on your commute, or based in your own home, may afford you more time with your child. But convenience is far down the list as a primary factor. We are not talking about only making your life easy, but making your child's life more wonderful through your choice.
- *Licensing and accreditation.* The program should meet local licensing regulations; but this only means that they have met minimum standards for care. Accreditation is a voluntary process in which programs show they have met a higher standard of care. The National Association for the Education of Young Children (NAEYC) is the highest standard in the child-care industry. Many good home-based centers do not qualify, however, and these distinctions don't apply to nanny or babysitter care.
- *Cost.* Obviously this is an important factor—but it's not as important as some people think to identifying an ideal situation. You don't always get what you pay for. Rates at an impressive new center may reflect the mortgage on the building or extensive recruitment for new staff. The granny in a humble home down the street may cost a fraction as much, but be fully available to meet your child's needs.

   One thing worth paying for, however, whatever the type of care, is a guarantee that one consistent individual will give your baby lots of individualized attention and responsive care. A private nanny or a setting with a low child-to-caregiver ratio can be expensive. Face time with a baby is worth the investment, even if it seems like you're allocating precious time and money to something so "ordinary." Rest assured: Science is telling us that it's more important to invest in high-quality care from birth to two than it is to save up and spend that money on a fancy preschool or kindergarten.

## 2. Interview the Actual Caregiver

Usually the first—and last—stop at a child-care center is a visit with the director. This individual can offer useful information about how the center is organized, who the staffers are, and what turnover is like. But you must also insist on interviewing the actual person who will be responsible for your child. Remember, that relationship is paramount! Likewise, it's not enough to go on the recommendations of your best friend about a nanny, or the staffing agency that places the nanny.

If you're told this interview is not possible, or against center policy, don't accept this answer. Ask why. If the answer is that there are too many different people responsible for infants, that's a red flag.

Try to determine whether the person has enough time to love one more child. For example, a family day-care provider may have four children in her care, but if two are two-year-old twins, one is an infant, and another is in kindergarten and she ferries him to school and activities, she'll be very busy already meeting their needs and may not therefore be the best choice.

## 3. Observe the Caregiver

You also need to observe the caregiver with other babies, and then with your baby. Does she speak directly to children? Seem to genuinely enjoy them? Here are some factors that were documented in a 2005 National Institute for Child Health and Human Development's Early Child Care Research Network checklist of things to look for when observing a caregiver interact with a child. Some things they suggest watching out for:

1. Caregiver responds to the child's vocalization (responds verbally to what the child is saying or is trying to say, repeats the child's words, comments on what the child has said, or answers the child's question).
2. Caregiver asks the child a question. (Examples: "Are you hungry?" "Who is that?" "You're sleepy, aren't you?" "You like the green ones?")

3. Caregiver praises, says something affectionate to child. (Examples: "I love you." "You're a cutie." "You did it!")

4. Caregiver teaches the child. (Caregiver instructs the child: "This is a ball." "Say 'ball.'" "That's a ball.")

5. Caregiver directs other positive talk to the child; describes an object or event, comforts or entertains the child, sings a song, tells a story. (Examples: "We're going outside." "The bottle is totally empty." "I'm going to put your bib on.") A single sentence will do. Does not use negative talk (insults, criticizes, rejects, reprimands, teases, yells) or directive talk (giving orders).

These kinds of interactions are minimums to look for. Verbal exchanges that are even richer and more extended are, of course, even more desirable.

### 4. Share Your Expectations

There's an assumption on many new parents' parts that they are just the newbies at child care and the experienced center/nanny/sitter must be the expert. Caregivers *are* experts—at the way they've always done things. However, your caregiver may not really know some of the simple key things a baby needs, and if she does know them, she may not realize how critical those things she does well really are! She is very unlikely to understand *why*.

Here are some things you can suggest to your caregiver (whether at a center, in a home, or in your own home):

- Have toys on hand that encourage brain-based play, such as mirrors or tactile experiences, simple colorful books.
- Let her know how important her bond with your baby is. Let her know that you want to help to foster that bond. Emphasize your wish to have routines for your baby.
- Encourage tummy time. Most care providers now proudly explain that they know to put babies to sleep on their backs to help prevent SIDS. (Definitely a factor to verify.) But they may

not know about the extra need for deliberate tummy-time play as a direct result of that safety measure.

• What info you need at pickup. What do you want to know about your child: How attentive was he today? What new things was he interested in? What he ate? Did? Length of naps? Be specific and don't settle for a standard form that's always been used, if it's not what you want to know. A conversation is always better than a written record to pass on important information.

• Provide a copy of this book to help her be "on the same page" about early brain development.

### 5. *Don't Be Jealous*

Parents sometimes express reservations about their child-care choice that reflect a lack of awareness about what good care really is:

"I hate that the girl at the center saw Jake take his first steps instead of me."

"I'm worried that our toddler likes this place too much—she cries when we pick her up and never wants to leave."

"We fired Abby last week because the baby seemed too attached to her."

It's scary to leave your baby in someone else's care. Especially when your baby—and your own bond—is still fresh and new, it's easy to feel a little insecure. Many new moms confide that they fear their baby will fall in love with a child-care worker. And yet—this is exactly what you should wish for.

That may be a difficult concept to accept. But remember the importance of forming strong attachments. You should *want* your baby to fall in love with somebody else who is providing such important care. In fact, once you understand what's happening down in the "bagel" part of your baby's brain, this idea of your baby loving another becomes much easier to support.

What's more, just because your baby loves the person who feeds, changes, and plays with him during certain hours of the day doesn't mean he will love you less. Attachment is not an either-or proposition, and love is not a finite thing. Babies can, and should, form strong attachments to their primary caregivers, plural. Having these strong bonds goes a long way toward developing a capacity to love, period.

### 6. Choose Toddler Day Care the Bright Way

By age two, most of the key, basic brain wiring has been established, your child has a strong sense of self, and knows how to experience the joy and comfort of a loving relationship. Now his mind is focused on action and interaction. Although sensory input and initial brain wiring progresses from the back to the front of the brain, the action mode or output goes from the front of the brain to the back! We make our plans in our frontal lobes of what we want to do, what we want to play with, and how we will explore our environment and then engage our motor centers and move into ACTION. In a preschool or day-care center this move into action mode involves lots of increased social interactions with other kids and a wider circle of adults.

The standard checklists that describe what to look for in child care are a good road map to finding toddler or preschooler care. I'd like to stress a few brain-specific things to look for:

- *Caregivers who hug, let children climb in their laps, and otherwise touch.* As a legal precaution, some day-care centers now have a policy whereby staffers may not touch children. I think this is wrong in schools (where it's prevalent) and tragic in settings for young children. Touch is a primary way of communicating security, love, and attention to a young child. It shouldn't be a legal issue; it's a requirement.
- *Still "smallish" caregiver-to-child ratios:* 1:4 for twenty-four-month-olds, 1:7 for thirty-six-month-olds.
- *An ever-expanding variety of materials.* Especially important are tactile materials (a sand table or water table), blocks of all sizes, art supplies, dress-up and pretend-play props, music to move to, a playhouse area, outdoor play facilities, and of course lots of books!

- *A child-directed pace.* Toddlers' minds are working out different concepts at different times and paces. Montessori schools do a wonderful job of recognizing this; materials and open schedules are set up to reflect it.

## A Kristin Story This Time: Brain-Based Care

Even though I had experience being a mom with Jenny, I was still green when it came to thinking about preschool choices for my daughter Kristin. I stumbled accidentally on a Montessori preschool for her the way many parents pick programs: It was close to my house. Little did I realize what a brain-centered approach this would turn out to be, and it's a type of program I have no reservations recommending.

A few months into Kristin's time there, diligent mother (and schoolteacher!) that I was, I suggested to her teacher that maybe she should be encouraging Kristin to spend some more time on the language centers. I was nervous that Kristin showed no signs of being interested in reading. Day after day, it seemed that all she wanted to do was tinker in the math areas (which consisted of blocks, counting beads, sand table, and similar materials). Luckily her teacher calmly explained the Montessori philosophy: This was where Kristin's little brain wanted and *needed* to be at the moment, figuring out the physics about volume and measurement. The language work could come later. Sure enough, she eventually got around to reading and writing skills, but who knows if she would have turned out to be a neuroscientist if her brain had been discouraged from those days and days of spatial reasoning explorations!

### 7. Make Changes Thoughtfully

One of the most important things you can do regarding your child's care setting is to really watch your child's responses on a regular basis and respect them. Look. Listen. Is your child happy? After normal separation anxiety, does she go on to have a good day? If your child suddenly seems depressed, unhappy, or anxious, that's a big red flag.

If something doesn't "feel right," trust your instincts and invest in the hard work of making a change. All too often we get so busy that we keep putting changes off. Change is hard. Change takes energy. And energy is one of the rarest of commodities in a new parent's life. Yet, because the brain develops in ways that are *time sensitive*, with certain systems wiring at different times, you can't afford to wait if you're in a child-care situation that's not right. Take time off from your job if you must and go seek better care. Time and again I hear from families who, years after being given this advice about searching for the correct care for a child, and course-correcting if a first situation isn't right, seek me out to report that it was one of the most important things they learned as parents. They saw an immediate change in their child and in their own stress levels, too. The whole family benefits when child care is right! Invest.

# 12

## Bond-Builders Little Ones Love

> **Why we do a Bonding activity . . .**
> Bonding activities provide practice for caregivers in how to help a child feel safe, cared for, and loved. A child needs to know that there is *at least one person* in the world that he/she can depend on. Providing responsive, predictable care is critical for a child's healthy, early brain development.
> **Children who feel secure learn better.**

All activities you share with your child help promote bonding, but these have been chosen as especially rewarding in establishing a secure emotional start, as described in the preceding section. I want to stress that these activities are for fun and are not predictive of any problem if your child does not seem interested when you play them. Come back and try them at a later time. Have fun!

Following each activity, there are short sections that give you additional information to understand *why* certain kinds of activities have been shown to be helpful in developing a young brain:

- The *Brain Link* tells you how the activity can influence your child's brain now.
- The *School Link* tells you the potential impact on later school readiness.
- *Variations* are related kinds of activities that serve a similar function.

## BOND-BUILDERS FOR INFANTS (0 TO 6 MONTHS)
*Baby Book Talk (3 to 6 months)*
*Directions:*

- Choose a picture storybook about the love between parents and babies. Any children's book that's not an instruction-oriented book will work. A classic I love is *I Love You As Much* (Laura Krauss Melmed/Harper Festival). Also good: *Hugs and Kisses* (Roberta Grobel/Scholastic Cartwheel Books), *Mommy Loves Her Baby/Daddy Loves His Baby* (Tara Jaye Morrow and Tiphanie Beeke/HarperCollins Children's Books).
- Hold your baby in your lap with her back against your chest so she can see the pictures and watch as you turn the pages.
- Name the pictures. Describe them. Point out details. Tell your baby what's happening in the book. This is baby "book talk." Your baby may seem too young for this at first, but you are the most important person in her world and she loves hearing your voice and being in your arms.
- Follow the actions you see pictured—a kiss on the belly, a kiss on the feet—if they are part of the story. Express the emotions shown on the pages and the joy you feel when you spend time with your baby.
- Read together often this way!

*Brain Link:* Being read to in this way stimulates emotional, cognitive, visual, auditory, and motor connections in the brain. It also stimulates the parts of the brain that process and store language in the critical frontal and left temporal regions.

*School Link:* Begins to develop a sense of connection with others. Also develops your child's visual discrimination abilities and vocabulary, which are necessary for later reading.

*Variations:*

- Any reading time with a baby builds security. Dads especially may enjoy a book like *Baby Dance* (Ann Taylor/Harper Festival) because it features the development of the father-child relationship. Read part of the poem with enthusiasm, describe the dad's loving actions on the page (dancing, singing) and then try to perform the various actions.

## BOND-BUILDERS FOR BABIES (6 TO 18 MONTHS)
### "I'm Gonna Getcha!"

*This classic game has been studied extensively by Daniel Stern, M.D., a professor of psychology of the University of Geneva, Switzerland, and adjunct professor of psychiatry at the Cornell Medical School. Dr. Stern studies "micro-moments" in very young children's lives. He examines every-day care practices and games between parents and babies around the world, looking first for commonalities and then for ways to make sense of these scientifically. This game shows your baby's computer-power brain!*

*Directions:*

- Move in close, and with a big smile, begin near the baby's belly button and start slowly creeping your fingers up toward his chin saying, "IIIII'm gonna getcha. . . ."
- Then STOP and freeze for a few seconds. *Stopping is critical to this game.*
- Start again from where you left off, slowly finger-crawling toward the baby's chin saying, "IIIIII'm gonna getcha . . . ." Then again, you stop.
- Then start once more from where you left off, again slowly finger-crawling toward the baby's chin saying, "I'm gonna getcha. . . ." Except that this time you suddenly skip the pause that the baby has now come to anticipate, having calculated when it will come. Instead, you surprise him with a quick "GOTCHA!!!" while kissing him and nuzzling his face. You both laugh.

*Brain Link:* Babies everywhere love this game. Dr. Stern has shown why. The baby's brain quickly learns to predict when the next "I'm gonna getcha" is coming. His brain actually begins an unconscious computation of the statistical probability of when the next "I'm gonna getcha" will typically come. When Mom or Dad disrupts this pattern by jumping ahead, the baby is surprised and a little afraid (just a little) because this "GOTCHA" went against his mathematical computation! Being only slightly alarmed, yet clearly in the loving arms of his most secure relationship, a baby feels a thrill and is comforted at the same time. Fun stuff—and amazing brainpower! This game illustrates how the brain's *need to predict* starts very early. Being able to predict what comes next is another basic tenet of survival.

(Interestingly, Stern also tells us that dads—all around the world—typically play this game slightly differently with their infants than do moms. Dads jump ahead faster with the last . . . "GOTCHA!" This even shorter pause tends to alert and excite the baby more than when the moms do it.)

*My Photo Album*
*Babies love this activity so much you'll want to repeat it often.*

*Directions:*
- Find a small, easy-to-hold photo album with plastic sleeves (so your baby won't ruin the pictures) and put simple, easy to see family snapshots in it. Include the main characters in your child's life: family, friends, caregivers who interact with your child.
- Put your baby in your lap and turn the pages. Point to each picture and study it together: "Remember when Grandma came to our house and helped us paint your room?"

*Brain Link:* Discussing and reviewing the key people in a child's world helps her feel connected to others and adds to a sense of security and a sense of connectedness that builds confidence.

*School Link:* Helps develop the ability to regulate and control emotions. Also teaches new vocabulary words and concepts needed for later reading.

*Variations:*
- Walk around your home looking at framed family photos. Tell stories about the people in the pictures.
- Attach photos to your baby's mobile and make a separate mobile of photos with paper and yarn to hang in your baby's room (not over the crib or within grabbing reach).
- Make a photo display out of a montage of family pictures on a piece of cardboard you can attach to the back of the seat of the car for your baby to enjoy looking at on car trips.

### Hello Dolly and Bye-Bye Birdie
*Directions:*
- When your child first wakes up, greet her with "Hi" and a little wave. Make this part of your routine and continue to greet her this same way every time you can.
- Each time that you leave your child, be sure to say, "Bye-bye" and wave to her.

*Brain Link:* Consistent modeling and interaction teach how people act when we meet or leave them and helps to model the power of language. Consistent modeling is necessary to encourage imitation.

### Roll, Roll, Roll the Ball
*Directions:*
- Sit on the floor as close as necessary to your child. Have your child sit with his legs open.
- Roll a ball back and forth between you. Sing, to the tune of "Row, Row, Row Your Boat":

*"Roll, roll, roll the ball*
*back and forth it goes . . .*
*It's your turn to roll the ball*
*so roll, roll, roll, roll, roll. Yeah!"*

*Brain Link:* In addition to practicing large-motor skills, this kind of game teaches the concept of "turn taking" which will later be important in all kinds of interactions that require inhibition (waiting), from play to speaking.

*Variations:*
- Take turns tossing a bean bag or soft foam or rubber ball into a laundry basket or large cardboard box.

## BOND-BUILDERS FOR TODDLERS (18 MONTHS TO 3 YEARS)
### *Identifying Family Members*
*Directions:*
- Choose five dolls to represent a family. They can be a set of wooden dollhouse dolls, a mismatched collection, or paper dolls that you buy or make.
- Without talking, take out a plain place mat (see note at end of chapter).*
- Say, "Watch."
- Take out the dolls one at a time. Describe them as you put each on the placemat. For example, "Here is the child. He's wearing blue shorts. What are you wearing?" Talk about your child and the things he likes to do.
- Take out and describe the next doll. Create a relationship between the dolls that's similar to the friends and family members your child spends time with. For example, "Here is the grandma. She has gray hair. Does your grandma have gray hair? What do you like to do with Grandma?"
- Continue the discussion about other family members and friends using the other dolls.

*Brain Link:* Children like to talk about people who love them, which helps develop the emotional pathways of the brain.

*School Link:* Develops social and emotional stability necessary for school success. Also develops vocabulary and concepts needed for later reading and communication.

*Variations:*
- Share real-life stories about family members. Include funny events about your child's birth, first words, or past birthdays.
- Incorporate vocabulary about family members—where they live, what they look like—into everyday conversations with your child.
- Ask an older toddler to draw family members. Then discuss who each figure is and ask details about what your child knows about that person.

**Sweeping Like Mom or Dad**
*Directions:*
- Sit on the floor next to your child with a small hand broom and dustpan.
- Make a twelve-inch square on the floor with masking tape to draw attention to your proposed "work area." Drop some shredded paper on the floor (not just in the square) from an empty bag.
- Say, "Watch."
- Slowly sweep the paper into the square. Then put the dustpan inside the square and sweep the paper into the dustpan. Dump it back into the empty bag.
- Then say, "Now it's your turn." Spread the shredded paper over the floor again. If your child has problems sweeping, coach by guiding his hand to sweep the paper into the square, then the dustpan. Remember to praise his accomplishments.

*Brain Link:* Older toddlers learn a lot from watching grown-ups and copying what they do. Sweeping is a good example of an activity that children love learning to do that also provides sensory input. This activity stimulates the sensory-motor strip that controls finger, hand, and wrist movements.

*School Link:* Develops large- and fine-motor control needed later for controlling a pencil for handwriting. Improves spatial awareness and problem solving, as well as patience and tenacity needed as prerequisites for school tasks.

### Build a Hideaway
*Directions:*

- Put a large blanket over a card table to make a tent.
- Encourage your child to bring his toys and dolls inside.
- Ask if you can enter.

*Brain Link*: Encourages child to feel secure when in safe, fun environments that can be shared with loved ones. Leads to feelings of competence and confidence.

*Variations:*

- Take an extra-large cardboard box. (Be sure all staples are removed.) Turn it upside down and cut a door and window.

### Playing Doctor or Dentist
*Directions:*

- Set your child on a table and have him remove his T-shirt and shoes. Using a pretend doctor kit, "listen" to his heart with the stethoscope. Use a tongue depressor and flashlight to look in his mouth.

- To play dentist, have your child sit in a chair. Use a mouth mirror and flashlight and ask him to "Open wide."
- Talk about real medical visits as you play to help your child feel more comfortable in the real situation.

*Brain Link:* Pretend playing different roles helps reduce anxiety and increases comfort levels in a real situation.

### Your Teddy Can Do It!
*Toddlers love playing and pretending with dolls and stuffed toys. A favorite doll can be a useful tool when introducing your child to a new skill or situation.*

*Directions:*
- Model the new activity with the doll or stuffed toy before you try to do it with your child.
- For example, if you are going to teach your child how to ride on a tricycle, put his teddy bear in the seat first.

*Brain Link:* Pretending gives a visual example to help calm any fears your child may have about trying something new, reducing stress levels. Modeling and imitation are important for early learning.

### Happy Birthday
*Directions:*
- On birthdays, start a tradition of getting out your child's baby book and looking through the book together.
- Tell your child about the day he was born and about the first time he smiled, crawled, and walked.

*Brain Link:* Telling fun, memorable stories about positive moments and events in your child's life boosts self-esteem and strengthens the bond between the child and the family.

## Cocooning

### Directions:

- Pretend you and your child are caterpillars in a cocoon of blankets or a sleeping bag. Lay quietly, closely touching, and sing softly.
- After a few moments, pretend you are two beautiful butterflies breaking out of a cocoon. Throw off the covers and "fly" around the room.

*Brain Link:* Builds strong connections of comfort and love by sharing fun moments. Activates the central centers of the brain where emotions are processed as well as the motor strip that controls movement.

---

\*The purpose of the place mat is to show the child *where* and *when* to pay attention. The place mat is a visible, concrete cue that you want your child to pay attention to the work (which is really *play*) that you are doing together. Consistently using the place mat eventually teaches a young child how to direct his attention. Show excitement and anticipation as you spread out the place mat. By doing this consistently, pleasure and anticipation become associated with paying attention. See also page 80.

# PART FOUR

## Communication

## WHAT THE SCIENCE SAYS: LANGUAGE GROWS THROUGH EXPOSURE

To understand why communication is so critical that I call it the third cornerstone of brain power for a child, along with attention and bonding, it's helpful to see just what your child's brain does with all those words you speak around her.

For a long time it was thought that babies were born with a capacity for comprehending and speaking that somehow "switched on" at a certain age (the so-called *language instinct*). Language is so complex, it was reasoned, that it would otherwise be impossible for babies to learn to understand and talk as quickly as they do. Until the 1970s, language researchers didn't even study babies until they'd begun to babble. But researchers now feel convinced that babies learn language starting at birth and that they learn based on what they are exposed to. Recent work shows that it's the incredible computational power of the brain that enables them to do so. In a few short years, a child masters the sounds, words and meanings, and proper grammar and syntax of his native tongue, all thanks to some amazingly sophisticated mathematical computations made by the brain as it decodes and sorts sounds. In a process called *neural commitment,* the neurons in the brain pick up on the patterns in one's language and become tuned to them. From the first moments of life, early brain structures begin to change, wiring up according to the language and sounds heard in each child's particular environment. If your baby hears Polish, or Swahili, or English every day, those word sounds and grammatical patterns are what his brain gets practice hearing and will eventually reproduce.

Imagine, for example, a baby born in Japan. She will grow up using a very different-sounding language from children born in India, Croatia, Kenya, or Peru. Yet healthy babies everywhere start out with brains that have the exact same language potential. They each have the ability to detect sounds from any language, all those intricate stresses and pronunciation nuances that make native tongues so distinct (and so difficult for adults to learn). If you only spoke English and were to listen to someone speaking Polish, for example, you might not grasp all the complicated

# 13

# "C" Is for Communication: Why It Matters

Your baby's ability to succeed in life is directly tied in so many ways to her ability to communicate. Talking, listening, reading—they're all critical skills needed for school and beyond. But it's a myth that learning how to talk begins in toddlerhood, or that learning how to read begins in first grade. These skills, we now know, begin much sooner. Your baby was designed to communicate right from birth and depends on you to cultivate that ability.

"Communication" refers to the development of a language system and language skills: all of the information that's transmitted from one person to another by things like words, sounds, gestures, and the printed page. It's your baby's first word—and his first babbles, too. It's reading the word "CAT"—and also recognizing that the McDonalds' Golden Arches represents the letter "M," which in turn represents the actual restaurant. Communication can be singing, crying, laughing, or signing. Getting plenty of practice communicating early in life is directly connected to a child's proficiency at later skills, from reading to understanding computers.

You won't believe how easy—and rewarding—it is to set your child on this path to success.

consonant sounds that are not used in English, and it would take you a very long time to learn them. But your baby is born physically equipped to hear distinct language sounds of all languages.

By age one, however, a child loses the ability to hear sounds that are not found in his native language and, in turn, to easily pronounce them. What has happened? Sounds that are heard frequently strengthen those neurons that are tuned to those specific sounds, and neurons not receiving input "prune away" or get reassigned to process the most dominant sound patterns. This is why, for example, Japanese adult speakers who learn English often have trouble distinguishing the "l" sound (which is not found in their language) from "r." They have literally lost the ability to hear and say the "l" sound as being different from the "r" sound. However, children who consistently hear more than one language during this time period may become native bi- or trilinguals, as they retain the ability to hear the subtle and discrete sounds of these languages.

Sorting out and becoming attuned to these intricate language sounds (*phonemes*) happens with repeated exposure. The structures within your baby's brain that process language are literally shaped by what he hears. When you talk, your child's brain listens . . . and learns . . . and *physically changes and grows*. It processes everything you say and is influenced by it. In essence, *babies' brains develop in relationship with other brains*.

"Other brains," including yours, are critical. As the next chapters will show, you can't just play a continuous tape of Shakespeare or French to reap the effect of changing your baby's brain. It turns out there is something uniquely essential (and wondrous!) about live interactions in building language. Communication is a very interactive process!

## YOUR BABY'S BRAIN IS WIRED TO INTERACT

To me, one of the most amazing new insights is how primal the drive to communicate is. Language development begins *in utero*, as the fetus hears the distinct cadences, intonations, and pitches of his mother's voice (and to a lesser extent, his father's and others', as well as environmental sounds such as music). Language *use* begins as infants have verbal interactions with family and caregivers. That's when babies can hear those once-muffled voices in high-fidelity and observe how the mouth and tongue work to create these unique sounds. Eventually, as they gain motor control over their vocal and breathing apparatus, babies also start to mimic the sounds they hear and the mouth and tongue movements they see.

Cooing and conversing with your baby is more than a pleasure—it's a biological imperative. A baby's brain is driven to interact. In fact, researchers have established that from birth, infants recognize and prefer:

- The sound of the human voice to all other sounds
- The sound of their mother's voice to other all other female voices
- The cadence/tonal qualities of their native tongue
- Familiar music (including music they have heard frequently in the womb)

"But how do you know what a baby who can't talk or control movements is thinking?" I'm always asked. That's a natural thing to wonder. Developmental scientists are able to gauge what infants notice, perceive, and in some cases, know, through some interesting research methods. One way is to track visual eye gaze through a camera connected to tracking equipment. Another is by recording changes in their sucking patterns. It's been known for decades that infants are able to control their sucking movements long before they can control other motor movements, such as reaching. So scientists design experiments that rely on this capability. For example, to assess the recognition of a familiar native language versus an unfamiliar language, researchers give the baby a pacifier that's attached to a computer that can analyze the frequency and intensity of the sucking, and show that infants will suck harder and more frequently when they hear familiar voices, sounds, songs. When the infant hears an unfamiliar voice, sound, or song he slows down his sucking response and also reduces the intensity of his sucking.

Researchers have refined our understanding of how the brain processes language partly by studying deaf infants and toddlers. It used to be thought that the so-called auditory processing area of the brain was programmed to receive input only from sound. Yet in working with deaf infants of deaf parents who routinely use standard sign language, in order to understand how and where in the brain these babies process the signing they see, Dartmouth's Laura-Ann Petitto, Ph.D., discovered something fascinating in 2000: Even though the babies can't hear, the auditory processing areas of the brain are active! They light up on a functional MRI (fMRI) when a deaf parent signs to a deaf child.

Using a computerized camera-enhanced tracking system connected to babies' hands and feet, Petitto also videotaped early hand movements in both hearing babies (ages seven to ten months) and deaf babies of the same age who were raised with signing. Although all the babies made movements with their hands and feet when they were excited, only those in the signing group exhibited a repetitive set of specific hand motions in a specific "box" area right in front of them known to be used to communicate in sign language—basically they were babbling with their hands. Indeed, deaf babies begin to babble in sign language at the exact same age hearing babies babble the sounds they hear in their native language (seven to eleven months). In fact, they reach all the same language milestones at the same ages as hearing children, such as first word (eleven to fourteen months), stringing together two words (sixteen to twenty-two months), and later the use of more complex sentences structures.

Petitto's discoveries mean that the language areas of the brain are not primed only for sounds and speech, per se, but for regular, repetitive, organized communication of any kind. Human beings have an overriding need to communicate, even when some of the systems ordinarily used for this task (hearing, speech) may be impaired. Babies thrive on early experience with language's rhythmical patterns. "It's as if the brain doesn't care," Petitto says, "as long as the input is systematic!"

## LANGUAGE DEVELOPMENT AND THE BRAIN

The chart on the following page links physical behaviors you will notice in your child with descriptions of what's happening simultaneously in brain development and associated language development.

| Age in Months | Neural Development | Language Development |
|---|---|---|
| **0–2** | Brain stem fully functional<br><br>Rapid neural-synapse development reinforced by repeated stimulation | Cries<br><br>Throaty sounds to coos, vowel-like sounds |
| **3–5** | Synapse development in cerebrum and in the parietal and occipital lobes allows for better vision and eye-hand coordination | Babbling—sound play<br><br>Experiments with range of tones and volume<br><br>Becomes more vocal when hearing others talk<br><br>Makes some consonant sounds |
| **6–8** | Neural pathways have formed sound template for native languages(s)<br><br>Begins to hear syllables, then distinct word boundaries. | Learns to make new sounds by changing shape of mouth<br><br>"Echolalia"—word-like sounds emerge<br><br>Babbling resembles conversation-like tone "vocables" |
| **9–12** | Hippocampus becomes fully functional.<br><br>Ability to determine and remember cause-effect.<br><br>Ability to retain words increases. | May respond to name<br><br>Begins to use gestures<br><br>Learns meaning of words by hearing them in context<br><br>May begin to use words<br><br>"Holo-phrases"—one word represents whole idea–sentence |
| **13–18** | Synapses in prefrontal lobe expand rapidly<br><br>Child now able to plan and think logically | Uses gestures<br><br>Large receptive vocabulary<br><br>Follows simple request<br><br>Points to body parts<br><br>Enjoys being read to—likes to hear or label objects, story characters |
| **19–24** | Full cortex consumes twice as much energy as adult<br><br>Synapses' density almost twice that of adult<br><br>Synapses not stimulated will wither—a process called neural-pruning | Language explosion: Child may learn 7 to 12 new words a day—linguists call this "fast-mapping"<br><br>Begins to use sentences<br><br>Enjoys songs, finger plays, storybooks |

From Christie, J., Enz, B. J., & Vukelich, C. *Teaching Language and Literacy: Pre-School through the Elementary Grade* (Third Edition). Facilitator's Guide. Published by Allyn and Bacon, Boston, MA. Copyright © 2007 by Pearson Education. Adapted by permission of the publisher.

## WHAT YOUR RESPONSES TEACH

Communication is, by definition, a two-way street. While babies are figuring out their native language(s), their parents are similarly engaged in becoming "interpreters" of another tongue, the universal baby language—crying. Crying is the chief way a baby communicates hunger, fatigue, fear, pain, or a need to be with you. Responding to cries and, over time, figuring out what's wrong and fixing it, does more than build security and strong attachment. Every time you respond quickly to your baby's cries and other messages, you provide positive reinforcement that aids his understanding of the role of language. The same thing happens when you respond to your baby's social smiles (which begin around four to seven weeks). If he could describe his thinking, he'd say, *Okay, I get it. When I cry, you soothe me. When I laugh, you laugh back.*

This nonverbal communication speaks volumes:

- It shows him he can use sounds to express his needs because when he does, that need will then be met. Remember, the brain likes patterns.
- It helps him figure out the rudimentary volley of conversational turn-taking: my turn, your turn, my turn.
- It builds trust, security, and attachment, by making the child feel like his "words" are important.
- And when you respond, your voice helps his brain to process sounds and figure out a particular language.

## DEVELOPING COMMUNICATION:
## WHAT *YOU* CAN DO AT DIFFERENT AGES

Because young children differ in when they reach developmental milestones, I strongly recommend that instead of focusing on what a child does or does not do (that is largely out of your control), that you focus on what YOU, as the caregiver, can actually do to promote language development and communication with your child. The particulars of how to do many of the behaviors listed in this chart will be explained in the four chapters that follow.

## Infants: 0–6 Months

Use *parentese* intentionally to stimulate distinct language-processing areas of the brain and extend infant's attention span.

Talk frequently all day long, describing actions and objects that are encountered in the daily routine (while dressing, changing, feeding, shopping, cleaning, preparing meals, etc.).

Modulate voice and facial expressions and vary intonation to match levels of enthusiasm, emotion, and meaning.

Talk face-to-face at a distance at which infant can clearly see your mouth and facial expressions as you speak.

Use a second language naturalistically if you are bilingual.

Introduce music at different times throughout the day and sing simple songs.

Hang photos for the infant to look at while in a crib, carriage, car seat, or on the floor to encourage early visual discrimination.

## Babies: 6–18 Months

At the beginning of this stage (6–9 months), sometimes use *parentese* intentionally to stimulate distinct language-processing areas of the brain and extend baby's attention span, then transition to child-directed speech in a conversational tone and speed.

Talk frequently all day long, describing actions and objects that are encountered in the daily routine (while dressing, changing, feeding, shopping, cleaning, preparing meals, etc.).

Modulate voice and facial expressions and vary intonation to match levels of enthusiasm, emotion, and meaning.

Talk face-to-face at a distance at which baby can clearly see your mouth and facial expressions as you speak.

Use a second language naturalistically if you are bilingual.

Introduce music at different times throughout the day and sing simple songs.

Hang photos for the baby to look at while in a crib, carriage, car seat, or on the floor to encourage early visual discrimination.

Deliberately point out and label objects by their name (e.g., light switch, door, cupboard, dish, etc.).

Deliberately point out and label simple attributes of objects (e.g., smooth, rough, hot, big, square, round, blue, red, striped, wet, etc.).

Deliberately point out objects that are the same, or different in one dimension (e.g., smooth/rough, hot/cold, big/little, up/down, over/under, open/shut, wet/dry, etc.).

| |
|---|
| Deliberately label and discuss feelings (e.g., tired, hungry, happy, mad, hurt, etc.). |
| Treat any signs of ear infections quickly by getting medical help. |
| Hold baby and read plastic, cardboard, or cloth books daily in order to share new words and repeat reading familiar books that the baby enjoys. |
| Frequently read rhyming stories or play with rhyming words with the baby, pointing out how/where words sound alike and sound different (e.g., rat, hat, sat, bat, etc.). |
| Provide building blocks for stacking to foster eye-hand coordination needed for writing. |
| Provide opportunities for the baby to pick up tiny pieces of bread, Cheerios, banana, etc., for practice with fine motor skills. |
| Introduce books with one or two sentences per page. |
| Allow baby to turn pages of cardboard book. |
| Play while reading (e.g., act silly by making animal sounds). |
| Invite participation by asking, "What does the dog say?" or ask baby to point to real life objects pictured in his favorite books. |
| Read the same book or story over and over. |
| Hold baby close while reading. |
| Make facial expressions while reading. |

## Toddlers: 18 Months–3 Years

| |
|---|
| Talk frequently all day long, describing actions and objects that are encountered in the daily routine (while dressing, changing, feeding, shopping, cleaning, preparing meals, etc.). |
| Modulate voice and facial expressions and vary intonation to match levels of enthusiasm, emotion, and meaning. |
| Emphasize eye-to-eye contact when talking directly to the toddler to assure understanding. |
| Use a second language naturalistically if you are bilingual. |
| Introduce music at different times throughout the day and sing simple songs. |
| Hang photos for the toddler to look at while in a crib, carriage, car seat, or on the floor to encourage early visual discrimination. |
| Deliberately point out and label objects by their name (e.g., light switch, door, cupboard, dish, etc.). |
| Deliberately point out and label simple attributes of objects (e.g., smooth, rough, hot, big, square, round, blue, red, striped, wet, etc.). |

Deliberately point out objects that are the same, or different in one dimension (e.g., smooth/rough, hot/cold, big/little, up/down, over/under, open/shut, wet/dry, etc.).

Deliberately label and discuss feelings (e.g., tired, hungry, happy, mad, hurt, etc.).

Treat any signs of ear infections quickly by getting medical help.

Hold toddler and read plastic, cardboard, or cloth books daily in order to share new words and repeat reading familiar books that the toddler enjoys.

Frequently read rhyming stories or play with rhyming words with the toddler, pointing out how/where words sound alike and sound different (e.g., rat, hat, sat, bat, etc.).

Provide building blocks for stacking to foster eye-hand coordination needed for writing.

Provide opportunities for the toddler to pick up tiny pieces of bread, Cheerios, banana, etc., for practice with fine motor skills.

Introduce books with one or two sentences per page.

Allow toddler to turn pages of cardboard book.

Play while reading (e.g., act silly by making animal sounds).

Invite participation by asking, "What does the dog say?" or ask toddler to point to real life objects pictured in his favorite books.

Read the same book or story over and over.

Hold toddler close while reading.

Make facial expressions while reading.

At the end of this stage, begin simple music "lessons" on keyboard or violin.

Sing favorite songs and introduce new songs that incorporate simple actions and movements that correspond (e.g., "I'm a little teapot" or "The itsy bitsy spider").

Promote reading print in the environment (restaurant signs and logos), food and product labels, and street signs.

Ask open-ended questions (e.g., "What do you think will happen next?").

Read enthusiastically—take on different voices and experiences (e.g., The Three Little Pigs and the Wolf, Goldilocks and the Three Bears, etc.).

Follow toddler's lead. Identify and discuss what toddler talks about. Find and read more books on those subjects.

# 14

# Everyday Talk: Thank Goodness It's Cheap!

- WHEN SHOULD I START TALKING TO MY BABY? WHAT SHOULD I SAY?
- IS IT OKAY TO USE BABY TALK?
- WHAT IF MY CHILD'S CAREGIVER DOESN'T SPEAK ENGLISH WELL?
- SHOULD I CHECK OUT FOREIGN LANGUAGE CLASSES OR TAPES?
- WHAT ABOUT TEACHING MY BABY SIGNING?

Everybody's searching for the next great brain booster. Well, scientists have found it—and it's accessible to every family, guaranteed to improve intellectual development and prevent certain kinds of learning problems later in life. And to reap its benefits, you don't have to buy a thing—or even learn any special new technique. In fact, it's free. And it's right under our noses (literally!): Talk.

Simply talking to a baby is so key to brain development that in the journal *Pediatrics* in 2001, Steven Berman, M.D., then president of the American Academy of Pediatrics, asked all members to share this important finding with moms and dads of newborns. "We need to start by implementing programs in our practices that motivate parents and other caregivers to talk with and encourage their young children," he wrote. "It is not enough to merely do developmental screening." Perhaps given time constraints on busy pediatric practices, however, I seldom hear from new parents that his request has been widely heeded. That's too bad, because this simple advice makes such a big, direct, and immediate difference. When my colleagues at New Directions Institute for Infant Brain Development and I teach this same message to parents, they're usually delighted to discover they have the power to influence their child's intellectual growth in such a simple way. What's more, when we conduct follow-up interviews, they report that they deliberately speak far more to their children now.

Talk may be cheap, but for young children it is priceless.

## WHAT THE SCIENCE SAYS: THE NUMBER ONE IQ BUILDER

The sheer amount of words spoken to a child from birth to three has a direct impact on later testable IQ. Imagine that! It doesn't matter what you say, or in what language. Whether you're just talking about what happened to you at work that day, or reading the words from a book, all kinds of spoken words count!

The seminal study by Betty Hart, Ph.D., and Todd Risley, Ph.D., took place in the mid-1990s, when a University of Kansas team followed forty-two families of various socioeconomic backgrounds for over two and a half years, from when their children were seven to nine months old until they were three. Dutiful graduate students actually sat in families' homes counting the number of words spoken in the home. They also noted tone of voice and whether the words were emotionally positive or negative. Later, the research team evaluated how the total amount of words spoken was related to each child's future IQ scores. The more words spoken in the home (in a positive tone), the higher the IQ scores were at age three—regardless of socioeconomic status. By age four, children in the language-richest homes had heard *thirty-two million more words* than those in the more language-impoverished homes. The study showed that kids who are exposed to more language, from birth, wind up, on average, smarter. Higher IQ was also associated with speaking style; the children who heard a more positive tone, had more conversational interactions, and were asked rather than ordered (who were the same children as in the more-talk homes) tended to score higher on intelligence tests.

Researcher Billie Enz, Ph.D., at Arizona State University, has compared ways that families might actually differ in their language patterns during typical mother-baby interactions. Her research confirms there are huge differences in the amount of talk in American homes. Compare three sample interactions:

**Mom 1:** *Okay, Crystal, let's eat.*

**Mom 2:** *Okay, Paulie, it's time to eat our lunch. Let's see what we are having? Yes, let's have carrots.*

**Mom 3:** *Okay, Teryl, it's lunchtime. Are you hungry? Mommy is so hungry! Let's see what we have in the refrigerator today. What is this? It's orange. Could it be peaches? Could it be apricots? Let's see!! See the picture on the jar? That's right, it's carrots.*

You can see which child is likely to develop the largest vocabulary. Talking to a child builds vocabulary and enhances concept development, factors that contribute largely in standard IQ assessments. The amount of words spoken, over time, makes a big difference. Although there were differences that fell along economic status in this University of Kansas talk-IQ study, *some of the children* who were from the poorest homes economically had the highest IQs. The amount of talk directed to a child in positive tones, along with your attention and love, proves to be a strong buffer against economic distress.

Below is a list of the comparisons between different groups showing the cumulative differences in the number of words recorded in a one-hour period of time.

| *Words* | *Hour* |
|---|---|
| 616 | Group A |
| 1,252 | Group B |
| 2,153 | Group C |

The graph on page 220 shows the relationship found between the amount of talk and later testable IQ.

Talking to a baby develops two types of language:

1. *Listening (receptive).* This means your child understands what you say. ("Point to Daddy's mouth!") This ability develops long before speaking. When a child is spoken to and read to

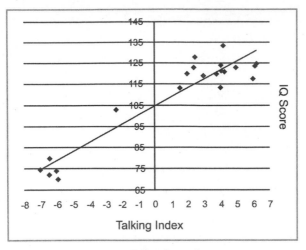

*Figure 9. Talk: More is better.*

The talking index represents a combination of the amount and quality of talking in the family: High positive scores represent environments in which there was a lot of high-quality speech; high negative scores represent less enriched environments.

frequently, receptive language often develops early. For example, you can tell when a seven-month-old understands what you're talking about by following her eye gaze when you mention a person or an object she's become familiar with. Once your child is mobile (crawling or walking), this becomes increasingly easy to observe. Ask your young toddler to bring mommy's purse, and off she'll go to find it. All new parents marvel at how "smart" their little one is when they see how much they already understand in such a short time!

2. *Spoken (expressive).* Most children begin to speak real words around age one. Within months after their first birthdays, most children are able to convey their intentions with single words. ("No!" "Mine!") More complex, rule-driven communication usually emerges between the ages of two and three, when children are able to construct sentences of two or more words. By three, many children have hundreds of words in their speaking and listening vocabulary. Language acquisition explodes.

## THE BABY STEPS OF LEARNING TO TALK

In order to learn to talk, a baby's brain must decode speech in four progressive and interactive ways:

1. *First, babies must learn the rhythmical properties of their language.* This refers to how the pattern of stress falls on different syllables. By two months old, infants can tell the difference between languages with different stress patterns, such as English and Japanese. As infants become more and more familiar with the properties of their native language, their skills are refined and they can tell the difference between languages with the same stress patterns, such as English and Dutch. By five months old, infants can even tell the difference between different dialects of English, such as American and British! At the same time, babies are also tuning their neurons to process only those sounds of speech (phonemes) that are present in their native language.

2. *Next, babies learn the words in the language.* In a continuous stream of speech, it's sometimes hard to tell where one word ends and the next begins. Think about how the words all seem to jumble together when you listen to a foreign language. Babies' brains amazingly use statistical probabilities to pick up the patterns in language to tell where the word boundaries are, a process called *word segmentation*. Some time between six and twelve months of age, the brain has matured enough to begin to distinguish syllables, which soon enables that brain to detect word boundaries. In the phrase "pretty baby," for example, the syllable "ba" occurs *more often* with "by" than it does with "ty" so that the word is "baby" and not "tyba." Prior to this, *doyouwantyourbottle?* was a pleasant tune, but was not explicit communication. After word boundaries become apparent, babies will hear distinct words: *Do / you / want / your / BOTTLE?*

3. *Then, babies learn the units of grammar in the language.* Just as they learned which syllables combined to form words, they now figure out which words combine to form phrases and sentences. Again, it's the

computational power of the brain that picks up on the patterns in what's heard. There are a lot of cues that babies use in order to learn the words and grammar of their native language. And the more you talk to your baby, the more experience with those cues your baby will have to help him learn.

4. *Simultaneously, words begin to take on meaning.* As sounds become words that are frequently used in context to label a specific object, the acquisition of word meaning begins. Parents instinctively help this process when they label objects in a child's environment:

> "*Where is Momma's* **nose**? *That's right! Okay, whoa Robby!*
> *Please be gentle with Mommy's nose!*"
> "*Where is the* **butterfly** *Annie? Can you find it in the book?*"

At this stage of development, babies usually recognize and have cognitive meaning for words such as *bottle, mama*, and *daddy*. Their receptive or listening vocabulary grows rapidly, though it will take a few more months before their expressive or oral language catches up.

Throughout the processes described above, the hippocampus becomes increasingly functional. Located near the center of the brain, the hippocampus is part of the limbic system and is the part of the brain that helps to index and file memories. As it matures, babies are able to form memories and recall labels for familiar objects/people, remember where objects are located, and recall what happens at specific locations, for example, shots at the doctor's office or a cookie at the bakery. As the hippocampus develops and more elaborate neural networks are created, a single word can come to call up many related ideas. The brain is able to catch in a *neural net* all of the related ideas that the brain has stored away.

## HOW WORDS HELP ORGANIZE THE BRAIN

New words help a baby or toddler to construct his reality; what it's like to be alive in this particular place, with this particular family, with this particular gender, in this particular body. The brain must learn quickly, because there is so much to know. With so much happening at any given moment, so many sensations bombarding the brain with input, the brain efficiently simplifies things for itself in order to better categorize the incoming information and preserve what's most important. Your child's brain conserves energy to continue to learn so rapidly by forming concepts and storing the gist of what his experiences add up to. To do this, it creates a *schema,* or theme for "how it goes." Brains of young children start making new schema that help to sort repeated experiences into "bundles" that store information about how the world works in general ways.

Consider, for example, the way a child learns the concept of "cat." When a baby first sees a cat, he studies it cautiously and carefully. Hopefully a caring adult will label this new thing: "This is a cat." The next time the baby sees a cat, because he has some familiarity with this thing, he will still study it, but for less time than he did the first time he saw it. The graph below shows how rapid this learning curve can be!

The child quickly comes to understand what a *cat* is. And he will know "that thing" as a cat for the rest of his life. This process of sorting helps explain why a young child will also *over-generalize* about other small, four-legged furry things; the first time he sees a small dog . . . yes,

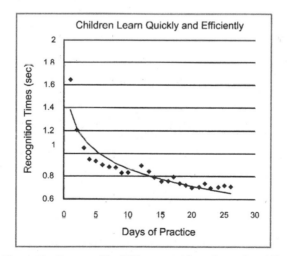

*Figure 10. Concepts like "What a cat is" are learned rapidly.*

you guessed it, he may proudly say, "Cat!" With adult assistance, categories like these become clarified and refined. Before long, if he has the interest and the opportunity, he can differentiate a bobcat from a Manx cat, a lion from a tiger, and so on.

The learning curve shown in Figure 10 is typical of most human learning:

- lots of effort in the very beginning,
- additional effort in the beginning,
- repeat, repeat,
- repeat with little effort,
- "I know it!" . . . forever.

Each schema develops through exposure and experience: A cat seen in a book, a big cat seen at the zoo, a pet cat to touch, as well as *The Cat in the Hat*. The context of a sentence or conversation and tone of voice also help a learning brain sort out meaning.

At the end of the first year, the prefrontal cortex, the brain's seat of forethought and logic, forms synapses at a rapid rate. This creates an increased capacity for learning that, along with better physical dexterity, leads to increased curiosity and exploration and a deep desire to understand how things work. It's this neural readiness, in combination with countless hours of repetition and playing with sounds through babbling and verbal exchanges with loving caregivers, that allows most children to begin speaking their first words, though there may be great variation of the amount of words young children speak.

Enough talking! Let's get right to the strategies:

## THE BRIGHT IDEAS: EVERYDAY TALK
### 1. *Talk Early, Talk Often!*
You should talk to your baby right from the start, long before she shows any sign of babbling to herself. Learning to talk is not a matter of being formally instructed in nouns, verbs, and vocabulary words; it's a matter of hearing natural conversation directed to you, over and over and over.

Here's some guidance about common concerns:

### "My Baby is Just a Newborn; What's a Good Age to Begin?"

Immediately. A newborn can pick out her mother's voice and routinely distinguish fine differences in speech patterns that exist in spoken language. By six months, a baby can imitate many of the sounds spoken around him. Don't get hung up on thinking about speech as something a baby is "taught" or "learns." Just do it and she will follow along as she grows.

### "I don't Know What to Say."

What you say is less important than simply that you talk, using a positive tone and positive words as much as possible. Some ideas:

- *Narrate your day.* "We had a nice day visiting, didn't we? I liked seeing Grandma. She loves you sooo much! Now we're driving home on this overly busy road, and then we'll get to see Daddy and have dinner. Won't that be great?"
- *Play "show and tell".* "Do you need a diaper? Okay, here's a nice fresh diaper. Oh my yes, you needed a change, didn't you!" You can use this kind of descriptive conversation when you're feeding, dressing, or bathing your baby; cooking; driving in the car—no matter what you're doing.
- *Read aloud to your child.* Reading works just as well as conversation in exposing your child to new words and sentence structure. (More specific information on that follows in Chapter 15, "Everyday Reading.")

### "I Feel Weird."

When parents find it awkward to talk to a baby who can't talk back, it's often because they have little prior experience with babies or they haven't seen other adults interacting with little ones in this way. When people thought babies were just lumps of clay, it might have made sense for them to say very little directly to the baby. Given what we now know about how the neurons in the brain are absorbing and reacting to the sounds your baby hears, however, feeding your baby with words is as essential as nourishing him with foods. There are many things that new parents must do that feel odd or unfamiliar (like changing diapers or soothing crying); it just goes with the territory, you do it because you know it's what's right for your child.

"I'M NOT A NATIVE ENGLISH SPEAKER."
Because I'm based in Arizona, I often encounter Spanish-speaking parents who say they are careful not to use too much Spanish around their babies because they want them to grow up understanding English. They figure, with the best of intentions, that they will wait until their child learns English from a proper teacher, in school. As a result, mistakenly, they don't talk very much to their baby or toddler. They are so relieved when I share this information about the tremendous value of talk . . . in *any* language. Hearing more than one language early in life will not stunt your child's ability to become proficient in either, or both, languages. (And, as I'll explain at the end of this chapter, hearing two languages can actually have benefits.)

Another example: Non-English-speaking nannies may be reluctant to speak in their native tongue to their young charges—or sometimes are instructed by their employers to use only English—and feeling awkward, wind up speaking little to the child. This is not a benefit and can be a huge drawback.

It's far more important for a child to hear spoken words—in any language—than not to hear normal language and communication. Silence is "deafening" because it doesn't give the brain practice in listening to the stresses and patterns of speech. It doesn't matter whether that speech is English or something else. It's also best for a child to hear the language that the speaker is most fluent in. In order to pick up on all the nuances of a language—again, any language, it doesn't matter which—you want the child to be able to hear consistent grammar and proper pronunciation. When non-English speakers try to limit their speech to English that they're sort of shaky with, the baby is more likely to have difficulty learning language. Better to learn the language a parent or caregiver is fluent in first and then pick up English later, or ideally, be simultaneously exposed to multiple languages (such as a parent and a caregiver speaking different languages, or two parents who have different native languages). Whatever language you would normally say *I love you* in is the language you should be speaking routinely to your young infant and toddler. They will transfer to English when needed. Young children learn a second language easily.

### "Is there such a Thing As Talking too Much?"

Yes—though only if you carry the advice to the extreme. As with all brain-related advice, I suppose I need to insert a caveat: Remember a young child needs downtime. *Quiet* downtime! Don't chatter away when your child seems tired or distressed. You shouldn't talk a blue streak or read books aloud to fill in the natural silent spaces of your day.

Also remember that in order to learn about language your child needs to understand that conversation is a process of give and take. Even before your child can speak to answer you, be sure you include natural pauses in your talk. As early as when babbling begins (six to eight months), your baby will learn to fill in the pauses with his own coos. You can get quite a fun "chat" going this way.

### 2. Say It in Parentese

There's a scene I love in the old movie *Three Men and a Baby* when Tom Selleck reads a sports magazine aloud to a baby on his lap. "What are you reading?!" someone just off-camera asks skeptically. "It doesn't matter what I read," he replies self-assuredly in the same singsong way that he'd used to read. "It's the tone I use . . . Now, where were we?" It's meant to be a gag, but when Selleck points out that it's the tone of voice and the amount of direct attention given that the baby responds to, not the specific words, he's right!

All around the globe, new parents speak to their infants in the same singsong way: "OOOOhhh, loooook at youuuuuu! You're a great, biiiig bay-beee!" This speech pattern is called *parentese*. And there's a biologically good reason for it. We speak in parentese because that's exactly the tone, pitch, and speed a baby's brain can hear!

You use the same actual words you normally do (not babbles or nonsense syllables), but you:

- speak more *slowly,*
- enunciate more deliberately and with greater emphasis,
- speak in a higher pitch, and
- elongate vowel sounds, particularly the long vowel sounds in words

You don't really need to "learn" parentese. You probably can't help it! It's a speech pattern parents use naturally in response to careful observation of what a baby seems to pay attention to the most. Infants will only pay attention to input they can process. We modify *our* behavior in response to what our baby shows us she likes. Because parents have always loved their babies and watched them so meticulously, they learn from their baby what she will attend to. I think it seems like magic . . . that we adapt our behaviors based on what our child is showing us. Just let yourself go with it!

By the way, studies from neuroscience show that this style of speaking parentese perfectly matches the auditory processing speed that a very young infant can hear. Infants hear best those sounds that are slower in speed, higher in frequency, clear and distinct! This shows that families closely watching their tiny infants, no matter in what culture around the world, have figured out what scientists can now confirm, though they knew it long before neuroscientists could explain it. Parentese is one of the first among many natural instincts that you can learn to trust. Watch, watch, watch. Infants *tell you* what they like, what they hear, what they need.

Don't confuse parentese with baby talk. Baby talk consists of nonsense sounds: "Ooh, ohh, baby-waby. Ga ga ga gaga goo goo." Although you may sometimes have fun using nonsense sound while playing, and it can be reinforcing to your baby to hear you mimic his/her ever-increasing number of babbling sounds (*ma-ma-ma*) baby talk doesn't teach the pattern-seeking brain about how actual language works. Parentese, on the other hand, is *regular* speech modified to match the processing capabilities of what your baby hears. It is everyday words and usual sentence structures slowed down and exaggerated so that your baby can more easily process that input.

Interestingly, no one has to direct you when to resume typical speech tones and speed as your baby gets older; you will naturally and unconsciously adjust according to the cues you get from your child. This happens slowly, almost imperceptibly, but one day you will suddenly note that little Charlie is a fully capable language listener!

### 3. Take Turns with Your Baby

A key part of the development of language is understanding that words and sounds are used to communicate some kind of shared meaning between two people. At an amazingly early age, a baby develops an anticipation of turn-taking in a typical conversational volley between two people. You can see this with a baby of just a few months old. When she coos or babbles, reply; she'll "talk" back to you. You are teaching her that conversation is a back-and-forth interaction. Stanford University researcher Susan Johnson, Ph.D., devised a clever experiment to show that a pre-verbal child understands that conversations are a two-way process of turn-taking. First a researcher speaking in English carried on a conversation with a faceless blob of a puppet making only nonsense noises. The child had never seen the researcher or the blob before. After witnessing just two or three short exchanges, a fourteen-month-old automatically began to turn her head toward the next "speaker" in anticipation of his (or its) response. Then the researcher left the room and the child sat alone with the blob. She soon initiated a noise and, to her surprise, the blob responded; she babbled again, this time looking right at it waiting for its reply. A conversation between them ensued that was perfectly modeled after the observed reciprocal "conversation" of the original scenario with the researcher.

You can use puppets (whether store bought or homemade) with your child to give additional practice in language learning and the art of communication. Because children are attracted by the novelty of the puppet, they will often pay close attention to it. Your baby, as young as one year old, may enjoy "conversations" with a puppet. As Johnson's research shows, the puppet does not have to be particularly lifelike. Any "talking" puppet will do. (See Puppet Play, in Chapter 7: "Attention-Builders Little Ones Love.")

### 4. Create a Talking Home
Opportunities for everyday talk exist all through your house. A researcher at Arizona State University, Billie Enz, Ph.D., is an authority on early learning and pre-literacy, and she suggests these ideas for taking advantage of talk opportunities:

**Bedroom Talk**
- Talk about toys' colors, textures and special features: "Wow! Look at how Tickle Me Elmo is moving!"
- Label and describe clothes, talk about their color, style, and textures. "Today we are wearing a warm, wooly sweater because it's cool outside."
- Sing songs, such as the *Barney* "Clean Up" song, as you pick up the room.

**Bathroom Talk**
- Label and describe what's happening during a bath: The slippery soap, warm water, bubbles in the water, the tickle of having toes washed.
- Talk about water toys in the tub: The duck floats, the cup pours, the fish toy squirts.
- Sing bathtime songs, like "Rubber Ducky."

**Family Room Talk**
- Read storybooks.
- Occasionally watch children's videos together and discuss the characters: "Which Teletubby do you like best?" "What color is he?" "Can you dance like that?"
- Ask your child to pick up toys by describing them: "Jose, please pick up the toy that has four blue wheels."

**Kitchen Talk**
- Describe the food you are preparing: Color, texture, smell, and taste.
- Talk about how small you are cutting the pieces, how the food is cooked.
- Narrate what you're doing as you set the table.
- Let your child play with kitchen goods such as wooden spoons, pots, unbreakable dishes, or measuring cups and spoons: Talk about their relative sizes and the sounds they make when you tap on them.
- Demonstrate using "please" and "thank you" while sharing food at the table.

### 5. *Support Your Child's Language*

Children's early attempts to use sentences need thoughtful support, not critical correction. You will hear many "mistakes" mainly because of the trial-and-error way that the child's brain is working to decipher language. (The development of mouth muscles to form various sounds is another factor.) Parents can best support their child's attempts to communicate through what linguists call "extensions and expansions."

*Extensions* include responses that incorporate the essence of a child's sentence but transform it into a well-formed sentence. For example, when a child says, "Ree stor-ee," you can respond, "Do you want me to read the storybook to you?" When parents and caregivers use extensions, they model appropriate grammar and fluent speech—helping to extend a child's vocabulary.

*Expansions* gently reshape the child's efforts to reflect grammatically appropriate content. For example, when your child says, "We goed to Diseelan," instead of correcting her ("We don't say 'goed,' we say went"), you can expand her language by initially confirming the intent of her statement while modeling the correct form, "Yes, we went to Disneyland."

Parents in all cultures have been observed to encourage language development in these and other ways. Notice, in the list on page 232, how many of the following supports you already offer naturally in the course of daily conversation.

**Expansions:** Recast the child's efforts to reflect appropriate grammar. Doing this helps to introduce and build new vocabulary.

> **Child:** *Kitty eat.*
> **You:** *Yes, the kitty is eating.*

**Extensions:** Restate the child's telegraphic speech into a complete thought and possibly add new information.

> **Child:** *Kitty eat.*
> **You:** *Kitty is eating food.*
> **Child:** *Kitty eat.*
> **You:** *The kitty is hungry.*

**Repetitions:** Aid the development of new sentence structure by repeating all or part of the child's comment.

> **Child:** *Kitty eat.*
> **You:** *Time for the kitty to eat. Time for the kitty to eat.*

**Parallel talk:** Describe the child's actions. This is a way to model new vocabulary or grammatical structure:

> **Child:** *Kitty eat.*
> **You:** *Jimmy is watching the kitty eat.*

**Self-talk:** Describe your actions. Like parallel talk, it models vocabulary and grammar.

> **You:** *I'm feeding the kitty.*

**Vertical structuring:** Use questions to encourage the child to produce longer and more complex sentences.

**Child:** *Kitty eat.*
**You:** *What is the kitty eating?*
**Child:** *Kitty eat cat food.*

**Fill-ins:** Structure the conversation so the child must provide a word or phrase to complete the statement.

**Adult:** *The kitty is eating because she is—*
**Child:** *Hungry!*

From Christie, J., Enz, B. J., & Vukelich, C. *Teaching Language and Literacy: Pre-School through the Elementary Grades* (Third Edition). Published by Allyn and Bacon, Boston, MA. Copyright © 2007 by Pearson Education. Adapted by permission of the publisher.

### 6. Build a Bilingual Brain (Now or Later)

If you speak more than one language, or your child's caregiver does, you don't need to change a thing. It used to be thought that bilingual children might have slower speech development because they had to sort through the confusion of two languages. In reality, when the words a child knows in both languages are added together, they're usually within the normal range expected for a child at that age. The truth is, if two languages are naturally spoken in the home routinely, a young brain can easily accommodate learning both simultaneously. What's more, we now know that bilingual children actually perform certain cognitive tasks better than monolingual kids. Researchers like Laura-Ann Petitto, Ph.D., at Dartmouth College think that having to process two different languages places more computational demands on a young brain, which, in effect, speeds it up. Adele Diamond, Ph.D., at the University of British Columbia, agrees that bilingual kids, because they have to adapt to a new set of rules in each language as they switch back and forth, have practice in learning to inhibit—not pay attention to—a previously learned set of rules. This skill of "switching" develops the prefrontal cortex of the child's brain, pushing it to mature earlier. Also, according to Suzanne Flynn, Ph.D., at Massachusetts Institute of Technology, children who speak two languages may also be better able to abstract information (pull general rules from specific examples) because they learn that the names of objects are arbitrary. For example, a child growing up with English and Spanish would learn that a blouse can also be a *shirt*, or in an "alternate code" it can be a *camisa* or a *blusa*.

But what if you don't happen to have a native speaker of a foreign language handy around your child every day—should you get one? If babies are primed to absorb more than one language early in life, does it follow that the best time to enroll your child is a foreign language course is in infancy and toddlerhood? Should you invest in some tapes or videos designed to teach babies Spanish, Russian, or Chinese? No, no, and no. Although the science does suggest that being introduced to languages before age three makes them easier to pick up, it is not the case that Spanish, Russian, or Japanese should be part of every baby's "curriculum." If you happen to hire a nanny who speaks a foreign language with your baby, that can be a great way to start your child on the path to bilingualism. But remember that if your child stops speaking that language once she begins formal schooling, the benefit will not be one that lasts. If a child has little opportunity to *use* a foreign language with some regularity, the ability to distinguish different stresses and sounds falls away over time; they are not imprinted on the brain forever.

Even if you miss that early window to expose your child regularly to another language, you can still give him this advantage later in life. Many elementary and middle-school curriculum offerings now feature foreign languages, and children can do very well in these classes. The language areas of the brain remain quite plastic and kids can learn a new language with near-native proficiency fairly easily all the way up until puberty, if they have regular practice hearing and speaking it. Again, *regular use* is the key. A toddler class that teaches Mandarin might be fun, but unless your child spends a lot of time in the rest of childhood around Mandarin-speaking people, speaking the language himself, he's not likely to effectively retain much of what he picks up.

Studying foreign languages, whether from infancy if circumstances make that possible or later in school, has practical benefits aside from building a dexterous brain. In a world where commerce, travel, and education are now so readily available to cultures in a free society, learning other languages is fast becoming a necessity. My personal attempts to learn Spanish as a fourteen-year-old and German as a seventeen-year-old allowed me to understand that *late*-adolescence language learning can be difficult. As a result of those struggles, I decided to be sure that my daughter Kristin, raised in Phoenix, would be bilingual. Happily, her school system offered Spanish from kindergarten through high school; age five was early enough to begin learning another language, especially because she did so every year thereafter and the school lessons were supplemented by a summer living in Spain as an exchange student. She's now definitely bilingual and even enjoys reading novels in Spanish—such is the power of the young, language-facile brain!

## What About Sign Language?

In recent years teaching a baby to sign has become a popular pastime for parents. Many believe it makes their baby smarter by establishing communication at an earlier age than when oral speech typically develops.

To date, I know of no replicable studies with solid evidence that learning signs can boost a baby's IQ or lead to earlier speech. It is my opinion that future studies may well end up showing a positive relationship because many believe that language itself evolved from an earlier gesture system. What your child can definitely learn from using sign language is an understanding that he can play an active role in communication. This kind of knowledge does have value. Knowing signs to express hunger or interest can lessen a baby's frustration, for example. Smoother interactions in turn facilitate bonding by helping both child and parent feel more relaxed, less anxious. Being less anxious can lead to many positive outcomes, thus, enhanced early learning and language milestones may be more directly related to the enhanced relationships in a baby's life than to the signing itself.

Your child is born communicating. The most important thing a parent can do to encourage learning and language development is to create a secure, predictable environment that is filled with language and contains a balance of routines and exposure to new experiences.

## 7. Be Alert for Lags

While the process of learning to talk follows a predictable sequence, the age at which children say their first word or talk in sentences can vary widely from one child to another. Developmental guidelines refer to the age *most* children do something; if your child does not, it's not necessarily a sign of a problem. But language development is an important thing to keep tabs on because while physical maturation is easy to observe, cognitive development is less obvious. Language development provides one indication that a child's cognitive abilities are developing normally.

If a child's language is delayed more than two months past the upper age limits, tell your doctor. Hearing difficulty or hearing loss, for example, often cause delays that can be easily treated, especially if handled early.

## TYPICAL LANGUAGE DEVELOPMENT

| Age in months | The majority of children will develop the following language skills by the ages indicated. If a child does not demonstrate these behaviors by these ages, it is important for parents to seek medical guidance. |
|---|---|
| 0–3 | • Majority of communication consists of crying as larynx has not yet descended |
| | • Turns head to the direction of the familiy's voices |
| | • Is startled by loud or surprising sounds |
| 3–6 | • Begins to make cooing sounds to solicit attention from caregivers |
| | • Begins to play with voice |
| | • Observes caregiver's face when being spoken to, often shapes mouth in a similar manner |
| 6 | • Responds to his or her name |
| | • Responds to human voices without visual cues by turning head and eyes |
| | • Responds appropriately to friendly and angry tones |
| 12 | • Uses one or more words with meaning (this may be a fragment of a word) |
| | • Understands simple instructions, especially if vocal or physical cues are given |
| | • Is aware of the social value of speech |
| 18 | • Has vocabulary of approximately 5–20 words |

| | |
|---|---|
| | • Vocabulary made up chiefly of nouns |
| | • Much jargon with emotional content |
| | • Is able to follow simple commands |
| 24 | • Can name a number of objects common to his surroundings |
| | • Combines words into a short sentence—largely noun-verb combinations |
| | • Approximately two thirds of what child says should be understandable |
| | • Vocabulary of approximately 150–300 words |
| | • *My* and *mine* are beginning to emerge |
| 36 | • Is using some plurals and past tenses—"We played a lot." |
| | • Handles three word sentences easily—"I want candy." |
| | • Has approximately 900–1000 words in vocabulary |
| | • About 90 percent of what child says can be understandable |
| | • Verbs begin to predominate, such as "let's go, let's run, let's climb, let's play." |
| 48 | • Knows names of familiar animals |
| | • Names common objects in picture books or magazines |
| | • Knows one or more colors and common shapes |
| | • Can repeat four digits when they are given slowly |
| | • Can usually repeat words of four syllables |
| | • Often engages in make-believe |
| | • Extensive verbalization as he carries out activities |
| | • Understands such concepts as longer, larger, when a contrast is presented |
| | • Much repetition of words, phrases, syllables, and even sounds |

From Christie, J., Enz, B. J., & Vukelich, C. *Teaching Language and Literacy: Pre-School through the Elementary Grades.* (Third Edition). Published by Allyn and Bacon, Boston, MA. Copyright © 2007 by Pearson Education. Adapted by permission of the publisher.

## When Talking Stops

Here's a fairly common scenario: A young toddler who has begun using simple sentences has a bad ear infection. Antibiotics clear it up and the child seems fine. But something isn't right. Maybe the parents notice the sound being turned up louder on the TV, or the fact that the child does not come quickly when called. The child doesn't respond unless she's

# 15

# Everyday Reading: Dr. Seuss Had It Right

- DOES IT REALLY MATTER WHETHER YOU READ TO A BABY OR TODDLER?
  - WHAT'S A GOOD AGE TO START?
- HOW DOES READING ALOUD TO A CHILD HELP HER?
  - WHAT KINDS OF BEGINNER BOOKS ARE BEST?

Reading a classic like *The Cat in the Hat* aloud to your child is one of the wonderfully fun things you get to do as a mom or dad. But it's more than a pleasure. Just as with being talked to, being read to helps "tune" individual bundles of neurons in a critical part of the growing brain, which will make your child better able to learn to speak and one day read himself. It's these thousands of hours of parent-child interactions, from the moment of birth through the preschool years, which provide the foundation for both language and literacy.

By now you've most likely heard that "reading is fundamental." But what does that really mean in infancy and toddlerhood? Many parents of under-threes who I have met aren't sure how this advice applies to them. So, let's first clear up some common misunderstandings about the "read to your child" campaign:

*"I thought it wasn't a good idea to push a child—*
*can't reading wait 'til kindergarten?"*

Reading to your child doesn't mean *teaching her how to read*. Nothing in neuroscience suggests it's useful to hook a one-year-old on phonics or run alphabet skill drills with a two-year-old. In fact, there's little developmental advantage to learning how to read before school. (Some kids do, and that's fine. But early reading is not consistently linked to advanced intellectual performance later.) Reading *to* a child, on the other hand, expands the total number of words your child hears, processes, and knows, which we now know to be critical to overall intelligence. Being read to also paves the way for skills involved in actual reading later.

### "My baby isn't even talking yet!"

Don't wait until your child asks you to read a story. The habit of sitting down quietly with a shared book is a practice you can start early. Practically speaking, I find it most helpful to wait until a child is about four months old for lap reading; before this a baby can enjoy the sounds of your voice, but he lacks the visual acuity to really see the pages and enjoy the colors, and he can't yet reach out and touch the pages. By six to seven months, his full range of vision is well established, and soft cloth or plastic books can already be favorite "objects" in a baby's world. What is significant is that you begin a ritual of reading that, *because it starts early*, becomes just a natural part of your child's daily experiences.

### "I don't know what to read."

In the beginning, it doesn't matter much what you read. With the proper tone and use of parentese, you can interest your four-month-old in just about anything you need to be reading! Directions for how to operate your new-fangled grill will do just fine at first. Your goal is to expose him to words and sounds. By six months, a baby's brain has already created permanent neural networks that recognize the subtle sounds and rhythmic patterns of his/her native language(s). By about twelve months, however, babies usually recognize and have cognitive meaning for words that are frequently used in their home. Their receptive or listening vocabulary has grown rapidly and they're ready to delight in storybooks made for children.

Theodore Geisel, a.k.a. Dr. Seuss, who loved to play with language, word patterns, and initial word sound changes, is one of my favorite children's authors because his stories are both fun to hear and activate the very parts of the brain that detect both pattern and change. Children of all ages love Dr. Seuss books for their three R's: rhythm, rhyme, and repetition.

Another kind of book that babies and toddlers love is one with clear, simple, colorful pictures. As you point to the colorful images, your little one's eye gaze will hopefully follow and you can begin to explain and elaborate about each image. It doesn't matter very much whether there are lots of words actually printed on the page—your descriptions and elaborations become the story. This chapter is full of many other suggestions for what to read, and how.

## WHAT THE SCIENCE SAYS: READ EARLY

We often discover what helps all children through examining what happens when there are problems. Recent longitudinal studies on common reading difficulties such as dyslexia conducted by Yale University's Bennett Shaywitz, M.D., and Sally Shaywitz, M.D., for example, show that at the base of a slowness to read efficiently is an auditory processing deficit—an inability to hear the small differences in speech sounds. It's in the auditory cortex (where sound is processed), that brains are wired to hear certain frequencies and tonal differences. The dyslexia research shows that children who have difficulty *hearing* subtle differences in sounds (phonemic awareness) also have difficulty *reading* those same words in print.

Reading to a child is one prevention strategy that provides auditory stimulation when the brain particularly needs it. Within the first three years of life, your child's brain is particularly alert to *changes* in sounds.

For years, children who had trouble learning to read by ages seven to ten heard harsh messages like, "If you would just work harder, you could learn this!" Brain scans of both groups of readers show, however, that the total amount of activation in the brain of a typical reader and a dyslexic is almost the same. The dyslexic is just using the wrong parts of the brain to try to accomplish the task! The dyslexic reader is using the frontal lobes, literally trying to "figure out the code" anew each time he is confronted with the task, instead of processing reading in the normal

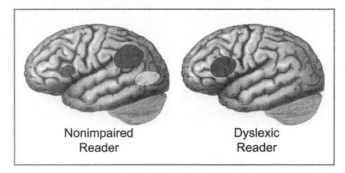

*Figure 11. A neural signature for dyslexia: Underactivation of neural systems in the back of the brain.*

At left, nonimpaired readers activate neural systems that are mostly in the back of the left side of the brain; at right, dyslexic readers underactivate these reading systems in the back of the brain and tend to overactivate frontal areas.

areas more toward the back portions of the brain (vision and sound association areas). Remember: The areas in the back of the brain develop greatly in the years from birth to age five. Experiences that "retrain" the brain (by extensive therapies under the supervision of skilled specialists) to activate in these more effective areas in the left hemisphere have been shown to be able to change the brain. That's good news. Even better news I think is that easy prevention practices like reading lots of rhyming books and singing rhythmic songs and repeating simple games involving "playing with words" when kids are preschool (birth to age five) *can do the same thing*.

A second thing that reading even simple picture books does for your child is to increase the total number of words he hears. For example, there are multiple words for couch—*sofa, chaise, lounge*—and you may not otherwise use them in daily life. Books also introduce objects that may not appear in a child's everyday life: *giraffe, freight train, jungle, snow*. Being exposed to new and more words and objects increases a child's concept development. Importantly, reading also exposes your child to different emotional tones and feelings connected with the words.

Why not just play books-on-tape 24/7, you might wonder? Because simply hearing isolated words without human interaction does not replicate the complex variety of things that happen when a child is read to. Reading is one of the single best activities you can provide your child in part because it beautifully blends all three of our ABCs of Early Brain Development:

- *Attention.* Talking to your child with interest and enthusiasm about the picture and the story holds and increases his attention span.
- *Bonding.* Nothing is as wonderful as snuggling next to mom or dad and reading. This act alone helps children feel more secure and loved, allowing them to relax and be more receptive to learning.
- *Communication.* Parents who read to their child introduce new vocabulary and reinforce familiar concepts. Sharing a book with a child gives the child lots to think and talk about.

It's this direct interaction between child and adult that seems to be the crux of learning language. Across the world, for example, babies and toddlers ask parents or caregivers to label objects in their environment through such means as pointing and grunting. *("Dat? Dat?")* Typically most adults (or older siblings) oblige. Psychologists call this human event *shared visual attention* (earlier referred to as joint attention), and it appears to be necessary for vocabulary development. In 2003, University of Maryland researcher, Amanda Woodward, Ph.D., and colleagues reported tests of seven- to nine-month-olds under two conditions. In both conditions, researchers introduced an unknown object and gave it a nonsense name. In the first condition, the researcher and child shared a joint visual gaze at the object while the researcher labeled it. In the second condition, the researcher looked away while labeling the new object. Later in the day, the child was asked to locate the object from a group of similar objects. Results showed that children were quickly able to correctly identify and locate objects that were introduced in the first condition (joint visual gaze) but had difficulty identifying objects that were introduced in the second condition. These findings suggest that children need the support of others in highly specific ways to learn new vocabulary. In other words, the child and adult need to share a visual "embrace" when the new object is labeled. Reading a book together with your child in your lap is a natural way for this to happen.

You are your child's first literacy teacher. That word—"literacy"—sometimes intimidates parents because while everyone wants their child to become a successful reader, not all parents feel confident that they know what's involved in teaching a child to read. But literacy is actually a long journey that starts with pre-reading activities. Exposing your child to books and printed material everyday gives him the rudimentary concepts needed to begin the process of literacy. The pre-literacy concepts in the Bright Ideas that follow are simple, but important.

## THE BRIGHT IDEAS: READING

### 1. Read Often (4 months and beyond)

Ideally, reading should be a daily experience—not a special event. Young children have short attention spans, so it's better to read for short periods of time (five minutes), two or three times a day instead of thirty minutes all at once. Building reading into your nap time, bedtime, or playtime routines ensures that it's a regular part of every day.

Besides giving the brain's auditory system a workout and growing your child's vocabulary, reading conveys many other fundamental lessons:

- *Print is different from pictures.* One of the first concepts about literacy that children learn, usually by age three, is the distinction between print and visuals. This distinction is true of writing as well. If you ask a three-year-old to write their name, the markings they make will be quite different from those they make when asked to draw a picture. This distinction is important because it establishes a separate "identity" for print and allows a child to begin learning about its functions and structure.

- *Print has meaning.* Researchers have found that by three, many kids expect print to be meaningful. You can see this in the way they point to words on signs, cereal boxes, or menus, and ask, "What does that say?" Older toddlers also often make marks on paper and then tell you, "This says . . ."

- *Print is functional.* Print can be used to get things done in daily life, like figure out what food to order, learn about a preschool field trip, wish someone a happy birthday, or make food with a recipe.

- *Phonemic awareness and phonics.* Phonemic awareness refers to a child's ability to hear the beginning, middle, and ending sounds of words, which most children begin to have by age three. Phonics is the ability to consistently link specific sounds to specific letter symbols. Most kids don't connect letter-sound relationships until five or six, although being read to frequently provides the kind of exposure that sets up this ability.

- *The conventions of print.* Decoding print involves learning a series of basic rules: We read from left to right, top to bottom; words have spaces between them, and there's a specific terminology about reading: *letter, word, page, cover,* and so on. Most kids learn the conventions of print just by watching and participating when their parents read books to them.

### 2. Choose Variety—and Familiarity (ages two and beyond)

Remember that the brain is "turned on" by both the familiar and the new. You'll want to make a large amount of books available to your child, adding more and more new titles as he grows. The public library is a wonderful opportunity for checking out several new books each week without having to spend any money. Used bookstores often have extensive children's collections as families recycle books their own children have outgrown. If you belong to a mother's group, consider starting a book swap that rotates books between members.

It's also a good idea to invest in some books you can have on hand to read over and over. Children learn new things each time they hear a story and look at the pictures. Repeated reading often encourages children to retell the story in their own way.

Set aside a special place for your child's books at home, ideally in his room or in a nook in his play space. Have an armchair or beanbag chair handy where you can snuggle together. The book area should be easily accessible to your child; the more often he passes his personal library as he plays with his toys, the more likely he'll stop to select a book to read with you or look through on his own.

Older toddlers love to burrow with books in a reading nest (old comforter and pillows tossed together) or a story tent (throw a sheet over a table and use a flashlight).

### 3. Encourage Hands-on Book Play (6 months to 3 years)

At first, babies are more interested in gnawing or ripping a book than looking at the pictures or hearing the words. This is age-appropriate behavior. Don't discourage it. Remember the mouth and the hands are important vehicles through which a baby's brain collects data about the world and its operating principles. By "manhandling" books along with other playthings, your child also experiences them as a normal and enjoyable part of his world. And by being able to hold the book or turn the pages when you read together, your child stays involved in the reading experience. Remember that it is totally natural for your baby to randomly turn the pages at first, often going backward or back and forth. There's no need to force your young reader to proceed in a linear fashion.

Keep those associations positive by offering your child books that can't get torn. There's nothing wrong with reading more delicate hardcovers or your own childhood favorites, but if you're constantly saying, "Gentle!" or "Don't touch!" the fun gets leached right out of the experience.

Best bets:

* Sturdy, board books
* Cloth books
* Plastic books (great for bathtub reading and play)

### 4a. Provide a Print-Rich Environment (18 months and beyond)

Not all reading requires books! Toddlers become aware of print in their world as early as eighteen months of age. By three, many children recognize and know the meanings of common product labels, restaurant signs, and street signs. Even if children do not say the correct word when attempting to read such print, they usually will come up with a related term. For example, when presented with a Pepsi can, the child might say, "soda" or "Coke."

The ability to read relies on our brain's ability to substitute symbols for real objects. From twelve to thirty-six months, normal brain maturation allows young children to develop the ability to substitute a picture of an object for the real object. Shortly after, the brain is able to further substitute symbols—letters and words for a picture of an object. This ability is called *representational thinking*. Learning to read is dependent upon the brain's ability to mentally substitute a symbol for the "real" thing.

Being exposed to environmental print (EP) helps this process along. EP refers to print that occurs in real-life contexts, such as the word "Cheerios" on a cereal box or the "McDonald's Golden Arches" towering like a giant "M" in front of the restaurant. First a child attends to the entire context of the environmental print: the combined impact of logos, colors, shape, pictures, size, such as the bulls-eye sign that's part of the Target stores signage, the bright yellow Cheerios cereal box with pictures of *Os*, the McDonald's arches. As they grow older, children become able to recognize increasingly "decontextualized" forms of print. Between two and three, children who live in a print-rich environment have learned:

- A photograph of a cat is not the same thing as a real cat, but is a representation of a real cat.
- The sounds that make *cat* actually stand for the picture of the cat or the real cat.
- A string of symbols is not just a bunch of squiggly lines, but stands for a word *cat*, which in turn stands for a picture of a cat or the real cat.

### 4b. Use Environmental Print to Gauge Representational Thinking (age 3 and beyond)

Initially, young children attend to the entire context of EP—logos, colors, shape, and size—rather than to just the print letters that make up a word. Research has revealed that there is a general developmental progression of EP recognition:

- Level 1: Actual three-dimensional object (such as a Goldfish crackers package or a small tub of Play-Doh)
- Level 2: Two-dimensional color picture of a complete logo, stylized color "word art" text from logo
- Level 3: Two-dimensional black-and-white-picture of logo, black-and-white "word art" text from logo
- Level 4: Two-dimensional black-and-white standard print of the word (Goldfish, Play-Doh).

A typical three-year-old will have close to 100 percent success at level number one and will easily recognize the actual object: "I can read that . . . it says Play-Doh." When shown a laminated card of the logo at level number two, he may also report successfully, "It says Play-Doh." At level number three or four, however, when the supports of the color of the logo or the shape of the text word art design are gone, he may not be able to tell you what it says. Parents can easily tell where their child is on this continuum and can begin to play simple word/letter games that will encourage careful visual discrimination that can prepare a child for the next "level." (See EP games in Chapter 17: "Communication-Builders Little Ones Love.")

### 5. Elaborate and Ask Questions While You Read (18 months and beyond)

Countless studies confirm that one of the most effective way parents can help children learn to make the connections between the spoken and written word is through storybook reading. Unfortunately, researchers found that many parents become frustrated with story time when their child doesn't respond enthusiastically.

The solution is *dialogic reading*, a way of reading with children that engages them throughout the story time. As the name indicates, it means having a dialogue about the story as you go along. To do this, periodically pause to ask your child to:

- Describe the illustrations ("What is that silly duck wearing?")
- Describe what they think is happening on the page ("How many frogs are trying to help this duck? Let's count them.")
- Predict what might happen next ("What kind of animals do you think will be on the next page?")
- Personalize ideas ("Remember when you were on the swing at Grandma's? Tell me about it)."
- Share feelings about things in the story ("Did that make you sad? Me too.")

When two- and three-year-olds in a 1994 Head Start study were exposed to dialogic reading at home and at school over the course of a year, they scored higher in many areas of literacy development than those who received standard reading experiences. For example, they experienced a 93 percent increase in their ability to link sounds and letters—a critical pre-literacy skill.

### 6. Play While You Read (6 months and beyond)

You'll enrich the reading experience—and cause your child to attend longer—if you have a little fun with it:

- *Be enthusiastic.* Don't use a monotone. Make it seem like there's no place else you'd rather be, and no more riveting story than the one right in front of you.
- *Give the characters different voices.* You don't have to give an Oscar-worthy performance. Simply changing the pitch, accent, or pace of your reading adds helpful variety.
- *Put on a "play."* Creative dramatics is informal dramatizing with no printed script or memorized lines. Pick a familiar story, such

as a fairy tale or favorite book, with dialogue and action—characters who say and do something. Props are optional. For example, you and your child can pantomime the bowls, chairs, and beds in *Goldilocks and the Three Bears*, or pretend a chair is the bridge and a stuffed animal is the troll in *The Three Billy Goats Gruff.*

*7. Choose Books That Match Your Child's "Brain Level" of Engagement*
Almost any reading is good reading for a child. But certain kinds of books will grab your child's interest longer because they are tailored to his stage of cognitive development. You can literally feed the brain the kinds of experiences it craves through your choice of reading materials.

Here's a quick look at the development of a "reader":

**Stage 1: Attending to pictures, but not forming stories:** The child looks at the pictures in the book, labeling or making comments about them, but does not need to make up an integrated story that links her ideas together. At this stage, she can be fascinated by single isolated photos of objects, animals, and people without much reference to a storyline.

**Stage 2: Attending to pictures, forming oral stories:** The child looks at the book's pictures and creates her own story that weaves across the pages. Although the child's intonation makes it sound like she is telling a story, the listener has to actually see the pictures in order to follow along.

**Stage 3: Attending to pictures, forming written stories:** The child reads by looking at the book's pictures, and the child's wording and intonation sound like reading. The listener does not usually have to see the pictures to follow the story.

**Stage 4: Attending to print.** The child attends to the print rather than to the pictures when attempting to read the story. She points to printed word configurations as she recounts and retells the story she already knows, but is not actually reading each word.

## Best First Books

A child's first library (including both bought and borrowed titles) should include a mix of the following kinds of books:
(Many of these titles belong to a series with companion books in a similar style, which makes the related titles great choices, too.)

### INFANTS (BIRTH TO 6 MONTHS)
*Books with High Contrast Colors and Crisp Graphics:*
*White on Black.* Hoban, T. (1993). New York: Greenwillow Books.
*What Is That?* Hoban, T. (1994). New York: Greenwillow Books.
*Baby Animals Black and White.* Tildes, P. (1998). Watertown, MA: Charlesbridge Publishing.

### BABIES (6 TO 18 MONTHS)
*Books with Color and Very Simple Images:*
*Colors.* Shooter, H. (2003). New York: DK Publishing.
*Spot Looks at Colors.* Hill, E. (1986). New York: Putnam Publishing Group.
*Brown Bear, Brown Bear, What Do you See?* Martin, Jr., B. (1992). New York: Henry Holt.
*I Love Colors.* Miller, M. (1999). New York: Little Simon.
*Happy Colors.* Weeks, S. (2001). New York: Reader's Digest Children's Books.
*Little Blue and Little Yellow.* Lionni, L. (1995). New York: Mulberry Books.

*Books with Textures (Tactile Experiences Add Pleasure to Reading and Boost Sensory Explorations):*
*Sunny Day Activity Book.* Minneapolis: Manhattan Toy.
*Baby Brain Box Touch and Learn.* Carrington Brain Research.
*Touch and Feel: Baby Animals.* Kindersley, D. (1999). New York: Dorling Kindersley Publishing.

*That's Not My Teddy.* Watt, F. & Wells, R. (1999). London: Usborne Publishing Ltd.
*Kipper's Sticky Paws.* Inkpen, M. (2001). London: Hodder Children's Books.
*Night, Night Baby.* Birkinshaw, M. (2002). London: Ladybird Books.

*Books That Encourage Object Labeling:*
*Touch and Feel: Clothes.* Kindersley, D. (1998). New York: Dorling Kindersley Publishing.
*Match Shapes with Me.* Hood, S. (1999). New York: Reader's Digest Children's Books.
*Baby Faces.* Miller, M. (1998). New York: Little Simon.
*Buster's Bedtime.* Campbell, R. (2000). London: Campbell Books.
*The Going to Bed Book.* Boynton, S. (1995). New York: Little Simon.
*Froggy Gets Dressed.* London, J. (1992). New York: Scholastic.

## TODDLERS (18 MONTHS TO 3 YEARS)
*Interactive/Lift-the-Flap Books (a more advanced kind of tactile experience):*
*Baby Dance.* Taylor, A. (1999). New York: Harper Festival.
*Where is Baby's Belly Button?* Katz, K. (2000). New York: Little Simon.
*Fit-A-Shape: Shapes.* (2000). Philadelphia, PA: Running Press.
*Where's My Fuzzy Blanket?* Carter, N. (2001). New York: Scholastic Paperbacks.
*Where Is Baby's Mommy?* Katz, K. (2001). New York: Little Simon.
*The Wheels on the Bus.* Stanley, M. (2002). Bristol, PA: Baby's First Book Club
*Touch and Talk: Make Me Say Moo!* Greig, E. (2002). Bristol, PA: Sandvick Innovations.
*Quack, Quack, Who's That?* Noel, D. & Galloway, R. (2002). London: Little Tiger Press.

**Books That Label Familiar People, Emotions, and Actions (name the emotions as you read):**

*Winnie the Pooh: Feelings.* Smith, R. (2000). New York: Random House–Disney.

*WOW! Babies.* Gentieu, P. (2000). New York: Crown Publisher.

*Faces.* Miglis, J. (2002). New York: Simon Spotlight.

*Where the Wild Things Are.* Sendak, M. (1988). New York: HarperTrophy.

*Alexander and the Terrible, Horrible, No Good, Very Bad Day.* Viorst, J. (1987). New York: Aladdin Library.

*The Selfish Crocodile.* Charles, F. & Terry, M. (2000). New York: Scholastic.

*Glad Monster, Sad Monster: A Book About Feelings.* Emberley, E. & Miranda, A. (1997). New York: Scholastic.

*No David!* Shannon, D. (1998). New York: Scholastic Trade.

**Books with Rhyme and Rhythm:**

*Each Peach Pear Plum.* Ahlberg, A. & Ahlberg, J. (1978). London: Penguin Books Ltd.

*Moo, Baa, La La La.* Boynton, S. (1982). New York: Little Simon.

*Down By the Bay.* Raffi, & Westcott, N. B. (1990). New York: Crown Publishers.

*Five Little Ducks.* Raffi (1999). New York: Crown Publishers.

*Five Little Monkeys Sitting in a Tree.* Christelow, E. (1993). St. Louis, MO: Clarion.

*This Old Man.* Jones, C. (1990). New York: Houghton Mifflin Co.

*The Itsy Bitsy Spider.* Trapani, I. (1993). Watertown, MA: Charlesbridge Publishing.

*Find the Puppy.* Cox, P. (2001). London: Usborne Publishing Ltd.

**Books that Encourage Scribbling as a Part of Pre-Literacy Writing:**

*Crayon World.* Santomero, A. (1999). New York: Simon Spotlight.

*Figure Out Blue's Clues.* Perello, J. (1999) New York: Simon Spotlight.

*Blue's Treasure Hunt Notebook.* Santomero, A. (1999). New York: Simon Spotlight.
*Harold and the Purple Crayon.* Johnson, C. (1981). New York: Harper Collins.
*Get in Shape to Write.* Bongiorno, P. (1998). New York: Pen Notes.
*Messages in the Mailbox: How to Write a Letter.* Leedy, L. (1994). New York: Holiday House.

*Books That Use Environmental Print:*
*The M & M's Counting Board Book.* McGrath, B. B. (1994). Watertown, MA: Charlesbridge Publishing.
*The Cheerios Play Book.* Wade, L. (1998). New York: Little Simon.
*Pepperidge Farm Goldfish Counting Fun Book.* McGrath, B. B. (2000). New York: Harper Festival.
*Kellogg's Froot Loops! Counting Fun Book.* McGrath, B. B. (2000). New York: Harper Festival.
*The Sun Maid Raisins Playbook.* Weir, A. (1999). New York: Little Simon.
*The Oreo Cookie Counting Book.* Albee, S. (2000). New York: Little Simon.
From Vukelich, C., Christie, J., & Enz, B. J. *Helping Young Children Learn Language and Literacy: Birth through Kindergarten.* (Second Edition) Published by Allyn and Bacon, Boston, MA. Forthcoming 2008 by Pearson Education. Adapted by permission of the publisher.

## 8. Let Your Child See You Read

Remember "monkey-see, monkey-do?" Modeling yourself handling books, magazines, and newspapers, valuing books, and exchanging books at the library, can go a long way in helping your child to want to be a reader. Although the brain is primed to learn language naturally and is perfectly equipped for the task, there is nothing inborn in a brain that is equipped for reading. Historically, learning to talk is natural, reading is not. The more you can make reading a natural part of life, the easier the learning task of becoming a reader will be.

# 16

## Everyday Music: Mozart Myths and Facts

- CAN JUST LISTENING TO MUSIC MAKE A CHILD SMARTER?
- CAN MUSIC IN BABYHOOD IMPACT LATER SCHOOL SKILLS?
- WHAT KINDS OF MUSIC EXPERIENCES ARE BEST FOR MY CHILD?
- SHOULD I ENROLL MY CHILD IN MUSIC LESSONS?

Brahms, Bach, and Beethoven pushed Barney tunes aside in 1993 when University of California at Irvine researchers reported that college students who had listened to Mozart sonatas for a few minutes before taking a test performed better than students who had listened to a different kind of music or no music at all. This finding was quickly, if illogically, extrapolated to mean that even younger minds must stand to benefit all the more from hearing classical music. Since public policy makers are as eager for a quick fix as anyone, soon state-funded preschools in Florida were being required to play the classics. In 1998, Georgia governor Zell Miller secured private funding to provide every newborn in his state with a CD of music by Mozart, Schubert, Vivaldi, and others. Today, dozens of music CDs are marketed to parents of babies and young children with the promise of boosting brainpower.

Despite the hype, the "Mozart effect"—the notion that just listening to classical music boosts mental aptitude—is not real. It won't hurt your child one bit if you turn on some classical music, though the main benefit for you both is probably relaxation. (Not a bad thing!) Playing soothing classical music has been shown to calm babies and aid the development of a sense of timing and rhythm, and all kinds of music are a great way for a child to learn basic concepts such as *longer* versus *shorter, softer* versus *louder*, and *fast* versus *slow*. But simply listening to a CD of Mozart (or any other classical composer) won't significantly change the structure, capacity, or ability of your child's brain in any lasting way.

Where music does seem to have a relationship to brain development is in the actual *playing* of it. Many studies now show a positive connection between musical training and verbal memory, for example. Others show clear, visible differences in certain brain structures in adult musicians that are not evident in non-musicians.

Here's what's really known about changing brain capabilities and music, followed by a few suggestions of how to wisely (and sanely) introduce music into your child's life.

## WHAT THE SCIENCE SAYS: MUSIC, MAYBE

The music-IQ bandwagon got rolling as the result of a happy accident. In the early 1990s, a graduate student of physicist Gordon Shaw, Ph.D., at University of California at Irvine wondered what brain waves would sound like. He took EEG brain wave patterns of a person focused on a complex math problem and fed the patterns into a music synthesizer. The results sounded just like classical music! (So much so that some have speculated whether child prodigy composers, such as Mozart himself, may have simply been listening to their own brain wave patterns—literally writing out the music in their heads!) A theory emerged from the Irvine research team that if brain waves emitted during complex tasks sound like classical music, maybe that particular type of music could evoke a specific brain wave pattern that would, in turn, enhance complex brain abilities.

To explore this idea, Shaw and collaborator Fran Rauscher, Ph.D. (currently a neuroscientist at the University of Wisconsin), conducted the now-famous experiments with results dubbed "the Mozart effect." They hypothesized that the patterns of classical music could help activate the neural firing patterns of the brain used in spatial reasoning, which have similar patterns to the music. College students listened to Mozart's "Sonata for Two Pianos in D Major" for ten minutes before taking a spatial-reasoning test; two control groups heard either white noise or British techno-pop. The students who listened to the Mozart music scored significantly better on tests of spatial reasoning than did the other two groups.

This beneficial effect only lasted a brief ten minutes, however. While interesting, this temporary boost doesn't imply that listening to Mozart sonatas makes a person smarter in any lasting way. It simply shows that listening to Mozart sonatas boosts one type of problem-solving ability in a controlled setting of the type set up by Rauscher. No one has exactly replicated the results either. At the very least, it's now clear that the original results should never have been applied to babies. There are not yet any studies showing that listening to classical music causes babies to get smarter.

Much more promising is the research on instrumental music training. Plenty of *correlational* evidence associates music training with increases in certain kinds of memory (verbal memory in particular) and with spatiotemporal reasoning. But scientists are just beginning the kind of necessary long-term, expensive, and tightly controlled longitudinal studies that will enable them to answer the questions that such associations bring up: Does learning to play a musical instrument *cause* lasting brain changes that result in improved test scores? Which kinds of lessons? What kinds of academic subjects could get a boost?

That such a link exists seems like a reasonable, if premature, conclusion. It seems reasonable because of the prior neuroimaging evidence of studies done on adults. Harvard's Gottfried Schlaug, M.D., Ph.D., has clear brain scan evidence that the adult brains of professional musicians and non-musicians are very different. For one thing, the *corpus callosum,* the communication bridge between the two hemispheres, is larger in musicians than in non-musicians. Having a larger corpus callosum may result in enhanced communication between the two halves of the brain. Secondly, most typical *non*-musician's brains are very asymetrical, with the left hemisphere, where language is centered, being naturally larger than the right hemisphere. By contrast, in a typical musician's brain, the left and right hemispheres are more evenly matched in structure and size. The right hemisphere in musicians is therefore larger than in non-musicians. The right hemisphere controls the left hand, and the left hand has to do a lot of work in music. The areas in the right hemisphere

that are larger in musicians are those responsible for planning and executing movement, as well as those for hearing. The *cerebellum*, which
plays a role in the coordination and timing of sequential movements,
also shows a higher relative cerebellar volume in musicians as compared
to non-musicians; it, too, is larger.

## MUSIC TRAINING AND THE BRAIN

A research team funded by the National Science Foundation (NSF) is
looking for more direct answers in an important long-term study. Ellen
Winner, Ph.D., at Boston College, along with Gottfried Schlaug, and
colleagues, began by imaging the brains of five- to seven-year-olds before
they ever had a music lesson. Then they divided the sample into three
groups of about forty kids each. Some children are receiving music instruction (keyboard or violin), others are receiving a comparable amount
of one-to-one attention through foreign language instruction for equal
amounts of time, and a third group receives no instruction. Over the
study's three- to five-year span, the researchers are looking at three things:
Direct measures of learning of music skill (gains in finger movements,
notation reading, etc.), indirect influences of music on other non-music
areas (math reasoning, phonological awareness), and measures of brain
changes through anatomical and functional MRI scans.

The study, at this writing almost half finished, is investigating two
opposing hypotheses:

1. Are the differences previously noted between musicians' and non-
   musicians' brains due to the fact that young kids are learning to play
   music and are practicing skills with their fingers (coordinating hand-
   eye movements) and exercising their memory more? If true, these
   factors combine to *cause* the brains of these young children to develop
   and to function differently.

2. Or do kids differ biologically *before* they start taking music lessons
   and possess a genetic bias to music (music aptitude/talent) that draws
   them to study and practice music?

Though complete answers won't emerge for several years, there are already preliminary findings. In the *initial baseline* scans (before any groups received any training), researchers found no discernable structural differences in the brains of the three groups, and no cognitive differences, either. Kids who take music lessons do not start out with a brain that is different. After just fifteen months, however, the scientists *did find differences* both in brain structure and in music-related measures. The differences involved brain regions, in fact, that control the left hand. There were also differences in the development of music skill (finger movement, note reading, and so on), as you might predict. Math skills of the music group were also slightly improved over the controls. This is still solely correlational data; the researchers can't yet determine cause.

I think that the functional imaging data is the most interesting. During tasks that require rhythm discrimination and melody processing, the children in the music-training group used more of their temporal lobes, which means they may be using more of their auditory cortex. Scientists also found more activation in the cerebellum in the music group, but no change for the control group.

Personally, I think that it *is* the playing of the instruments that causes all of these differences and brain changes, and I have thought so for years because of what I know about how brains operate. Think of what's involved in studying music: You have to move your hands and fingers independently; you have to be able to combine small perceptual units into larger musical phrases; you have to translate the notation you see on the score into motor movements of your hands; your memory demands are critical, as you have to remember longer and longer musical phrases; and you have to be able to make very fine discriminations among sounds and among rhythms. That's a lot of brain effort!

I also know that the brain is a pattern-seeking organ. That's one of the brain's basic operating principles, to look for patterns. Music *is* pattern: Repeating tones, rhythm, sequences. Brains respond readily to this kind of patterned, repetitive input. Given what we know about the timing of early brain development, I wish children as young as three had been included in the NSF study. My guess is that the resulting data would be even stronger.

## MUSIC TRAINING AND READING

One of the most promising ideas coming from research on the topic of music training and the brain is the evidence that the *attention system* may be so activated while learning music that it accounts for some overall gains in other academic areas. Paula Tallal, Ph.D., at Rutgers University is conducting studies that attempt to evaluate the effects of auditory training, which includes music training, on brain organization for language. The research team is trying to see if the cause of core phonological deficits (inability to hear differences in sound units) observed in language-learning impairments are those that involve temporal change in auditory brain regions; they test to determine if slow auditory processing may lie at the root of impairments in the language system. In addition to improved auditory rapid processing of sound that musical training obviously impacts, other factors such as improved attention and improved sequencing skills are likely to be key factors because these may, in turn, have an impact on improved language and literacy skills.

There has also been some evidence from Katie Overy, Ph.D., who spent several years collaborating with Gottfried Schlaug on various neuro-imaging studies of musical processing, that music training, particularly rhythm training, can improve phonological awareness. A study she conducted showed enhanced phonological skills in dyslexic children when they studied music. Phonological awareness is the ability to listen to sounds and break them up into various parts. This ability is helpful to later reading skills. Poor phonological ability has been identified as a key problem in dyslexia, so it may be that music training could actually help reading.

## MUSIC TRAINING AND MATH

A meta-analysis (large-scale review) of many prior studies led by Lois Hetland, associate professor of art education at the Massachusetts College of Art and a research associate at Project Zero, found only six "good" studies that looked at the question of music training and improvement of spatial skills. She feels confident that kids who have musical training by experimenting with musical instruments in formal instruction do improve on the spatial skills and that it is not a temporary finding. Again, from my perspective, this is understandable given that piano and violin playing require extensive coordination and use of the left hand (which corresponds to the right hemisphere). Increased blood and nutrients flow to those areas that are being used more and, knowing how brains work in general, it seems perfectly logical that such increased *use* would cause *growth*. Interestingly, the areas known to process many math concepts are located in the parietal regions near the motor strip of the brain where finger movements are controlled.

## THE BRIGHT IDEAS: MUSIC

### 1. Start with Singing (birth to 3)

For all the lab emphasis on formal music training, don't overlook a terrific free, easy way your child can experience music with you: Singing. Although I know of no scientific studies being done on the impact of singing on brain reorganization, behavioral studies do show that infants (age six to nine months) will sustain their attention to adults while they sing to a child just as much as they will when an adult reads to the child. I also know that lullabies are used worldwide to help calm infants. The languages they are sung in may differ, but the essence of the song is always the same. A lullaby:

- Contains few pitches
- Repeats simple melodic patterns
- Has rhythms that closely match the rocking and swaying motions used to soothe fussy infants.

Here's the best part: Your child could care less whether you can carry a tune. Singing lullabies and nursery rhymes is a great way to expose your child to the patterns in music. As your child gets older, she can start to sing and clap along with you, building motor control and coordination between sounds and actions.

Invest in a good Mother Goose book to remind yourself of the basic rhymes. You'll be surprised how easily the sing-song tunes of "Mary Had a Little Lamb," "Little Bo-Peep," and "Hickory, Dickory, Dock," come back to you.

Some fun ways to build singing these classics into everyday routines:

- While driving in the car, sing "The Wheels on the Bus"
- While cooking in the kitchen, sing "Pat-a-Cake, Pat-a-Cake, Baker's Man"
- While watching the rainfall from the window, sing "The Itsy Bitsy Spider"
- While looking at stars together, sing, "Twinkle, Twinkle Little Star."

### 2. Introduce Finger Play (age 6 months to 3 years)

As your baby grows, you can combine the pleasure of music with simple games. Common finger play rhymes such as "Five little monkeys jumping on the bed" provide practice for the brain's responsiveness to repetitive, rhythmic input. Some of my favorite finger-play songs:

- "The Itsy Bitsy Spider"
- "Pat-a-Cake, Pat-a-Cake, Baker's Man"
- "Where Is Thumbkin?"
- "This Little Piggy"
- "Ten Little Indians" (or "Ten Little Children")
- "Head and Shoulders, Knees and Toes"

Another way to foster imagination and communication about emotion through music is to construct little stories around instrumental music (without lyrics) with your child. Perhaps as the music plays in the fast portion, you talk about a happy little mouse scurrying across the floor to get a piece of cheese, and during the slow portion, there is a little baby being rocked to sleep. Use your imagination to start a story that you and your child can begin to build on together, and make up hand motions to carry your story along.

Use the following music-development chart to spark other ways to expand the fun in music for your child.

## Typical Musical Development

This chart purposely covers broad age spans. It's not meant to be a checklist of milestones. Use it to see an overview of how musical interest grows naturally and to note what kinds of things your child may be interested in as she grows:

Birth to nine months:
- Recognizes parents' voices from birth
- Begins to listen attentively to sounds
- Is calmed by human voices
- Starts vocalization (imitating sounds heard)

Nine months to two years:
- Interested in every kind of sound
- Begins to discriminate among sounds to be able to hear small differences
- May respond to changes in pitch
- Begins to respond to music with repetitive movements such as clapping
- Most attracted to music that is strongly rhythmic such as marches and rock and roll

Two to three years:
- Creates spontaneous songs
- Sings parts of familiar songs
- Recognizes instruments by sight such as drum, piano, trumpet
- Responds more enthusiastically to certain songs
- Strong physical response to music such as swaying, jumping, imitation of fast dance movements

Peeking ahead: Three to four years
- Gains better voice control
- Likes songs that play with language
- Enjoys making music with a group and alone
- Likes physical activity with music (such as dancing or hopping)
- Begins to learn concepts such as loud and soft, fast and slow.

*3. Consider Music Training (two-and-a-half to three years and beyond)*
Given the evidence, I do recommend music lessons for an older toddler, if you're interested and can afford it. I especially like Suzuki violin. Early lessons include standard rhythm "chants" your child plays on his own tiny violin. The strategies emphasize learning by listening, not formal notation for tots. The "Chitty Chitty Bang Bang" tempo drill may sound harsh and irritating to you after the twentieth time you've heard it, but it's actually going a long way toward "making music" in your child's brain.

Your child's interest and enthusiasm should always be your guide when considering musical instruction. Some suggestions:

- **When he's two or even three, expose your child to music being played right in front of him.** Not faraway exposure as in a concert hall—just a friend or other student or child who is playing an instrument. This will help give you an idea of your child's innate interest level. You can also buy a toy piano or keyboard. My daughter Kristin, for example, first saw the violin at age two when my mother took her to a local street fair. At one of the booths they had a small stage with a child playing the violin each time the curtain opened, which was initiated when you put a quarter in a nearby jar. Kristin was mesmerized watching a young girl play simple Suzuki violin songs over and over. Mom was eventually out of quarters! Not long after that, my mom urged me to sign Kristin up for similar lessons—and this was back when I had never even heard of such a thing! She began Suzuki violin within a few months and continued for several years. Later, now as an adult, she has resumed taking lessons and still enjoys playing. It's a fascinating question, whether some brains are born predisposed for musical interest and aptitude, or whether it's the musical exposure that shapes the brain. Or both.

- **Choose an instrument appropriate to a toddler.** Suzuki violin programs, for example, use very small-sized violins for beginners. Some children can be introduced to piano on smaller keyboards until they are big enough to physically play a regular piano. The greatest amount of research has been done on the piano and the violin and the studies show gains in a variety of cognitive skills in those who persevere in their training. Other instruments that may contain some of the same elements present in the piano and violin may offer similar benefits. We just have little research to support it.

- **Don't push it.** If your child starts dreading lessons, protesting about playing, or otherwise shows resistance, you'll create more negative associations with music than you will build brain connections. Remember that the brain seeks what is pleasurable; if musical training is not fun, your child won't get the benefit from it.

- **Overall music programs, such as Kindermusik, can give a good, broad introduction to music.** Children who participate will have experiences with rhythm and movement in connection with various types of music. Because these sessions are usually large groups, there is generally less pressure on the child than individual instrumental training settings. I think most kids learn a lot from such programs.

- **Don't feel guilty if your child does not have musical instruction, or if you cannot afford it.** While I recommend formal music education, I do so cautiously, because I am not suggesting that every child needs to do this, or that if a child does not he will be at a great disadvantage. Plenty of smart neuroscientists out there never took a single piano lesson! If it is too inconvenient, or you cannot afford lessons, there is no harm in waiting until your child goes to a public school where they may offer music classes. The brain's tremendous capacity to change and learn (plasticity) is so basic, that a child in elementary school will also benefit by most, if not all, of the critical aspects of music training throughout childhood.

### 4. Listen in Moderation (birth to 3)
Your baby is liable to enjoy any kind of music. Because classical composers are especially relaxing, it's a nice idea to make them part of a short

nighttime or nap time ritual. Please don't overdo, however. It seems strange to have to say this, but I've met well-intentioned parents who keep classical music on in the background 24/7. This is not a good idea. Children need a break from performance and from input. The brain needs time free of background noise. Music can be as overdone as can other forms of stimulation.

Better: Play music intentionally to accomplish specific things, such as:

- During transitions (playtime to meals, playtime to bed)
- For calming during quiet time
- Changing the pace when things are too energetic or not energetic enough.

I also question whether it's in our societal best interest to promote music simply as a tool to advance other cognitive areas. Music should foremost be one of life's pleasures! Phrases like, "The music just soothes my soul" and "It's music to my ears," speak to the intense emotion linked inextricably to music. The pure joy that many of us find in playing an instrument or singing can never be minimized by only linking this experience to an interest in brain power. For all we know, the real power of music is *to emphasize our humanity*, not our IQ.

# 17

# Communication-Builders Little Ones Love

---

**Why we do a Communication activity . . .**

Communication activities provide practice for caregivers in helping a child to learn to listen carefully to the sounds of language. Also, young children can learn to enjoy being read to. Research shows that it is important to be able to hear the differences in sound units (known as phonemic awareness). This ability to both hear small differences in sounds and notice small differences in letter formations impacts later success in learning how to read!

*Children who can easily recognize words*
*and their meanings learn better.*

---

**Why we do a music activity . . .**

Research also shows that frequent musical involvement, which includes listening to music, saying rhymes, singing songs, and playing musical instruments can be important to later intellectual development. Music brings many different learning elements together by developing physical coordination, timing, discipline, confidence, memory, language, and imagination.

*Children who participate in music training learn better.*

---

Like the activities in the preceding chapters, these games provide more opportunities to develop practice with language, sounds, music, and patterns. I want to stress that these activities are for fun and are not predictive of any problem if your child does not seem interested when you play them. If this happens, come back and try them at a later time. Have fun!

Following each activity, there are short sections that give you additional information to understand *why* certain kinds of activities have been shown to be helpful in developing a young brain:

- The *Brain Link* tells you how the activity can influence your child's brain now.
- The *School Link* tells you the potential impact on later school readiness.
- *Variations* are related kinds of activities that serve a similar function.
- *Reminders* link you back to main ideas expressed in this book.

## COMMUNICATION–BUILDERS FOR INFANTS (0 TO 6 MONTHS)

### Foot Rattles

Many baby stores sell infant socks with small rattles carefully sewn into the sock or bootie. If you have a pair, notice how attentive your baby is to the sounds he can make!

*Directions:*
- When your baby is alert and playful, put the foot rattle socks on her feet.
- Watch your baby as she enjoys noticing the sounds of the rattles on her feet.
- Encourage her to "find" each foot by lifting and gently shaking the baby's foot.
- Enjoy as she discovers that the rattle sound seems to be under her control. Have fun.

*Brain Link:* This activity stimulates auditory, visual, and motor connections in the brain. Also stimulates the parts of the brain that process and store language.

---

Note: In the first few months, be sure to use a very exaggerated, slow, expressive form of talk (known as *parentese*) when you play to help capture your infant's attention. To learn more about parentese, see page 227.

*School Link:* Develops listening skills necessary for sound and music enjoyment, and encourages the ability to gain self-control.

### Body Parts . . . with Added Rhyme and Rhythm (Starting at about 3 Months)

Directions:

- Find a children's book that has rhymes and that has either large pictures of people's faces or that discusses body parts. A few I like: *Eyes, Nose, Fingers and Toes; The Foot Book; Hand, Hand, Fingers, Thumb.*
- Hold your baby in your lap with his back against your chest, or face him sitting in his infant seat so he can see the pictures and watch you turn the pages.
- Read the book about body parts with enthusiasm. If you are reading a rhyme (like in the Dr. Seuss books) be sure to emphasize the singsong rhyme and rhythm. Young children love to hear the "beat" of rhyming books.
- Point to the pictures and describe them, then point to the same body part on you.
- Encourage your baby to touch or grab hold of your ears, mouth, hair, nose, and fingers. The more your baby's hand-eye coordination improves, the more accurate his grasp will become.

*Brain Link:* This activity stimulates emotional, cognitive, auditory, visual, and motor connections in the brain. Also stimulates the parts of the brain that process and store language.

*School Link:* Reading rhymes develops the listening discrimination skills necessary for pre-reading. You're also encouraging a love of books, necessary for later formal education.

*Reminder:* The brain is a pattern-seeking organ. A young child's brain searches for patterns while listening and looking. Books that rhyme and follow a pattern quickly become favorites.

*Silly Songs*
   *Directions:*
- When you are doing daily routines with your infant, take time to sing. You can make up your own words and rhythms. For example, when changing a diaper, you could sing (to the tune of "The Muffin Man"):

> *It's time to change your diaper now, your diaper now, your diaper now. Oh, it's time to change your diaper now, so early in the morning!"*

- Be as silly and creative as you want to be. Your baby will love it, even if you sing off-key.

*Brain Link:* Singing, especially with lots of rhythm and rhyme, helps your baby learn about the sounds of language.

*Reminder:* Most children love to repeat *familiar* songs and stories. Repetition is a key factor in effective learning. Each time your baby hears a repeated pattern, that pattern becomes stronger. Each repetition results in a stronger memory.

*Peekaboo (3 months and beyond)*
This classic game is a valuable exercise in pre-reading because it helps teach **object permanence**, a precursor to symbolic representation, a concept necessary for later reading.
   *Directions:*
- Hold a small blanket or cloth across your face to "hide" momentarily from your infant.
- "Pop out" from behind the cloth and say, "Peekaboo," surprising your baby.
- Laugh and smile as you reappear each time you play.

A baby's love of this game is universal and provides "exercise" in letting your baby safely learn that people and things still exist, even when out of sight.

*Variations:* Enjoy playing peekaboo differently each time: With your hands, with clothing, behind a chair, behind a book, behind a toy. Play both "Where's baby?" as well as "Where's mommy?"

## COMMUNICATION–BUILDERS FOR BABIES (6 TO 18 MONTHS)

### Noticing Color Differences

The concept of visually noticing differences in objects and pictures in a book is an important start in noticing more subtle differences in letter formations that will become significant much later when learning to read. You can begin this process by pointing out similarities and differences from an early age. One of the best places to start is by comparing colors.

This activity is for a baby who can sit up. You can use colored plastic links (available at toy stores), blocks, or other toys that come in sets with several different colors and have multiples of each color.

*Directions:*
- Sit your baby on the floor. In front of her, put down a plain place mat* (see note at end of chapter) to help focus her attention. (If your baby starts to play with the place mat, put it away for now and start this "focus" activity a few months later.)
- Take six to eight colored links and mix them up. Say, "Waaaatch!"
- Slowly, quietly, and deliberately, match the links by color. Put two links of the same color next to each other. Continue the process until all the links are matched into sets. Check to make sure your baby is watching closely.
- Then mix the links back into a group and place one color on the place mat. Say, "Now, it's your turn."
- Wait for your baby to make a match. Coach *if necessary* by directing your baby's hand to the correct link. Continue until all the matches are made.
- Then mix them up again. Take an orange (or one other color) link, set it on the mat and say, "Find another orange one." Coach *if necessary*.
- Continue this way until your baby has matched all the links.

*Brain Link:* Stimulates the visual part of the brain as well as the parietal lobe, where many math concepts such as one-to-one matching develop.

*School Link:* Helps with pattern matching necessary for later identifying letters, numbers, and symbols needed for one-to-one correspondence in both reading and math.

*Variations:*
- Match things in your home: Find everyday household items for your baby to match such as socks, mittens, shoes, vegetables, fruits, animal crackers. Identify and discuss their colors and shapes.
- Match things in the environment: Take a walk and collect rocks, leaves, and flowers. Identify and discuss them. Place objects of the same color in pairs next to each other.

*Reminder:* Children can be taught to see the similarities and differences in objects and in images. You can encourage your child to carefully observe the world.

### Personalized Nursery Rhymes

Invest in a sing-along CD (such as *Wee Sing Nursery Rhymes and Lullabies*, Pamela Beall and Susan Nipp/Price Stern Sloan) or a nursery-rhyme book to re-familiarize yourself with the classics.

*Directions:*
- Listen to the CD. Choose the song most familiar to you.
- Use the song manual as a guide to sing for and with your baby.
- Sing with enthusiasm and drama.
- Incorporate your baby's name into rhymes where you can, such as in "Mary Had a Little Lamb," you can sing, "*Billy* had a little lamb." Another example:

*Pat-a-cake, pat-a-cake, baker's man*
*Bake me a cake as fast as you can!*

*Roll it and pat it and mark it with a B*
*And throw it in the oven for [baby's name] and me!*

When your baby coos and gurgles back at you, she is aware of the smile on your face and is learning that talking and singing are two-way communications. Later, your baby may start to try to sing with you.

*Brain Link:* This activity stimulates emotional, auditory, and visual connections in the brain. Also stimulates the parts of the brain that process and store language.

*School Link:* Develops basic concepts, including new vocabulary words that are needed for comprehension tasks when reading.

*Variations:*
- As your baby gets older, sing with some pauses or hesitation, giving your baby time to respond by filling in the appropriate word or sound.
- Add simple instruments to beat out the rhythm of songs.
- Dance and act out rhymes with your baby.
- Record your baby talking or singing. Play it back for him to enjoy.

### Reading that Inspires Talking

Visit your public library and enlist the help of the children's librarian to show you the many choices of books that encourage interactions. For this young age, also find books that include familiar objects, often with only a few objects on a page. A bird, a shoe, a cup. A plot or a sequence is not important yet.

The goal of reading books at this age is to begin a **dialogue** about the things in the book. Clear, simple pictures allow your baby to see easily what you both are talking about. Two examples that I like include: *Snuggle Time Activity Book*, Discovery Toys, and *Peekaboo Zoo: A Lift-the-Flap Book*, Susan Hood and Simone Abel/Learning Curve International.

*Directions:*

- Hold your baby in your lap with his back against your chest, or face him sitting in his seat so he can see the pictures and watch you turning the pages.
- Choose a book that is soft and interactive that is full of multiple textures and surprises. If the book includes interactive elements like lifting a flap to reveal a hidden object begin by saying, "Lift up the flap . . . peekaboo . . . look . . . there's a [whatever is hiding there]."
- Your baby can learn to help turn the pages.*
- Tell what is happening in the book. Describe the textures and colors. Label the objects and people on each page.
- Stop and interact with your child by encouraging him to touch the book. We call this interaction with the baby "book-talk." Have fun interacting with your baby as you read.

*Brain Link:* Book-reading activities stimulate emotional, auditory, and visual connections in the brain. Also stimulates the parts of the brain that process and store language.

*School Link:* Develops phonemic discrimination skills necessary for pre-reading. Also develops a love of books necessary for later formal education.

*Reminder:* Continue to describe and label familiar everyday objects found in your child's environment. Research indicates that the *more words* that infants and toddlers hear in their everyday environment, the greater their understanding and use of concepts will be later on in school. Label and discuss ideas. Whenever possible, link your descriptions to experiences the child is having every day. These experiences will change as the child grows, so remember to extend and expand a little each day!

---

* Note: At this early age, one of the most important "skills" that young children need to begin to develop is how to hold a book, how to turn pages, where to begin reading, and how to progress from the beginning to the end of the book. Literacy specialists emphasize these skills and label them as pre-reading.

*Beginning Environmental Print: Play with Real Objects*

Use real objects during dramatic play. Use objects for house play, restaurant play, or grocery play. Save the following kinds of items:

- plastic drink bottles (empty juice boxes, plastic soda bottles)
- empty cookie boxes, cereal boxes
- restaurant bags (McDonald's or Burger King bags)
- cartoon paper plates (*Pokemon, Blue's Clues*)
- Band-Aid boxes and items you use every day in your home

While you are playing, encourage your child to name the logos or say the names of the food labels on the boxes. Show him your pleasure with his ability to "read!"

*Brain Link:* Activates the ability to make associations in the cortex between the physical object and the entity that is represented.

*School Link:* The ability to understand that a symbol can represent an object or an idea is a critical pre-reading skill.

## COMMUNICATION-BUILDERS FOR TODDLERS (18 MONTHS TO 3 YEARS)

*Toy Phone Talk*

Young children learn language from repetition, mimicking, and adult modeling. Children learn quickly from adults about talking on the phone. Often a baby will begin to babble when given a toy phone. Later, as a toddler, the child will begin to talk using words and sentences with a toy or real phone.

*Directions:*
- Give your child a toy telephone. Pick up your own cell or cordless phone to begin a simple conversation. Say, "Hello."
- Wait. If necessary, say to your child, "Say 'hello' to me."
- Say, "What is your name?" Wait.
- Continue a short, fun conversation.
- Use your "phone time" to introduce new words and concepts to your child. You may find that your child will express himself

more freely when using a prop like a toy phone than when trying to speak directly to you.

*Brain Link:* This activity stimulates the auditory and motor connections in the brain. Also stimulates the parts of the brain that process and store language.

*School Link:* This improves your child's ability to communicate, which is necessary for all areas of the school curriculum.

*Variations:*
- Encourage your child to talk with family members and friends on the real phone.
- Teach the emergency number 911. Review and practice it often. Many very young children have successfully brought needed help to a family member in distress because they had practiced this procedure often.

### Sequencing Snap-Lock Beads

Pattern detection is an important precursor to learning to read. Reading is built on patterns and the ability to detect similarities in items and to sort by similar characteristics.

*Directions:*
- Sit beside your toddler on the floor or at a table or high chair. Spread out a plain place mat* (see note at end of chapter).
- Take child-safe, colorful snap-lock beads and say, "Watch."
- Snap two different colored beads together, such as red and yellow. (If your beads come in different shapes, focus only on color for this exercise.)
- Say, "Now, it's your turn. Can you put yours together in the same way?" Wait for your toddler to snap together the same two colored beads. *If necessary,* coach your child. Assist him in snapping the beads by guiding his hand to select and snap the bead correctly. Continue until he succeeds. Praise each successive step.

- Now make a sequence or pattern and ask your toddler to replicate it. Say, "Make a set just like this one." At first, you may need to reduce the number of beads in the sequence for your toddler to have success. Later you can increase the number of beads. Again, praise effort and accomplishments.
- Later, unsnap the beads and mix them up and say, "Now, it is your turn to make a pattern for me to make." Wait and coach, *if necessary*. After you have done this a few times, hesitate and occasionally make mistakes to encourage your toddler to correct and assist you.

*Brain Link:* The brain is a pattern-seeking organ. A young child's brain searches for patterns while observing and interacting with objects. Matching and sequencing activities stimulate the visual areas of the brain.

*School Links:* Develops dexterity, sorting skills, and eye-hand coordination. Helps develop concepts and problem solving necessary for later reasoning in math, reading, and writing.

*Variation:*
- Use colored O-shaped cereal, such as Froot Loops, to make a short, easy pattern: Red, blue, red, blue. Encourage your child to make the same pattern. Slowly make patterns longer or more challenging, but ensure that your child remains at a 90 percent success rate. Success leads to a love of repeating the task!
- Find items around the house that can be sequenced by color, shape, or size: toy blocks, cars, dolls, dishes, animals, crackers, or boxes. Toddlers also love to pull out shoes to play this sequencing game: mommy's shoe, daddy's shoe, mommy's shoe, daddy's shoe. And it will occupy your toddler for quite a long time!

### Make Texture Dominoes
Here's a game that encourages sorting.

*Directions:*
- Using cardboard, cut small rectangles similar to a domino. Paste two different textures on the surface of the domino, one on each half, such as different fabrics (corduroy, felt, silk, beaded material), sandpaper (with different degrees of roughness), rubber, smooth wallpaper, and so on.
- Put the dominoes in a bag.
- Let your child pick one to start.
- Demonstrate by putting your hand into the bag to feel around and to find the texture that matches the first half of the "domino." Place it end to end with the one your child selected to start.
- Let your child take a turn. He will love this feel-and-match game.

*Brain Link:* The brain is a pattern-seeking organ. A young child's brain searches for patterns while observing and interacting with objects, this time using his sense of touch.

*School Links:* Develops dexterity, sorting skills, and eye-hand coordination. Helps develop concepts and problem solving necessary for later reasoning in math, reading, and writing.

*Variation:*
- Shape sorter products are a fun way for a child to make matches. One I like: Shape and Color Sorter (Lauri Learning Toys) because you can use it to sort the shapes on a pegboard by color or by shape.

### Sidewalk Chalk Talk
*Directions:*
- Find some large size colored chalk at a drugstore or art store. Model for your child how to mark with chalk on the sidewalk and even draw along with her on the concrete.
- Show her how to make lines and squiggles while you draw other pictures. Talk about the drawings.

- Try drawing a simple hopscotch square and play the game together.
- Also allow your child to freely experiment with the chalk.*

*Brain Link:* Drawing activities provide opportunities for children to learn dexterity, large- and fine-motor control, and eye-hand coordination, while increasing opportunities for meaningful language experiences.

*School Link:* Both large and fine motor control skills are important for many activities requiring the coordination of movements, including future writing skills.

*Variations:*
- You can also draw with jumbo-sized crayons on paper. With your hand around your child's guide him to the paper and show him how to "draw" and mark on the paper. Let him have the freedom to scribble. He will soon begin to ascribe meanings to his scribbling marks. Encourage this. It is the beginning of his understanding that he can communicate meaning by the marks he makes on a page. (Again, it's normal for a toddler to mouth the crayon, so don't let him do this unsupervised.)

**Kitchen Drummers**
*Directions:*
- Have your child sit in a safe location in the kitchen.
- Hand her a large plastic bowl turned upside down and a pair of wooden spoons.
- Model for her how to beat out a sound on the bowl. Allow her to create all kinds of drumming "music" and rhythms with her instruments.
- Add pots and other kinds of bowls to make different sounds.

---

*Note: It's very normal for a toddler to try to put the chalk in her mouth. For this reason don't leave her alone with it as it's a *potential choking hazard.*

*Brain Link:* Singing and playing with musical toys stimulates cognitive and motor connections in the brain. Rhythm activities stimulate the areas of the brain used for pre-reading skills.

*School Link:* Recent research is connecting the ability to detect rhythm with improved early decoding skills in reading.

### Scribble Stories

It's important for your child to experience creative, kinesthetic pre-writing experiences. Early attempts to write indicate the achievement of an important cognitive milestone: It means your child understands that the squiggles he sees in a written word have meaning! This activity is geared to older toddlers.*

*Directions:*
- Sit beside your child at a table. Provide a large sheet of blank paper, a pencil, and/or markers.
- Say, "Go ahead, draw (or write) anything you wish!"
- When your child is finished, encourage him to describe the picture or writing. Say, "Tell me a story about your picture," or "Tell me what you wrote." Take notes while your child is talking.
- Read back what was said. Encourage him to extend his comments. Say, "Here is what you just told me. Did you want it to say anything else?"
- Print or type the story and attach it to the picture. Enjoy re-reading it together.

*Brain Link:* Stimulates the part of the brain that controls touch in the parietal lobe and in the sensory-motor strip. Also stimulates the part of the brain that processes language (temporal lobes).

---

*Note: There is no correct way to draw or begin to scribble-write.

*School Link:* Develops dexterity, and fine-motor control, and touch discrimination necessary for future writing skills, as well as visual and language skills that will be needed for school success.

*Variations:*
- Use another medium, such as crayons, finger paint.
- Use paint to draw on a large paper taped to a wall or floor, or onto the sidewalk.
- Encourage your child to scribble in a blank booklet (or blank paper folded and stapled into a book form) in order to make a book. Ask him to tell a story about each page. You may wish to write out the story below each picture.
- Develop a script for a photo album: As you look through family photo album, have your child dictate a story for each familiar photo. Write down the descriptions. Put them together in a stapled booklet or sequence each single page into the photo album.

**Stage Two of Environmental Print—Match Real Objects with "Logo Print"**
Tailor your items to the businesses in your area and products you use in your everyday life. Use logo images that can be downloaded from the internet to make your own matching cards for this game. Environmental Print Objects that you will need to collect include things like: Cheerios box, Peter Piper Pizza paper plate, McDonald's bag, Dairy Queen item, Target item, Play-Doh mini-can, Band-Aid packet, minature STOP sign you can make, Goldfish package. Then make nine small matching cards with the logos of each Environmental print concept.

*Directions:*
- Spread out the place mat* (see note at end of chapter).
- Set out one item at a time. As you do so, ask: "What is this?" If the child does not know, say the name of the item.
- Ask the child to repeat it. Continue until child has success with a few.

- Then lay out a few logo cards. At first, limit selections to *no more than* three cards.
- Hold up an item and ask the child to find the matching logo card. For example, say: "Can you find the McDonald's card to match the McDonald's bag?"
  If your child has trouble, model the activity or coach him in finding the card. Ask him to say the name of the item.
- Continue the process at a later time, adding one or more items, until the child can identify all ten items correctly. Praise each match. This is early reading!* Have fun!

*Variations:*

### Play Environmental Print Hunt!

1. Go on an *Environmental Print Hunt* together while grocery shopping or running errands.
2. Point out road signs, store signs, product logos, and fast-food logos. Say: "Do you know the name of this item?" After your child responds, praise him, repeating the correct word(s).
3. Later, tell your child the name of the beginning letter of the word. Also say the sound.
Remember this is early, informal reading. Have fun!

### Play Matching Card Games!

1. Choose a card from the deck and see if the child can match the Environmental Print item.
2. For more challenge, lay the cards out in a two card by two card grid (similar to a BINGO card) and have your child place the matching item on the card.
3. Later, make a three-by-three card grid.

---

* Note: A first step in learning to read is the concept that a symbol connects to and can substitute for an actual object. Over time, a child builds an awareness that symbols have meanings. Praise his first attempts to connect symbols with meanings.

---

* The purpose of the place mat is to show the child *where* and *when* to pay attention. The place mat is a visible, concrete cue that you want your child to pay attention to the work (which is really *play*) that you are doing together. Consistently using the place mat eventually teaches a young child how to direct his attention. Show excitement and anticipation as you spread out the place mat. By doing this consistently, pleasure and anticipation become associated with paying attention. See also page 80.

# Epilogue

My purpose in writing this book has been to take scientific information about early development and learning that has traditionally been circulated primarily through university settings and academic journals and move it into the hands of the people who need it the most . . . parents and care providers. Your personal investment of time and thoughtful planning into the care of your own child from birth through age three will reap rewards for both you and your child. Your maximum influence in "setting up" responsive, loving environments can reinforce that YOU are the person with the power to positively impact your own child's learning potential.

The communities in which you will raise your children, however, will matter as well. Every parent, every person caring for a young child should be given the opportunity to develop the skills to provide the kind of care that protects and nurtures the developing brain. At our organization in Arizona, New Directions Institute for Infant Brain Development, which is now a proud member of the family of agencies of Arizona's Children Association, we emphasize that the time has come to invest dollars and effort in order to provide an "upstream solution" for all children that can prevent the start of so many later learning and behavior problems. There is an old story that illustrates this approach:

*A man was walking along a swift river one day when he saw someone who was drowning and calling out for help. He jumped in to save the man. Now safely on the riverbank, he then saw another, and another, who were also calling out from downstream for help. He recruited his friends and neighbors to help him in the task of saving the ever-increasing number who were drowning. He called to another friend who was walking by and asked him to help. The man kept walking upstream. He asked why this man was not helping in this clear time of crisis. The man replied, "I am. I am going to the top of the stream to find out why they are all falling in, and to see if I can stop it."*

The work of New Directions Institute and the ideas contained in this book present an upstream solution that can prevent many of the costs of expensive rehabilitation and remediation that now occur downstream. Remedial reading programs, treatment of learning disabilities, drop-out prevention programs, juvenile justice, drug and alcohol rehabilitation, and incarceration are all costly to our society and can be painful for the children needing such services. In the United States, we are a caring society. We have always reached out to those clearly in need. It is time, however, to utilize science to aid in an early prevention strategy to elevate each child's capacity to learn and to stimulate every child's brain to be ready for formal schooling. I encourage you, therefore, to share this book and its messages with people close to you, and to advocate for better education for all caregivers and parents and for higher quality child-care services in your community.

Wonderful parents have always had a keen ability to react to subtle indicators as they raised a young child. The ability to "tune in" to a very young child is, in fact, deliberate, even though it may come naturally to many. Consciously, deliberately acting is key. It is the deliberate caring for the intellectual and emotional growth of infants and toddlers that we, at New Directions, are all about. If you are interested in information about our programs that can provide training to child-care businesses or community action committees, visit our Web site at www.newdirectionsinstitute.org, as well as other national non-profit Web sites listed in the Resources section.

Learning the specifics of *how* to take care of little children is pretty easy. Actually *taking care* of little children is difficult, particularly at first. Quality care *is* an investment of time. Time to learn and time to devote to responsive, consistent care.

> "It is the time you have wasted for your rose that makes
> your rose so important."
> "It is the time you have wasted for my rose," said the Little
> Prince, so he would be sure to remember.

I want to reassure you that the time you set aside to interact with your child will pay off. As a parent you can feel good about using the science-based, easy-to-remember ABCs of early learning (Attention, Bonding, and Communication):

- To remind yourself each day of things you can do to purposefully focus on ways to involve your child's Attention to things in his world, to encourage Bonding with people who love him, and to emphasize Communication with everyone he meets
- To evaluate your child's other care environments (for consistency with babysitters, day-care providers, and relatives who interact regularly with your child)

Once you realize that you are deliberately paying attention to healthy development, you can look forward to the enjoyment of watching your child grow and learn.

# Acknowledgments

There are several people I want to thank for helping me either directly or indirectly in writing this book. My daughter Kristin Stamm McNealy has served as my primary collaborator and editor, which allowed us to spend many hours reviewing not only the science of early development, but also the milestones of our lives together. By virtue of her birth, she literally gave me a reason to want to stay alive when life was looking joyless and grim many years ago, and she continues to be the wisest and nicest person I have ever met. Thank you, Kristin. I also thank Paula Spencer whose talent for writing and whose life experiences as a mother of four herself gave an added perspective to deliver many of the science-based messages in a "real" way. Additionally, I want to thank:

- My friend and faculty colleague Billie Enz, Ph.D., who started out once upon a time as my boss and who continues to guide me and share her amazing talents with me
- My friend and colleague at New Directions, Pamela Webb, who uses her good judgment and instincts to promote our work in the community
- My academic mentors, Raymond Kulhavy, Ph.D., a past Regents' Professor at Arizona State University, and Bill Stock,

Ph.D., who together taught me the importance of going to the primary source when reporting research, but who also insisted that I look for opportunities to make my research interests benefit the general public

- All of the people who have supported the work I've been doing at New Directions Institute over the years and who have recognized the wisdom of educating parents and child-care staff about healthy early brain development. Thanks to the Nina Mason Pulliam Charitable Trust and to Arizona Public Service for their partnership, investment, and decision to educate all their employees as well as community members throughout Arizona.

- Lauren Marino, my editor, who made the revision process so easy

- And, my Jenny, who has taught me that every person in this world has a right to be . . . that, regardless of whether they bring very little, or a lot when they arrive, each shows what it is to be human by just their very existence. Jenny will forever be my supreme teacher.

# Appendix

## BRAIN BASICS: A PICTURE GUIDE

The brain is part of the central nervous system. It has two hemispheres, each of which has four lobes. Different parts of the brain control different kinds of functions, but, almost always, many parts of the brain work together at the same time to produce our behaviors. The **occipital lobe** is concerned with vision. Some functions of the **temporal lobe** include hearing, language, memory, emotion, and complex visual perceptions. The **parietal lobe** is involved in sensory processes, attention, and language. The **frontal lobe** functions include reasoning, working memory, decision making, planning, language, and motor processes. The **sensory**

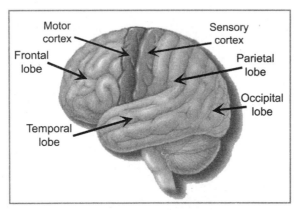

*Figure 12. Lateral view of the brain, showing the four lobes from the side.*

**cortex** is the main receptive area for the sense of touch. The **motor cortex** is involved in the planning and execution of movements.

The **limbic system** is critical for learning, motivation, memory, and emotion and is a grouping of many structures, including the amygdala, hippocampus, thalamus, hypothalamus, basal ganglia, and cingulate gyrus. The **amygdala** is involved in the processing and encoding of emotions, particularly of fear and aggression. The **hippocampus** is like a filing system that enables the formation of new long-term memories and their retrieval. The **thalamus** relays information coming from the senses to the different parts of the cortex and regulates one's level of awareness and activity. Just as the thalamus monitors external input, the **hypothalamus** regulates internal, automatic processes such as blood pressure, heart rate, and hunger. The **basal ganglia** are a group of nuclei that are important for movement and certain aspects of learning, such as sequence learning. One of its nuclei, the **nucleus accumbens**, is part of the reward pathway and is involved in pleasure and addiction. The **cingulate gyrus** is important for the allocation of attention. The **corpus callosum** is a band of fibers that connects the two hemispheres of the brain. The **cerebellum** is responsible for coordinating movement and cognitive tasks involving precise timing. The **brain stem**, at the base of the brain, connects the **spinal cord** with the hemispheres of the

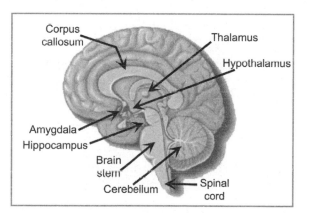

*Figure 13. Medial view of the brain, showing internal structures from the middle.*

brain and controls breathing, heart contraction, and other automatic processes.

## HOW WE KNOW WHAT WE KNOW

In research laboratories around the world, scientists are using the following types of technologies to learn about brain development and when and where certain capabilities to perform mental tasks develop:

### PET scans (Positron Emission Tomography)

PET scans indicate where the brain is working at a given time by tracking how the brain uses energy. A radioactive tracer chemical that closely resembles the brain's fuel, glucose, is introduced into the bloodstream. This chemical is then taken up into brain tissue, allowing researchers to measure the level of activity in various brain regions. In addition to measuring activity levels, when other types of tracer chemicals are used, researchers can measure blood flow, oxygen usage, and the release and binding of specialized chemicals that are used to communicate between neurons, called neurotransmitters. PET scans help to determine where in the brain specific mental functions take place. Because this technology utilizes radioactive components, children at any age are not routinely scanned except for research on important medical issues.

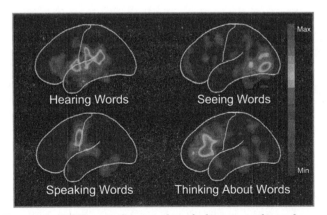

*Figure 14. PET images showing where the brain is working when a person is hearing, seeing, speaking, and thinking about words.*

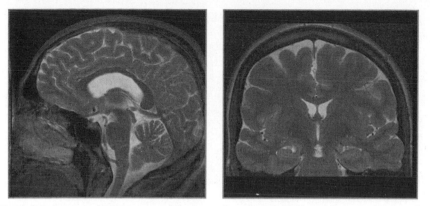

*Figure 15. Structural MRI images of the brain from the side (left) and from the front (right).*

### sMRI scans (structural Magnetic Resonance Imaging)

The structural MRI is a technique used to obtain detailed images of different types of brain tissue. The combination of a magnetic field and radio waves is used to generate computer images of the structure of the brain. Researchers are now using sMRI to better understand how different parts of the brain grow during development.

### fMRI scans (functional Magnetic Resonance Imaging)

Functional MRI scans can measure changes in blood volume and blood flow, and are most often used to measure the use of oxygen in blood, as neural tissue uses oxygen while performing various tasks. The magnetic properties of the blood change as oxygen is used and the fMRI scanner records these changes in the magnetic properties. Computers then generate images of areas of the brain that are using the most oxygen due to increases in neural activity. Because this technology provides an action picture of the brain "lighting up," it's being widely used to explore how the brain orchestrates everything from seeing and hearing to learning, memory, and language.

### EEG images (Electroencephalograms)

Newly refined EEG technology measures the electrical activity of neurons by recording from electrodes placed on the scalp. Computers

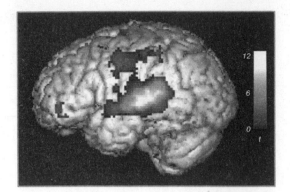

*Figure 16. Functional MRI image showing brain activation
in response to a person hearing a new language.*

"filter out" extraneous electrical background noise from the recordings in order to isolate specific brain activity and create images of electrical patterns of activity in the brain over time.

### Molecular imaging techniques
Using a variety of molecular and cellular imaging techniques, scientists can now study slices of the brain to explore how neurons make connections in real time at a microscopic level as well as how the signal is passed from one neuron to another across the synapse.

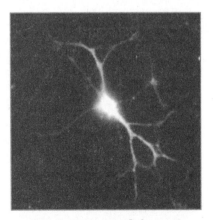

*Figure 17. A magnified neuron.*

In the rapidly developing field of neuroscience, there are many new techniques in the forefront—magnetoencephalography (MEG), transcranial magnetic stimulation (TMS), and optical imaging techniques like near-infrared spectroscopy (NIRS), for example—that will likely prove very useful in our learning even more about the brain and how it functions. Stay tuned, as you might, in the not-too-distant future, be hearing these acronyms, too, tossed around like household words.

# References with Brain Briefs

## CHAPTER 1

Balbernie, R. (2001). Circuits and circumstances: The neurobiological consequences of early relationship experiences and how they shape later behavior. *Journal of Child Psychotherapy.* 27(3): 237–255.

Benes, F. M. (1994). Development of the corticolimbic system. In: *Human Behavior and the Developing Brain.* (Dawson, G., & Fischer, K. W., eds.) New York: The Guilford Press.

Bennett, A. J., Lesch, K. P., Heils, A., Long, J. C., Lorenz, J. G., Shoaf, S. E., Champoux, M., Suomi, S. J., Linnoila, M. V., & Higley, J. D. (2002). Early experience and serotonin transporter gene variation interact to influence primate CNS function. *Molecular Psychiatry.* 7(1): 118–122.

Chugani, H. T. (1998). A critical period of brain development: Studies of cerebral glucose utilization with PET. *Preventive Medicine.* 27: 184–188.

Chugani, H. T. (1998). Biological basis of emotions: Brain systems and brain development. *Pediatrics.* 102: 1225–1229.

Cirulli, F., Berry, A., & Alleva, E. (2003). Early disruption of the mother-infant relationship: Effects on brain plasticity and implications for psychopathology. *Neuroscience and Biobehavioral Reviews.* 27: 73–82.

Diamond, M. & Hopson, J. (1998). Magic Trees of the Mind: How to Nurture Your Child's Intelligence, Creativity, and Healthy Emotions from Birth Through Adolescence. New York: Plume Books. *This book is a wonderful resource for anyone who has children or works with kids. The last third of the book is filled with suggestions for books to read, games to play, and activities that kids will love at various ages. Written in 1998, this is still a useful book rich with neuroscience information generated from the laboratory of leading neuroanatomist Marion Diamond, Ph.D., at University of California, Berkeley, where she has been instrumental in demonstrating that neurons sprout and branch in response to different types of stimulation. The book tells about studies showing that physical changes in the brain can result from an experience after the very first time that experience occurs! Tiny spines at the very ends of the neuron's branches (the dendrites) grow and alter their shape in response to use. One of Dr. Diamond's students has described the tiny spines themselves on these trees as looking like "three dimensional lollipops with a ball on a stalk," which reminds me of my favorite candy, the Tootsie Pop.*

*By studying these spines in other species, we've learned a lot about how they grow. A researcher named Richard Coss, Ph.D., discovered that in a honeybee, a single flight into a meadow for the first time causes spines to change from that Tootsie-Pop shape to that of an umbrella, an exciting discovery that was then replicated in other animals. These structures are so tiny that they're difficult to study, but it's thought that regular use can transform the original round shape into more of an umbrella shape, whereas with disuse the spines resemble a collapsed umbrella—microscopic physical proof of the power of first learnings!*

Eliot, L. (1999). *What's Going on in There? How the Brain and Mind Develop in the First Five Years of Life*. New York: Bantam Books.

Galvan, A., Hare, T. A., Parra, C. E., Penn, J., Voss, H., Glover, G., & Casey, B. J. (2006). Earlier development of the accumbens relative to orbitofrontal cortex might underlie risk-taking behavior in adolescents. *The Journal of Neuroscience.* 26(25): 6885–6892. *In this fMRI study, researchers scanned participants between the ages of seven and twenty-nine while they performed a task that gave them various amounts of reward (coins on the screen that correspond to extra money received after the scan) for their responses. They found that adolescents had exaggerated activity in a region involved in reward-seeking behavior (nucleus accumbens) relative to activity in the prefrontal cortex, a region involved in control and planning of behavior. These results suggest that it may be the case that this disproportionate activity in reward regions compared to behavioral control regions underlies the tendency during adolescence to act impulsively and to prioritize immediate over long-term gains.*

Gopnik, A., Meltzoff, A. N., & Kuhl, P. K. (1999). *The Scientist in the Crib: Minds, Brains and How Children Learn.* New York: HarperCollins.

Hensch, T. K. (2005). Critical period plasticity in local cortical circuits. *Nature Neuroscience.* 6: 877–888; Hensch, T. K. (2005). Critical period mechanisms in developing visual cortex. *Current Topics in Developmental Biology.* 69: 215–237; Wiesel, T., & Hubel, D. H. (1965). Extent of recovery from the effects of visual deprivation in kittens. *Journal of Neurophysiology.* 28: 1060–1072. *Here's one way we know that specific neural circuits develop in a predictable sequence, with periods in which they are most plastic and optimally receptive to influences from the environment. Researchers sewed shut one eye of a kitten and then examined how the developing visual cortex was affected. Surprisingly, there were many more connections in the cortex for the uncovered eye than for the closed eye, indicating that the structure and function of the cortex can be dramatically altered by experience while it's developing. Even after the eye was reopened, the kitten remained blind in that eye because the circuitry in the cortex had already matured and was not plastic enough to accommodate the incoming input from the recently opened eye.*

*The timing of the development of various structures and how long it lasts differs greatly across brain areas. The kitten had trouble regaining its sight because the visual cortex is one of the earliest to fully mature. But many other brain areas remain highly plastic throughout the lifespan. That's how fifty-year-olds are able to switch careers or eighty-year-olds can take up learning to play bridge.*

*Since the kitten study won the Nobel Prize back in the 1970s, scientists have continued to actively study this phenomenon. Now they're making great progress in determining the molecular signals that are responsible for this type of plastic reorganization in response to input during development. As a result of this research, the medical community has made changes in the timing of procedures such as the removal of cataracts from newborn infants. Traditionally, doctors had waited until the child was "bigger and stronger" to remove them, but based on the findings of this type of research, policies were changed and treatments are now given earlier.*

Huttenlocher, P. R. & Dabholkar, A. S. (1997). Regional differences in synaptogenesis in human cerebral cortex. *Journal of Comparative Neurology.* 387: 167–178.

Joseph, R. (1999). Environmental influences on neural plasticity, the limbic system, emotional development and attachment: A review. *Child Psychiatry and Human Development.* 29(3): 189–208.

Knudsen, E. I., Heckman, J. J., Cameron J. L., & Shonkoff, J. P. (2006). Economic, neurobiological, and behavioral perspectives on building America's future workforce. *Proceedings of the National Academy of Sciences.* 103(27): 10155–10162.

Maguire, E. A., Frackowiak, R. S. J., & Frith, C. D. (1997). Recalling routes around London: Activation of the right hippocampus in taxi drivers. *The Journal of Neuroscience.* 17(18): 7103–7110; Maguire, E. A., Gadian, D. G., Johnsrude, I. S., Good, C. D., Ashburner, J., Frackowiak, R. S. J., & Frith, C. D. (2000). Navigation-related structural change in the hippocampi of taxi drivers. *Proceedings of the National Academy of Sciences.* 97(8): 4398–4403; Maguire, E. A., Spiers, H. J., Good, C. D., Hartley, T., Frackowiak, R. S. J., & Burgess, N. (2003). Navigation expertise and the human hippocampus: A structural brain imaging analysis. *Hippocampus.* 13(2): 250–259. *These studies provide a fascinating illustration of neural plasticity. London taxi drivers, who have extensive training (lasting an average of two years) to learn the complex web of streets in the city, were given brain scans by scientists at the University College London along with a group of participants who were not taxi drivers. The taxi drivers were found to have larger posterior hippocampi than the non-driver participants. That's the part of the brain important for memory formation, and it is used during navigation and for storing spatial representations (like being able to picture the map of interconnecting streets in your head). The scientists also found that the more time a taxi driver spent on the job, the bigger this back part of the hippocampus grew, thus providing evidence that brain structure can change in adult humans in response to environmental demands.*

Perry, B. D., Pollard, R. A., Blakley, T. L., Baker, W. L., & Vigilange, D. (1995). Childhood trauma, the neurobiology of adaptation, and "use-dependent" development of the brain: How "states" become "traits." *Infant Mental Health Journal.* 16(4): 271–292. *This article provides an overview of the emotional, behavioral, cognitive, social, and physical consequences of childhood trauma. It highlights the predictable sequence and use-dependent nature of brain development and also emphasizes how the development of healthy, complex systems used for cognitive functioning is dependent on the healthy development of less complex systems used for emotional functioning.*

Shonkoff, J. P. & Phillips, D. A., eds. (2000). *From Neurons to Neighborhoods: The Science of Early Childhood Development.* Washington, DC: National Academy Press. *This book provides a comprehensive, detailed account of the research that has been conducted during the past several decades about early childhood development. Written by the Committee on Integrating the Science of Early Childhood Development (on behalf of the Board on Children, Youth, and Families of the National Research Council and the Institute of Medicine), this in-depth analysis of recent scientific findings highlights the importance of early life experiences and relationships in guiding healthy development and future successful outcomes. It is a long book, but it contains a wealth of fascinating information!*

Sowell, E. R., Delis, D., Stiles, J., & Jernigan, T. L. (2001). Improved memory functioning and frontal lobe maturation between childhood and adolescence: A structural MRI study. *Journal of the International Neuropsychological Society.* 7(3): 312–322.

Suomi, S. J. (2003). Gene-environment interactions and the neurobiology of social conflict. *Annals of the New York Academy of Sciences.* 1008: 132–139.

Sylwester, R. (1995). *A Celebration of Neurons: An Educator's Guide to the Human Brain.* Alexandria, VA: Association for Supervision and Curriculum Development.

Van Essen, D. C., Drury, H. A., Joshi, S., & Miller, M. I. (1998). Functional and structural mapping of the human cerebral cortex: Solutions are in the surfaces. *Proceedings of the National Academy of Sciences.* 95: 788–795.

Webb, S. J., Monk, C. S., & Nelson, C. A. (2001). Mechanisms of postnatal neurobiological development: Implications for human development. *Developmental Neuropsychology.* 19(2): 147–171.

Zero-to-Three: www.zerotothree.org; (Brain Wonders, Frequently Asked Questions section); Carmichael, A. (1990). Physical development and biological *attention! What did the researchers do to train these kids? They had them play computer games that required them to complete tasks such as: a) track a cartoon cat on the screen using a joystick, b) anticipate the movement of a duck across a pond on the screen by moving the cat to where they thought the duck would appear, c) pick a cartoon portrait out of several that matched the one they had just seen on the screen a few seconds beforehand, and d) to click as fast as possible when they saw a sheep on the screen, but not to click at all if a wolf appeared instead. Each of these tasks is thought to engage a different type of maintenance attention, and can be easily adapted into fun activities you can play with your child!*

Ruff, H. A. & Rothbart, M. K. (1996). *Attention in Early Development: Themes and Variations.* New York: Oxford University Press.

Sax, L. (2005). *Why Gender Matters: What Parents and Teachers Need to Know about the Emerging Science of Sex Differences.* New York: Broadway Books.

Sethi, A., Mischel, W., Aber, J. L., Shoda, Y., & Rodriguez, M. L. (2000). The role of strategic attention deployment in development of self-regulation: Predicting preschoolers' delay of gratification from mother-toddler interactions. *Developmental Psychology.* 36(6): 767–777.

Thapar, A., O'Donovan, M., & Owen, M. J. (2005). The genetics of attention deficit hyperactivity disorder. *Human Molecular Genetics.* 14(2): R275–R282.

Thompson, L. A., Fagan, J. F., & Fulker, D. W. (1991). Longitudinal prediction of specific cognitive abilities from infant novelty preference. *Child Development.* 62(3): 530–538. *In this study, infants were given an assessment of their preference for novel stimuli at five and seven months of age. They were then followed over time and given various tests of intelligence at one, two, and three years of age. Children who were more attracted to novel stimuli as infants were more likely to have higher IQs as well as to be more advanced on a variety of cognitive skills, such as verbal ability and memory.*

## CHAPTER 3

Alexander, G. & Hines, M. (2002). Sex differences in response to children's toys in nonhuman primates. *Evolution and Human Behavior.* 23: 467–479.

influences. In: *Handbook of Studies on Child Psychiatry.* (Tonge, B. J., Burrows, G. D., & Werry, J. S., eds.) New York: Elsevier. *These references explain about basic brain development and growth, and include how a baby's brain size is 25 percent of an adult's at birth, 75 percent before the child turns two, 80 percent by age three, and 90 percent by age five.*

## CHAPTER 2

Atkinson, R. C. & Shiffrin, R. M. (1968). Human memory: A proposed system and its control processes. In: *The Psychology of Learning and Motivation.* (Spence, K. W. & Spence, J. T., eds.) New York: Academic Press.

Barkley, R. A. (2006). *Attention Deficit Hyperactivity Disorder: A Handbook for Diagnosis and Treatment* (Third Edition). New York: Guilford Press.

Clohessy, A. B., Posner, M. I., Rothbart, M. K., & Vecera, S. P. (1991). The development of inhibition of return in early infancy. *Journal of Cognitive Neuroscience.* 3: 345–350.

Davenport, T. H. & Beck, J. C. (2001). *The Attention Economy: Understanding the New Currency of Business.* Boston, MA: Harvard Business School Press.

Driscoll, M. P. (2004). *Psychology of learning for instruction* (Third Edition). New York: Allyn and Bacon.

Eigsti, I.-M., Zayas, V., Mischel, W., Shoda, Y., Ayduk, O., Dadlani, M. B., Davidson, M. C., Aber, J. L., & Casey, B. J. (2006). Predicting cognitive control from preschool to late adolescence and young adulthood. *Psychological Science.* 17(6): 478–484.

Harman, C., Posner, M. I., Rothbart, M. K., & Thomas-Trapp, L. (1994). Development of orienting to objects and locations in human infants. *Canadian Journal of Experimental Psychology.* 48: 301–318.

Kahneman, D. (1973). *Attention and Effort.* Englewood Cliffs, NJ: Prentice-Hall.

Mischel, W., Shoda, Y., & Rodriguez, M. I. (1989). Delay of gratification in children. *Science.* 244(4907): 933–938.

My ADHD: Connecting Doctors, Parents and Teachers. www.myadhd.com

Porges, S. W. (1992). Autonomic regulation and attention. In: *Attention and Information Processing in Infants and Adults.* (Campbell, B. A., Hayne, H., & Richardson, R., eds.) Hillsdale, NJ: Erlbaum.

Posner, M. I. & Peterson, S. E. (1990). The attention system of the human brain. *Annual Review of Neuroscience.* 13: 25–42.

National Resource Center on AD/HD: A Program of Children and Adults with Attention Deficit/Hyperactivity Disorder. www.help4adhd.org. *This online resource is one of many in which information about ADHD can be found. Currently, ADHD affects between 3 to 7 percent of children, with boys being diagnosed three times as often as girls. There is a strong hereditary component to ADHD. In fact, an individual is five times more likely to have it if a first-degree family member has it (25 percent of first-degree relatives of a child with ADHD also had ADHD, whereas this percentage is only 5 percent in the control population, and if one identical twin has ADHD, the other twin will have it 80 percent of the time).*

New Directions Institute for Infant Brain Development. (2006). S.T.E.P.S. Curriculum.

Rankin, C. H. & Carew, T. J. (1987). Development of learning and memory in Aplysia. II. Habituation and dishabituation. *The Journal of Neuroscience.* 7(1): 133–143; Glanzman, D. L. (2006). The cellular mechanisms of learning in Aplysia: Of blind men and elephants. *Biological Bulletin.* 210: 271–279. *These studies review what is known about simple learning mechanisms in the marine snail, Aplysia. This organism, because it is very simple and primitive, has been instrumental in teaching researchers about how cells change in response to experience. One form of learning that has been particularly well studied in Aplysia is the habituation response, in which the snail's startle response to a stimulus that is neither rewarding nor harmful (say, a jet of water sprayed on it) is lessened each time the stimulus is repeated. Humans also habituate to repeated stimuli, such as the weight of our clothes on our skin or the noise of the ceiling fan in the background. Scientists are still actively studying habituation at the cellular, molecular, and behavioral levels in organisms such as Aplysia to eventually better understand mechanisms of learning in humans.*

Ratey, J. J. & Hallowell, E. M. (1994). *Driven to Distraction: Recognizing and Coping with Attention Deficit Disorder from Childhood to Adulthood.* New York: Pantheon Books.

Raz, A. & Buhle, J. (2006). Typologies of attentional networks. *Nature Neuroscience.* 7: 367–379. *This article reviews what is currently known about the attention system, including the brain anatomy of different components of the system. While many brain areas are engaged during the allocation of attention, researchers have learned that the alerting component utilizes the thalamus in the center of the brain, the shifting component, which involves orienting of the head and eyes, uses the inferior parietal and midbrain areas, and the maintaining component relies on the anterior cingulate gyrus in the frontal lobes. Furthermore, each component has been associated with different neurotransmitter systems that modulate their function, with the noradrenaline system involved in alerting, the cholinergic system involved in shifting, and the dopaminergic system involved in maintaining. While each component has been heavily studied as serving an independent function, the components operate in cooperation with each other to result in one's ability to seamlessly pay attention to the surrounding world.*

Rothbart, M. K., Derryberry, D., & Posner, M. I. (1994). A psychobiological approach to the development of temperament. In: *Temperament: Individual Differences at the Interface of Biology and Behavior.* (Bates, J. E. & Wachs, T. D. eds.) Washington, DC: American Psychological Association.

Rueda, M. R., Rothbart, M. K., McCandliss, B. D., Saccomanno, L., & Posner, M. I. (2005). Training, maturation, and genetic influences on the development of executive attention. *Proceedings of the National Academy of Sciences.* 102(4) 14931–14936. *A group of scientists from the University of Oregon tested whether or not it would be possible to boost children's attention span through training. About seventy-five kids (four- and six-year-olds) were brought in for evaluation of their attention span. The kids were then divided into two groups. One group took part in five sessions of attention training designed to boost the third component of the attention system: The ability to maintain attention on a task. A second group of children served as the control group, and received no attention training. When both groups of kids were tested, the training group displayed marked increases in attention span while the control group remained the same, indicating that it is possible to train the brain to i*

Brooks, R. & Meltzoff, A. N. (2005). The development of gaze following and its relation to language. *Developmental Science.* 8(6): 535–543.

Committee on Children with Disabilities. (2001). Technical report: The pediatrician's role in the diagnosis and management of autism spectrum disorder in children. *Pediatrics.* 107: 85–103.

Connellan, J., Baron-Cohen, S., Wheelwright, S., Batki, A., & Ahluwalia, J. (2000). Sex differences in human neonatal social perception. *Infant Behavior and Development.* 23: 113–118. *This study set out to determine whether differences between boys and girls in sociability is biologically or culturally driven. By using newborn infants (who have had no real postnatal experience) and examining the length of time they looked at either a human face or a moving mobile, the researchers concluded that the female preference for faces and the male preference for mechanical objects is biologically and likely neurologically based.*

Dapretto, M., Davies, M. S., Pfeifer, J. H., Scott, A. A., Sigman, M., Bookheimer, S. Y., & Iacoboni, M. (2005). Understanding emotions in others: Mirror neuron dysfunction in children with autism spectrum disorders. *Nature Neuroscience.* 9(1): 29–30.

de Haan, M. & Nelson, C. A. (1997). Recognition of the mother's face by 6-month-old infants: A neurobehavioral study. *Child Development.* 68: 187–210.

de Haan, M. & Nelson, C. A. (1999). Brain activity differentiates face and object processing in 6-month-old infants. *Developmental Psychology.* 35: 1113–1121.

di Pellegrino, G., Fadiga, L., Fogassi, L., Gallese, V., & Rizzolatti, G. (1992). Understanding motor events: A neurophysiological study. *Experimental Brain Research.* 91(1): 176–180.

Falck-Ytter, T., Gredeback, G., & von Hofsten, C. (2006). Infants predict other people's action goals. *Nature Neuroscience.* 9(7): 878–879. *This study investigated whether infants recruit the mirror neuron system to map an observed action onto their own motor representation of that action. Researchers followed the eye gaze of six- and twelve-month-old infants to see whether they exhibited proactive goal-directed eye movements when watching another person's hand move three toys into a bucket. The twelve-month-old's eye gaze moved to the bucket before the person's hand arrived there, as is the case in adults, but the six-month-old's gaze arrived at the bucket after the person's hand arrived. In the conditions when the toys moved into the bucket without a person's hand moving them, both groups of infants did not demonstrate proactive eye gaze to the bucket; they simply followed the toys. These findings indicate that, as infants develop sufficient control over their eye movements sometime during the second half of the first year of life, they also develop gaze behaviors that arise from understanding the action intentions of others—a skill that is most likely gained through the development and recruitment of the mirror neuron system.*

Farroni, T., Csibra, G., Simion, F., & Johnson, M. H. (2002). Eye contact detection in humans from birth. *Proceedings of the National Academy of Sciences.* 99(14): 9602–9605.

Filipek, P. A., Accardo, P. J., Ashwal, S., Baranek, G. T., Cook, E. H., Dawson, G., Gordon, B., Gravel, J. S., Johnson, C. P., Kallen, R. J., Levy, S. E., Minshew, N. J., Ozonoff, S., Prizant, B. M., Rapin, I., Rogers, S. J., Stone, W. L., Teplin, S. W., Tuchman, F. G., & Volkmar, F. R. (2000). Practice parameter: Screening and diagnosis of autism: Report of the quality standards subcommittee of the American Academy of Neurology and the Child Neurology Society. *Neurology.* 55: 468–479.

Gallese, V., Keysers, C., & Rizzolatti, G. (2004). A unifying view of the basis of social cognition. *Trends in Cognitive Sciences.* 8(9): 396–403.

Gallese, V., Fadiga, L., Fogassi, L., & and Rizzolatti, G. (1996). Action recognition in the premotor cortex. *Brain.* 119: 593–609.

Gazzaniga, M. S. (2005). Forty-five years of split brain research and still going strong. *Nature Neuroscience.* 6: 653–659.

Gazzaniga, M. S. (2000). Cerebral specialization and interhemispheric communication: Does the corpus callosum enable the human condition? *Brain.* 123: 1293–1326.

Hainline, L. (1978). Developmental changes in visual scanning of face and nonface patterns by infants. *Journal of Experimental Child Psychology.* 25(1): 90–115.

influences. In: *Handbook of Studies on Child Psychiatry.* (Tonge, B. J., Burrows, G. D., & Werry, J. S., eds.) New York: Elsevier. *These references explain about basic brain development and growth, and include how a baby's brain size is 25 percent of an adult's at birth, 75 percent before the child turns two, 80 percent by age three, and 90 percent by age five.*

## CHAPTER 2

Atkinson, R. C. & Shiffrin, R. M. (1968). Human memory: A proposed system and its control processes. In: *The Psychology of Learning and Motivation.* (Spence, K. W. & Spence, J. T., eds.) New York: Academic Press.

Barkley, R. A. (2006). *Attention Deficit Hyperactivity Disorder: A Handbook for Diagnosis and Treatment* (Third Edition). New York: Guilford Press.

Clohessy, A. B., Posner, M. I., Rothbart, M. K., & Vecera, S. P. (1991). The development of inhibition of return in early infancy. *Journal of Cognitive Neuroscience.* 3: 345–350.

Davenport, T. H. & Beck, J. C. (2001). *The Attention Economy: Understanding the New Currency of Business.* Boston, MA: Harvard Business School Press.

Driscoll, M. P. (2004). *Psychology of learning for instruction* (Third Edition). New York: Allyn and Bacon.

Eigsti, I.-M., Zayas, V., Mischel, W., Shoda, Y., Ayduk, O., Dadlani, M. B., Davidson, M. C., Aber, J. L., & Casey, B. J. (2006). Predicting cognitive control from preschool to late adolescence and young adulthood. *Psychological Science.* 17(6): 478–484.

Harman, C., Posner, M. I., Rothbart, M. K., & Thomas-Trapp, L. (1994). Development of orienting to objects and locations in human infants. *Canadian Journal of Experimental Psychology.* 48: 301–318.

Kahneman, D. (1973). *Attention and Effort.* Englewood Cliffs, NJ: Prentice-Hall.

Mischel, W., Shoda, Y., & Rodriguez, M. I. (1989). Delay of gratification in children. *Science.* 244(4907): 933–938.

My ADHD: Connecting Doctors, Parents and Teachers. www.myadhd.com

Porges, S. W. (1992). Autonomic regulation and attention. In: *Attention and Information Processing in Infants and Adults.* (Campbell, B. A., Hayne, H., & Richardson, R., eds.) Hillsdale, NJ: Erlbaum.

Posner, M. I. & Peterson, S. E. (1990). The attention system of the human brain. *Annual Review of Neuroscience.* 13: 25–42.

National Resource Center on AD/HD: A Program of Children and Adults with Attention Deficit/Hyperactivity Disorder. www.help4adhd.org. *This online resource is one of many in which information about ADHD can be found. Currently, ADHD affects between 3 to 7 percent of children, with boys being diagnosed three times as often as girls. There is a strong hereditary component to ADHD. In fact, an individual is five times more likely to have it if a first-degree family member has it (25 percent of first-degree relatives of a child with ADHD also had ADHD, whereas this percentage is only 5 percent in the control population, and if one identical twin has ADHD, the other twin will have it 80 percent of the time).*

New Directions Institute for Infant Brain Development. (2006). S.T.E.P.S. Curriculum.

Rankin, C. H. & Carew, T. J. (1987). Development of learning and memory in Aplysia. II. Habituation and dishabituation. *The Journal of Neuroscience.* 7(1): 133–143; Glanzman, D. L. (2006). The cellular mechanisms of learning in Aplysia: Of blind men and elephants. *Biological Bulletin.* 210: 271–279. *These studies review what is known about simple learning mechanisms in the marine snail,* Aplysia. *This organism, because it is very simple and primitive, has been instrumental in teaching researchers about how cells change in response to experience. One form of learning that has been particularly well studied in* Aplysia *is the habituation response, in which the snail's startle response to a stimulus that is neither rewarding nor harmful (say, a jet of water sprayed on it) is lessened each time the stimulus is repeated. Humans also habituate to repeated stimuli, such as the weight of our clothes on our skin or the noise of the ceiling fan in the background. Scientists are still actively studying habituation at the cellular, molecular, and behavioral levels in organisms such as* Aplysia *to eventually better understand mechanisms of learning in humans.*

Ratey, J. J. & Hallowell, E. M. (1994). *Driven to Distraction: Recognizing and Coping with Attention Deficit Disorder from Childhood to Adulthood.* New York: Pantheon Books.

Raz, A. & Buhle, J. (2006). Typologies of attentional networks. *Nature Neuroscience.* 7: 367–379. *This article reviews what is currently known about the attention system, including the brain anatomy of different components of the system. While many brain areas are engaged during the allocation of attention, researchers have learned that the* alerting *component utilizes the thalamus in the center of the brain, the* shifting *component, which involves orienting of the head and eyes, uses the inferior parietal and midbrain areas, and the* maintaining *component relies on the anterior cingulate gyrus in the frontal lobes. Furthermore, each component has been associated with different neurotransmitter systems that modulate their function, with the noradrenaline system involved in alerting, the cholinergic system involved in shifting, and the dopaminergic system involved in maintaining. While each component has been heavily studied as serving an independent function, the components operate in cooperation with each other to result in one's ability to seamlessly pay attention to the surrounding world.*

Rothbart, M. K., Derryberry, D., & Posner, M. I. (1994). A psychobiological approach to the development of temperament. In: *Temperament: Individual Differences at the Interface of Biology and Behavior.* (Bates, J. E. & Wachs, T. D., eds.) Washington, DC: American Psychological Association.

Rueda, M. R., Rothbart, M. K., McCandliss, B. D., Saccomanno, L., & Posner, M. I. (2005). Training, maturation, and genetic influences on the development of executive attention. *Proceedings of the National Academy of Sciences.* 102(41): 14931–14936. *A group of scientists from the University of Oregon tested whether or not it would be possible to boost children's attention span through training. About seventy-five kids (four- and six-year-olds) were brought in for evaluation of their attention span. The kids were then divided into two groups. One group took part in five sessions of attention training designed to boost the third component of the attention system: The ability to maintain attention on a task. A second group of children served as the control group, and received no attention training. When both groups of kids were tested, the training group displayed marked increases in attention span while the control group remained the same, indicating that it is possible to train the brain to improve attention! What did the researchers do to train these kids? They had them play computer games that required them to complete tasks such as: a) track a cartoon cat on the screen using a joystick, b) anticipate the movement of a duck across a pond on the screen by moving the cat to where they thought the duck would appear, c) pick a cartoon portrait out of several that matched the one they had just seen on the screen a few seconds beforehand, and d) to click as fast as possible when they saw a sheep on the screen, but not to click at all if a wolf appeared instead. Each of these tasks is thought to engage a different type of maintenance attention, and can be easily adapted into fun activities you can play with your child!*

Ruff, H. A. & Rothbart, M. K. (1996). *Attention in Early Development: Themes and Variations*. New York: Oxford University Press.

Sax, L. (2005). *Why Gender Matters: What Parents and Teachers Need to Know about the Emerging Science of Sex Differences*. New York: Broadway Books.

Sethi, A., Mischel, W., Aber, J. L., Shoda, Y., & Rodriguez, M. L. (2000). The role of strategic attention deployment in development of self-regulation: Predicting preschoolers' delay of gratification from mother-toddler interactions. *Developmental Psychology*. 36(6): 767–777.

Thapar, A., O'Donovan, M., & Owen, M. J. (2005). The genetics of attention deficit hyperactivity disorder. *Human Molecular Genetics*. 14(2): R275–R282.

Thompson, L. A., Fagan, J. F., & Fulker, D. W. (1991). Longitudinal prediction of specific cognitive abilities from infant novelty preference. *Child Development*. 62(3): 530–538. *In this study, infants were given an assessment of their preference for novel stimuli at five and seven months of age. They were then followed over time and given various tests of intelligence at one, two, and three years of age. Children who were more attracted to novel stimuli as infants were more likely to have higher IQs as well as to be more advanced on a variety of cognitive skills, such as verbal ability and memory.*

## CHAPTER 3

Alexander, G. & Hines, M. (2002). Sex differences in response to children's toys in nonhuman primates. *Evolution and Human Behavior*. 23: 467–479.

Brooks, R. & Meltzoff, A. N. (2005). The development of gaze following and its relation to language. *Developmental Science.* 8(6): 535–543.

Committee on Children with Disabilities. (2001). Technical report: The pediatrician's role in the diagnosis and management of autism spectrum disorder in children. *Pediatrics.* 107: 85–103.

Connellan, J., Baron-Cohen, S., Wheelwright, S., Batki, A., & Ahluwalia, J. (2000). Sex differences in human neonatal social perception. *Infant Behavior and Development.* 23: 113–118. *This study set out to determine whether differences between boys and girls in sociability is biologically or culturally driven. By using newborn infants (who have had no real postnatal experience) and examining the length of time they looked at either a human face or a moving mobile, the researchers concluded that the female preference for faces and the male preference for mechanical objects is biologically and likely neurologically based.*

Dapretto, M., Davies, M. S., Pfeifer, J. H., Scott, A. A., Sigman, M., Bookheimer, S. Y., & Iacoboni, M. (2005). Understanding emotions in others: Mirror neuron dysfunction in children with autism spectrum disorders. *Nature Neuroscience.* 9(1): 29–30.

de Haan, M. & Nelson, C. A. (1997). Recognition of the mother's face by 6-month-old infants: A neurobehavioral study. *Child Development.* 68: 187–210.

de Haan, M. & Nelson, C. A. (1999). Brain activity differentiates face and object processing in 6-month-old infants. *Developmental Psychology.* 35: 1113–1121.

di Pellegrino, G., Fadiga, L., Fogassi, L., Gallese, V., & Rizzolatti, G. (1992). Understanding motor events: A neurophysiological study. *Experimental Brain Research.* 91(1): 176–180.

Falck-Ytter, T., Gredeback, G., & von Hofsten, C. (2006). Infants predict other people's action goals. *Nature Neuroscience.* 9(7): 878–879. *This study investigated whether infants recruit the mirror neuron system to map an observed action onto their own motor representation of that action. Researchers followed the eye gaze of six- and twelve-month-old infants to see whether they exhibited proactive goal-directed eye movements when watching another person's hand move three toys into a bucket. The twelve-month-old's eye gaze moved to the bucket before the person's hand arrived there, as is the case in adults, but the six-month-old's gaze arrived at the bucket after the person's hand arrived. In the conditions when the toys moved into the bucket without a person's hand moving them, both groups of infants did not demonstrate proactive eye gaze to the bucket; they simply followed the toys. These findings indicate that, as infants develop sufficient control over their eye movements sometime during the second half of the first year of life, they also develop gaze behaviors that arise from understanding the action intentions of others—a skill that is most likely gained through the development and recruitment of the mirror neuron system.*

Farroni, T., Csibra, G., Simion, F., & Johnson, M. H. (2002). Eye contact detection in humans from birth. *Proceedings of the National Academy of Sciences.* 99(14): 9602–9605.

Filipek, P. A., Accardo, P. J., Ashwal, S., Baranek, G. T., Cook, E. H., Dawson, G., Gordon, B., Gravel, J. S., Johnson, C. P., Kallen, R. J., Levy, S. E., Minshew, N. J., Ozonoff, S., Prizant, B. M., Rapin, I., Rogers, S. J., Stone, W. L., Teplin, S. W., Tuchman, F. G., & Volkmar, F. R. (2000). Practice parameter: Screening and diagnosis of autism: Report of the quality standards subcommittee of the American Academy of Neurology and the Child Neurology Society. *Neurology.* 55: 468–479.

Gallese, V., Keysers, C., & Rizzolatti, G. (2004). A unifying view of the basis of social cognition. *Trends in Cognitive Sciences.* 8(9): 396–403.

Gallese, V., Fadiga, L., Fogassi, L., & and Rizzolatti, G. (1996). Action recognition in the premotor cortex. *Brain.* 119: 593–609.

Gazzaniga, M. S. (2005). Forty-five years of split brain research and still going strong. *Nature Neuroscience.* 6: 653–659.

Gazzaniga, M. S. (2000). Cerebral specialization and interhemispheric communication: Does the corpus callosum enable the human condition? *Brain.* 123: 1293–1326.

Hainline, L. (1978). Developmental changes in visual scanning of face and nonface patterns by infants. *Journal of Experimental Child Psychology.* 25(1): 90–115.

Iacoboni, M., Molnar-Szakacs, I., Gallese, V., Buccino, G., Mazziotta, J. C., & Rizzolatti, G. (2005). Grasping the intentions of others with one's own mirror neuron system. *Public Library of Science Biology.* 3(3): e79.

Iijima, M., Arisaka, O., Minamoto, F., & Arai, Y. (2001). Sex differences in children's free drawings. *Hormones and Behavior.* 40: 99–104.

Johnson, S. C., Slaughter, V., & Carey, S. (1998). Whose gaze will infants follow? Features that elicit gaze-following in 12-month-olds. *Developmental Science.* 1(2): 233–238.

Kanwisher, N. & Yovel, G. (2006). The fusiform face area: A cortical region specialized for the perception of faces. Philosophical Transactions of the Royal Society of Biological Sciences. 361: 2109–2128; McKone, E. & Kanwisher, N. (2005). Does the human brain process objects of expertise like faces? A review of the evidence. In: *From Monkey Brain to Human Brain.* (Dehaene, S., Duhamel, J. R., Hauser, M., & Rizzolati, G., eds.) Cambridge, MA: MIT Press; Gauthier, I. & Nelson, C. A. (2001). The development of face expertise. *Current Opinion in Neurobiology.* 11: 219–224; Haxby, J. V., Gobbini, M. I., Furey, M. L., Ishai, A., Schouten, J. L., & Pietrini, P. (2001). Distributed and overlapping representations of faces and objects in ventral temporal cortex. *Science.* 293: 2425–2430. *Neuroimaging studies have shown that a part of the brain called the* fusiform gyrus *is strongly activated when people view faces. There has been a large amount of research trying to clarify whether this region is specialized for face recognition, or whether it is specialized for making within-category discriminations, such as differentiating between similar objects or animals. Some studies have shown that the fusiform gyrus is also active, for example, when expert bird-watchers are asked to recognize different types of birds, which argues for this brain region as part of a* perceptual expertise network. *However, activity within the fusiform gyrus is still the strongest when participants are asked to recognize faces, and damage to this area can result in severe impairments in facial recognition. Whether or not the activity in the fusiform gyrus reflects a dedication of this region specifically to face recognition or to more general expert discrimination of objects, this line of research is demonstrating just how important the face is for humans, who rely on recognizing faces and facial expressions to process social and emotional information.*

Kaplan, E. & Bernardete, E. (2001). The dynamics of primate retinal ganglion cells. *Progress in Brain Research.* 134: 17–34.

Levine, D. N., Warach, J., & Farah, M. (1985). Two visual systems in mental imagery: Dissociation of "what" and "where" in imagery disorders due to bilateral posterior cerebral lesions. *Neurology*. 35(7): 1010–1018.

Lucas, A. (1992). Breast milk and subsequent intelligence quotient in children born preterm. *Lancet*. 339: 261–264.

Lucas, A. (1994). A randomized multicentre study of human milk versus formula and later development in preterm infants. *Archives of Disease in Childhood*. 70: F141–146.

Maurer, D., Lewis, T. L., Brent, H. P., & Levin, A. V. (1999). Rapid improvement in the acuity of infants after visual input. *Science*. 286: 108–110.

McClure, E. (2000). A meta-analytic review of sex differences in facial expression processing and their development in infants, children and adolescents. *Psychological Bulletin*. 126: 424–453.

Meltzoff, A. N. & Moore, M. K. (1977). Imitation of facial and manual gestures by human neonates. *Science*. 198(4312): 75–78.

Mondloch, C. J., Lewis, T. L., Budreau, D. R., Maurer, D., Dannemiller, J. L., Stephens, B. R., & Kleiner-Gathercoal, K A. (1999). Face perception during early infancy. *Psychological Science*. 10(5): 419–422.

Pfeifer, J. H., Iacoboni, M., Mazziotta, J. C., & Dapretto, M. Mirror neuron system activity correlates with empathy and interpersonal competence in children. (Paper under review).

Pollock, J. J. (1994). Long-term associations with infant feeding in a clinically advantaged population of babies. *Developmental Medicine and Child Neurology*. 36: 429–440.

Rizzolatti, G. & Craighero, L. (2004). The mirror-neuron system. *Annual Reviews in Neuroscience*. 27: 169–192.

Rogan, W. J. & Gladen, B. C. (1993). Breast-feeding and cognitive development. *Early Human Development*. 31: 181–193.

Sax, L. (2005). *Why Gender Matters: What Parents and Teachers Need to Know about the Emerging Science of Sex Differences.* New York: Broadway Books.

Stern, D. (2004). *The First Relationship: Infant and Mother. With a New Introduction.* Cambridge, MA: Harvard University Press.

Tuman, D. (1999). Sing a song of sixpence: An examination of sex differences in subject preference of children's drawings. *Visual Arts Research.* 25: 51–62.

## CHAPTER 4

Bransford, J. D., Brown, A. L., & Cocking, R. R. (1999). *How People Learn: Brain, Mind, Experience and School.* Washington, DC: National Academy Press.

Gazzaniga, M. S. (2005). Forty-five years of split brain research and still going strong. *Nature Neuroscience.* 6: 653–659; Gazzaniga, M. S. (2000). Cerebral specialization and interhemispheric communication: Does the corpus callosum enable the human condition? *Brain.* 123: 1293–1326. *The extensive research of Dr. Gazzaniga using patients who have part or all of the structure of the corpus callosum severed (split brain research) has revealed much about the function of the corpus callosum and the functions of each hemisphere in the normal brain. These articles, which review his findings, suggest that the left hemisphere tends to be specialized for language, creates a schema or story about events that goes beyond actual available information, and is crucial for making causal inferences about the world. The right hemisphere seems to be specialized for processing visual and perceptual information and creating a representation of the world based on what is perceived. The corpus callosum is important for coordinating activity between and linking the two hemispheres. The fibers of the corpus callosum have specific areas that are dedicated to the transfer of different types of information between the hemispheres, with the back part (posterior) transmitting basic sensory information and the front part (anterior) transmitting information about attentional resources and higher-level cognitive processes. While one hemisphere or the other may be more dominant for performing certain tasks, there is evidence that both hemispheres are used together most of the time. Additionally, there is a redundancy of processing such that, when the processing capabilities of one hemisphere are not adequate to perform a difficult task, the other hemisphere is recruited. This aids in an individual being able to direct their attention to tasks at hand and to solve problems successfully.*

Ginsburg, K. R. & the Committee on Communications and Committee on Psychosocial Aspects of Child and Family Health. (2006). The Importance of Play in Promoting Healthy Child Development and Maintaining Strong Parent-Child Bonds. *American Academy of Pediatrics Clinical Report.*

Needham, A. & Baillargeon, R. (1993). Intuitions about support in four-and-one-half-month-old infants. *Cognition.* 47: 121–148. *Infants are incredibly observant of their surroundings and learn quickly about the physical world. Researchers have demonstrated that infants as young as three- to four-months old already seem to understand, for example, that objects cannot be suspended in midair without support, that stationary objects move when they come into contact with objects that are moving, and that inanimate objects cannot start moving on their own without something to move them.*

*To make such discoveries, babies are often observed watching various set-up scenarios. We know that babies look longer at events or objects that they do not expect or recognize (such as novel objects) than at events or objects that meet their expectations or are familiar. In this type of study, experimenters would, for example, create physically possible scenarios (such as a hand placing a box onto a supporting platform) and physically impossible scenarios (such as a hand releasing a box that seems to float in the air next to a supporting platform). Four-month-olds are way more interested in watching what is happening with the floating box and look reliably longer at the impossible scenarios, demonstrating that they already know that this is not something that should be happening. It will take them years to label this concept as gravity, but these tiny infants have already learned what gravity means in their world.*

O'Doherty, J. P. (2004). Reward representations and reward-related learning in the human brain: Insights from neuroimaging. *Current Opinion in Neurobiology.* 14: 769–776; Knutson, B. & Cooper, J. C. (2005). Functional magnetic resonance imaging of reward prediction. *Current Opinion in Neurobiology.* 18: 411–417. *Reward circuitry [which includes the basal ganglia (particularly the ventral striatum), nucleus accumbens, orbitofrontal cortex and amygdala] has been found to play a role in reward processing in humans with regard to food, monetary rewards, and social rewards such as viewing happy faces. This circuitry is rich in neurotransmitters such as dopamine and norepinephrine. These two articles provide a wonderful review of how imaging research is elucidating the different function of each brain region within the reward pathway in the human brain.*

Perry, B. D., Hogan, L., & Marlin, S. J. (2000). Curiosity, pleasure and play: A neurodevelopmental perspective. *Haaeyc Advocate*.

Ruff, H. A. & Rothbart, M. K. (1996). *Attention in Early Development: Themes and Variations*. New York: Oxford University Press.

Teller, D. Y. & Bornstein, M. H. (1987). Infant color vision and color perception. In: *Handbook of Infant Perception*. (Salapatek, P. & Cohen, L., eds.) Orlando, FL: Academic Press.

## CHAPTER 5

Anderson, D. R. & Pempek, T. A. (2005). Television and very young children. *American Behavioral Scientist*. 48(5): 505–522.

Christakis, D. A., Zimmerman, F. J., DiGiuseppe, D. L., & McCarty, C. A. (2004). Early television exposure and subsequent attentional problems in children. *Pediatrics*. 113: 708–713. *In this study, researchers examined whether exposure to television between ages one and three is associated with attentional problems at age seven. When many other factors were taken into account (such as gender, ethnicity, amount of cognitive and emotional support in the home, etc.), the researchers found that each hour of television watched per day increased the risk of later attentional problems by 10 percent. The researchers highlight the need for more detailed research on this topic, in order to examine, for example, the impact of the type of television watched.*

Christakis, D. A., Ebel, B. E., Rivara, F. P., & Zimmerman, F. J. (2004). Television, video, and computer game usage in children under 11 years of age. *Journal of Pediatrics*. 145: 652–656.

Garrison, M. M. & Christakis, D. A. (2005). A Teacher in the Living Room? Educational Media for Babies, Toddlers, and Preschoolers. A background report prepared for The Henry J. Kaiser Family Foundation. *This report summarizes the educational claims that are made by electronic media products for children, and highlights that these claims have not been scientifically validated through research on children's learning outcomes. In fact, the authors report that, while some of the twenty-nine selected media products encourage parent-child interaction as a way to enhance their educational value, they found no published studies on the cognitive outcomes of any of those products or of any other commercially available in-home educational media products for children between zero and six years of age! In fact, some companies said that they don't conduct that type of research because it wouldn't influence sales and doesn't make economic sense. Nonetheless, in a recent survey, they found that 62 percent of parents said they thought educational toys like talking books are "very important" to children's intellectual development. From their perspective, the bottom line seems to be that, as a parent, you can buy these products, but don't be fooled into thinking that they necessarily are going to improve your child's intellectual growth.*

Green, C. S. & Bavelier, D. (2003). Action video game modifies visual selective attention. *Nature.* 423: 534–537; Green, C. S. & Bavalier, D. (2006). Enumeration versus multiple object tracking: The case of action video game players. *Cognition.* 101: 217–245. *In their most recent study, these researchers demonstrated that playing action video games increases one's ability to pay attention to multiple objects at the same time. The researchers compared video game players to non-video game players on two tasks in which participants either counted the number of squares on a screen or kept track of several moving circles on the screen after a cue telling them which circles to track had disappeared. Video game players outperformed the non-video game players, keeping track of two more objects than their non-playing counterparts. Interestingly, when non-video game players trained by playing thirty hours of a selected action video game, their performance on both test tasks improved. Because these tasks required the active allocation of visual attention, the researchers propose that video game playing can enhance visual short-term memory.*

Healy, J. M. (1999). *Endangered Minds: Why Children Don't Think and What We Can Do About It.* New York: Touchstone.

Kaldy, Z. & Sigala, N. (2004). The neural mechanisms of object working memory: What is where in the infant brain? *Neuroscience and Biobehavioral Reviews.* 28: 113–121.

Kuhl, P. K., Tsao, F. M., & Liu, H. M. (2003). Foreign-language experience in infancy: Effects of short-term exposure and social interaction on phonetic learning. *Proceedings of the National Academy of Sciences.* 100(15): 9096–9101.

Miller, G. A. (1956). The magical number seven, plus or minus two: Some limits on our capacity for processing information. *Psychological Review.* 63: 81–97. *In this article, cognitive scientist George Miller first described and characterized the extent and limitation of human working memory. Working memory is the part of the memory system that holds in mind for a brief period of time current information that may be needed to accomplish a task. Human beings can only attend to a small portion of the* *flood of information coming into their consciousness at a given time, and so there is a limited capacity of working memory, which has been called the magical number $7^{+ or - 2}$ bits of information (this is read as the magical number seven, plus or minus two bits of information). Human working memory span is remarkably small and unless you DO something with information as you are attending to it immediately, it will fade. Later neuroimaging research has shown that parts of the frontal lobes are active when a person is focusing on something they want to remember. Working memory limits, small though they are in adults, are even smaller in young children. And they develop slowly over time as the child grows and as their frontal lobes develop. Some estimates are that, starting at about age five, the limit may be as low as two bits, by age seven about three bits, by nine typically four bits, age eleven is five bits, age thirteen is six, and finally the adult capacity of seven is reached by about fifteen years of age.*

Restak, R. (2003). *The New Brain: How the Modern Age Is Rewiring Your Mind.* New York: Rodale Inc.

Rideout, V. J., Vandewater, E. A., & Wartella, E. A. (2003). Zero to Six: Electronic Media in the Lives of Infants, Toddlers, and Preschoolers. A report prepared by The Henry J. Kaiser Family Foundation and the Children's Digital Media Centers.

The Center on Media and Child Health, Children's Hospital Boston. (2005). The Effects of Electronic Media on Children Ages Zero to Six: A History of Research. A report prepared for The Henry J. Kaiser Family Foundation.

Wiecha, J. L., Peterson, K. E., Ludwig, D. S., Kim, J., Sobol, A., & Gortmaker, S. L. (2006). When children eat what they watch: Impact of television viewing on dietary intake in youth. *Archives of Pediatric and Adolescent Medicine.* 160: 436–442.

## CHAPTER 6

Anderson, J. R. (2000). *Cognitive Psychology and Its Implications* (Fifth Edition). New York: Worth.

Andreasen, N. C. (2005). *The Creating Brain: The Neuroscience of Genius.* Washington, DC: Dana Press.

Bloom, K. C. & Shuell, T. J. (1981). Effects of massed and distributed practice on the learning and retention of second-language vocabulary. *Journal of Educational Research.* 74(4): 245–248.

Debiec, J., LeDoux, J. E., & Nader, K. (2002). Cellular and systems reconsolidation in the hippocampus. *Neuron*. 36(3): 527–538.

de Haan, M., Mishkin, M., Baldeweg, T., & Vargha-Khadem, F. (2006). Human memory development and its dysfunction after early hippocampal injury. *Trends in Neurosciences*. 29(7): 374–381.

Donovan, J. J. & Radosevich, D. J. (1999). A meta-analytic review of the distribution of practice effect: Now you see it, now you don't. *Journal of Applied Psychology*. 84(5): 795–805.

Eichenbaum, H. (2006). The secret life of memories. *Neuron*. 50(3): 350–352; Suzuki, W. A. (2006). Encoding new episodes and making them stick. *Neuron*. 50(1): 19–21; Dudai, Y. (2006). Reconsolidation: The advantage of being refocused. *Current Opinion in Neurobiology*. 16: 174–178; Lee, J. L., Everitt, B. J., & Thomas, K. L. (2004). Independent cellular processes for hippocampal memory consolidation and reconsolidation. *Science*. 304(5672): 839–843. *These articles review the latest research on memory consolidation and reconsolidation, much of which has been done using experiments in rats. Memory consolidation, when experiences are transferred from short-term into long-term memory, is no longer thought to be a process that, once begun, is not influenced by subsequent experiences. Rather, researchers believe that it is a malleable process that can be influenced when a memory is recalled or another event is experienced, thus altering the original memory. This malleability of a memory after its reactivation occurs through a process called reconsolidation, which is thought to take place by different cellular processes than the original memory consolidation. Rats, for example, that have been trained to find a submerged platform in a tank of opaque, murky water can be made to forget how to do the task. If, after a "reminder" swim in which the platform is removed, they are given a drug that blocks hippocampal function and memory consolidation, they do not remember the location of the last platform that they had been taught to find. This suggests that a memory that should have already been consolidated (i.e., the location of the last platform) can be disrupted during reconsolidation by an interfering event (i.e., the "reminder" swim with no platform).*

Gomez, R. L., Bootzin, R. R., & Nadel, L. (2006). Naps promote abstraction in language-learning infants. *Psychological Science*. 17(8): 670–674.

Kahneman, D. (1973). *Attention and Effort.* Englewood Cliffs, NJ: Prentice-Hall.

Menzel, R., Manz, G., Menzel, R., Greggers, U. (2001). Massed and spaced learning in honeybees: The role of CS, US, the intertrial interval, and the test interval. *Learning and Memory.* 8: 198–208. *This article confirms for honeybees what teachers have long known is true for kids . . . that learning is most effective when there is time between learning sessions. When honeybees were conditioned to extend their proboscis to obtain a sugary solution in response to a stimulus (such as an odor, touch, or temperature increase), they learned to extend their proboscis faster and retained the memory longer and better when there was more space in between the learning sessions. Using honeybees to demonstrate this principle will allow researchers to delve deeper into the processes in the brain that account for this spaced learning effect.*

Rea, C. P. & Modigliani, V. (1985). The effect of expanded versus massed practice on the retention of multiplication facts and spelling lists. *Human Learning: Journal of Practical Research & Applications.* 4(1): 11–18.

Schacter, D. L. (2001). *The seven sins of memory: How the mind forgets and remembers.* Boston: Houghton Mifflin. *This captivating book, written by a renowned memory researcher, explores how the human memory system works by examining some common ways that it can lead us astray. The chapters focus on transience (how memories fade over time), absent-mindedness (how we won't remember something we didn't pay enough attention to), blocking (how we can sometimes not bring to mind or retrieve a fact that we are certain we know), misattribution (mixing up the source of a memory), suggestibility (allowing new information to intrude and cause us to remember something differently than it happened), bias (when we let our current point of view change how we remember an event), and persistence (the tendency to have memories intrude into our thoughts when we do not want them to). While delving into each of these "sins," the author also explains why these traits of the memory system can actually be valuable to us.*

## CHAPTER 8

Cushing, B. S. & Kramer, K. M. (2005). Mechanisms underlying epigenetic effects of early social experience: The role of neuropeptides and steroids. *Neuroscience and Biobehavioral Reviews.* 29: 1089–1105.

Dawson, G., Frey, K., Panagiotides, H., Hessl, D., & Self, J. (1997). Infants of depressed mothers exhibit atypical frontal brain activity: A replication and extension of previous findings. *Journal of Child Psychology and Psychiatry.* 38: 179–186.

Glaser, D. (2000). Child abuse and neglect and the brain—a review. *Journal of Child Psychology and Psychiatry*, 41(1): 97–116. *This article reviews what scientists have learned about the effects of child abuse and neglect on the brain. It outlines how the developing brain is shaped by early life experiences, and how, in turn, these neurobiological processes influence behavioral, cognitive, and emotional outcomes for children. The article covers how abuse and neglect can lead to the dysregulation of the stress response, reduced brain volume, as well as other biochemical, functional, and structural brain changes.*

Goleman, D. (1995). *Emotional Intelligence: Why It Can Matter More than IQ.* New York: Bantam Books.

Gunnar, M. R. (1992). Reactivity of the hypothalamic-pituitary-adrenocortical system to stressors in normal infants and children. *Pediatrics.* 90: 491–497.

Gunnar, M. R. (1998). Quality of early care and buffering of neuroendocrine stress reactions: Potential effects on the developing human brain. *Preventive Medicine.* 27: 208–211.

Knudsen, E. I., Heckman, J. J., Cameron J. L., & Shonkoff, J. P. (2006). Economic, neurobiological, and behavioral perspectives on building America's future workforce. *Proceedings of the National Academy of Sciences.* 103(27): 10155–10162.

Nelson, C. A., Zeanah, C. H., Smyke, A. T., Koga, S., Fox, N. A., Marshall, P., & Parker, S. W. (2001–present). Bucharest Early Intervention Project. More information about the project can be obtained from www.macbrain.org/beip.htm. *This ongoing longitudinal study is examining the effects of early experience on neurological, cognitive, emotional, and social development. By comparing three groups of children— children who are being raised in orphanages, children who are removed from orphanages and placed into high-quality foster care (with caretakers who are given parenting classes), and children who are raised by their own parents—the researchers aim to understand the effects of early deprivation as well as the effects of the timing of intervention to achieve maximal benefit for child outcomes. So far, it seems that the children who are placed into foster care exhibit fewer behavioral, attentional, and attachment problems than the children in orphanages, although they have more psychological problems than the children who are raised by their parents. The children in foster care also still have smaller brain volume in limbic structures that are devoted to emotional processing and that are among the earliest developing structures deep within the brain (as do the children who remain in the orphanages). That they exhibit such gains behaviorally indicates that there is compensation by and remarkable plasticity in other, later-developing brain regions. There is still much to be learned in the coming years as the study continues.*

New Directions Institute for Infant Brain Development. (2006). S.T.E.P.S. Curriculum.

Perry, B. D. (2003). Effects of traumatic events on children: An Introduction. The Child Trauma Academy. www.ChildTrauma.org.

Sapolsky, R. M. (1994). *Why Zebras Don't Get Ulcers: A Guide to Stress, Stress-Related Diseases, and Coping.* New York: W. H. Freeman and Company; McEwen, B. S. & Sapolsky, R. M. (1995). Stress and cognitive function. *Current Opinion in Neurobiology.* 5(2): 205–216. *Research by Dr. Robert Sapolsky, Professor of Biological Sciences, Neurology and Neurological Sciences at Stanford University, and Dr. Bruce McEwen, Professor of Neuroendocrinology at Rockefeller University, has been instrumental in showing the effects of stress hormones on the brain. They have demonstrated that a cycle of damage occurs with prolonged glucocorticoid exposure, whereby the glucocorticoids make the cells in the hippocampus vulnerable to death. The hippocampus, which plays a role in regulating the release of glucocorticoids, is then damaged and more glucocorticoids are secreted, further damaging the hippocampus.*

Shonkoff, J. R. (2005). Excessive stress disrupts the architecture of the developing brain. National Scientific Council on the Developing Child. Working Paper #3.

Shore, R. (1997). *Rethinking the Brain: New Insights into Early Development.* New York: Families and Work Institute.

Siegel, D. J. (1999). *The Developing Mind: Toward a Neurobiology of Interpersonal Experience.* New York: Guilford Press.

Teicher, M. H. (2002). Scars that won't heal: The neurobiology of child abuse.

*Scientific American.* 286(3): 68–75. *This article summarizes current research findings that maltreatment early in life can change the structure and function of the brain. These abuse-driven changes may underlie many of the psychosocial difficulties that manifest themselves as the child develops. In particular, the hippocampus and the amygdala, regions that are important for the formation and retrieval of memories and for process-ing emotions, respectively, are smaller in adults who have been neglected or abused as children. In addition, they display less integration between the two hemispheres (as a result of a smaller corpus callosum) as well as abnormalities in the cerebellum, which has many receptors for stress hormones. All together these changes can produce symptoms of depression, anxiety, hyperactivity, aggression, and impaired attention. Researchers now posit that these structural and functional differences may arise because of adaptations to an adverse environment, such as an exaggerated stress response, that end up being mal-adaptive in the sense that the brain is wired to be more aggressive, less emotionally sta-ble, less social, and less integrated between the right and left hemispheres.*

Teicher, M. H., Dumont, N. L., Ito, Y., Vaituzis, C., Giedd, J. N., & Anderson, S. L. (2004). Childhood neglect is associated with reduced corpus callosum area. *Biologi-cal Psychiatry.* 56: 80–85. *This article reports on the finding that the corpus callosum is 16.7 percent smaller in children who have been neglected or abused than in children who have not been neglected or abused.*

Uvnas-Moberg, K. (1998). Oxytocin may mediate the benefits of positive social interaction and emotions. *Psychoneuroendocrinology.* 23(8): 819–835.

Young, L. J. & Wang, Z. (2004). The neurobiology of pair bonding. *Nature Neuroscience.* 7(10): 1048–1054; Young, L. J., Murphy Young, A. Z., & Hammock, E. A. D. (2005). Anatomy and neurochemistry of the pair bond. *The Journal of Comparative Neurology.* 493: 51–57; Depue, R. A. & Morrone-Strupinsky, J. V. (2005). A neurobehavioral model of affiliative bonding: Implica-tions for conceptualizing a human trait of affiliation. *Behavioral and Brain Sciences.* 28: 313–350; Storm, E. E. & Tecott, L. H. (2005). Social circuits: Peptidergic reg-ulation of mammalian social behavior. *Neuron.* 47: 483–486. *These articles review current research about the neurochemistry of bond formation. The majority of this line of research has been conducted in a monogamous species of rodent, the prairie vole, whose males and females mate for life and parent their young together. Researchers have found that the neuropeptides oxytocin and vasopressin facilitate social recognition, and interact with the neurotransmitter dopamine to stimulate the pleasure pathways of the brain. There are other non-monogamous species of voles that do not form lasting pair bonds, perhaps due to a different level of receptors for oxytocin and vasopressin. It is believed that similar processes are at work in humans, and that a similar circuitry and receptor expression may underlie the strong familial bonds between mother and child, individual differences in the formation of sexual partner bonds, and other social bonds as well.*

## CHAPTER 9

Gillespie, L. G. & Seibel, N. L. (2006). Self-regulation: A cornerstone of early childhood development. *Young Children.* 61(4): 34–39.

Kagan, J. & Snidman, N. (2004). *The Long Shadow of Temperament.* Cambridge, MA: The Belknap Press of Harvard University Press.

Kristal, J. (2005). *The Temperament Perspective: Working with Children's Behavioral Styles.* New York: Paul H. Brookes Publishing Co.

New Directions Institute for Infant Brain Development. (2006). S.T.E.P.S. Curriculum.

Perry, B. (2005). Developing self-regulation: The second core strength your child needs to be human and protect himself from violence. *Early Childhood Today Magazine.*

Siegel, D. J. (1999). *The Developing Mind: Toward a Neurobiology of Interpersonal Experience.* New York: Guilford Press.

Thomas, A., Chess, S., & Birch, H. (1968). *Temperament and Behavior Disorders in Children.* New York: New York University Press.

Winberg, J. (2005). Mother and newborn baby: Mutual regulation of physiology and behavior—A selective review. *Developmental Psychobiology.* 47: 217–229.

## CHAPTER 10

Als, H. (1998). Developmental care in the newborn intensive care unit. *Current Opinion in Pediatrics.* 10: 138–142.

Als, H., Butler, S., McAnulty, G., Duffy, F., Conneman, N., Warfield, S., Huppi, P., & Rivkin, M. (2003). Effectiveness of individualized developmental care for preterm infants: Neurobehavioral and neurostructural evidence. *Proceedings of Society for Research in Child Development.*

Als, H., Duffy, F. H., McAnulty, G. B., Rivkin, M. J., Vajapeyam, S., Mulkern, R. V., Warfield, S. K., Huppi, P. S., Butler, S. C., Conneman, N., Fischer, C., & Eichenwald, E. C. (2004). Early experience alters brain function and structure. *Pediatrics.* 113(4): 846–857. *This study tracked whether a program of highly individualized care designed to mimic the environment in the womb could influence the health, physical growth, and brain development of pre-term infants in the neonatal intensive care unit. When compared with a control group, the infants who received the program of treatment showed enhanced brain structure and function, as well as being larger and healthier overall. The study is a powerful demonstration of how early experience can shape brain development.*

Als, H., Gilkerson, L., Duffy, F. H., McAnulty, G. B., Buehler, D. M., Vanden Berg, K., Sweet, N., Sell, E., Parad, R. B., Ringer, S. A., Butler, S. C., Blickman, J. G., & Jones, K. J. (2003). A three-center randomized controlled trial of individualized development care for very low-birth-weight preterm infants: medical, neurodevelopment, parent and care giving effects. *Journal of Developmental and Behavioral Pediatrics.* 24: 399–408.

Ayres, A. J. (2005). *Sensory Integration and the Child: Twenty-fifth Anniversary Edition.* Los Angeles: Western Psychological Services.

Field, T. (1986). Interventions for premature infants. *Journal of Pediatrics.* 109: 183–191.

Field, T. (1988). Stimulation of preterm infants. *Pediatrics in Review.* 10: 149–154.

Field, T. (1990). Alleviating stress in newborn infants in the intensive care unit. *Perinatology.* 17: 1–9. *This article reviews how touch interventions can improve newborns' reactions to being in the stressful environment of the intensive care unit, which is often noisy, bright, cold, and often involves painful procedures. Infants who were touched/massaged more gained more weight, were awake more, showed fewer startle responses, and scored higher on the Brazelton scale (an infant behavioral assessment scale).*

Field, T., Schanberg, S. M., Scafidi, F., Bauer, C. R., Vega-Lahr, N., Garcia, R., Nystrom, J., & Kuhn, C. M. (1986). Tactile/kinesthetic stimulation effects on preterm neonates. *Pediatrics*. 77: 654–658.

Hart, S., Field, T., Hernandez-Reif, M., & Lundy, B. (1998). Preschoolers' cognitive performance improves following massage. *Early Child Development & Care*. 143: 59–64.

## CHAPTER 11

The NICHD Early Child Care Research Network. (2005). *Child Care and Child Development: Results from the NICHD Study of Early Child Care and Youth Development*. New York: Guilford Press.

*Your Pregnancy & Birth* (Fourth Edition). (2005). Washington, DC: The American College of Obstetricians and Gynecologists and Meredith Books.

## CHAPTER 12

Stern, D. (2004). *The First Relationship: Infant and Mother. With a New Introduction*. Cambridge, MA: Harvard University Press.

## CHAPTER 13

Christie, J., Enz, B. J., & Vukelich, C. (2006). *Teaching Language and Literacy: Pre-School through the Elementary Grades* (Third Edition). New York: Allyn-Bacon (Addison-Wesley-Longman).

DeCasper, A. J. & Fifer, W. P. (1980). Of human bonding: Newborns prefer their mothers' voices. *Science*. 208: 1174–1176. *In this study, newborns could control whether they heard their mothers' voices or the voice of another female by sucking in different ways on a nonnutritive nipple. They sucked to hear their mothers' voices far more often than the other female voice, indicating that they show an early preference for their mothers' voices, an innate preference that may play a role in infant-mother bonding.*

Dehaene-Lambertz, G., Hertz-Pannier, L., & Dubios, J. (2006). Nature and nurture in language acquisition: Anatomical and functional brain-imaging studies in infants. *Trends in Neurosciences*. 29(7): 367–372.

Dehaene-Lambertz, G., Hertz-Pannier, L., Dubois, J., Meriaux, S., Roche, A., Sigman, M., & Dehaene, S. (2006). Functional organization of perisylvian activation during presentation of sentences in preverbal infants. *Proceedings of the National Academy of Sciences.* 103: 14240–14245. *Three-month-old infants were scanned with fMRI as they listened to sentences in their native language. The observed pattern of activity was already largely similar to the pattern that is observed in adults. This shows that early in life there is already a hierarchical organization within the brain for language, with the fastest brain response in auditory sensory areas and with slower responses in association or integration areas of cortex. Interestingly, the results also demonstrated that a region of the frontal cortex called Broca's area (which is necessary for the production of language) is active before the babbling stage begins, a finding that indicates that Broca's area is not only an area that governs the motor production of language, but one that aids the infant in learning the complex motor sequences needed for language production through interactions with perceptual brain regions. That the same brain regions are activated in immature infants with very little language experience and competent adult speakers indicates that there is a strong genetic bias for speech processing in these brain areas.*

Eimas, P. D. (1985). The perception of speech in early infancy. *Scientific American.* 252: 46–52.

Fernald, A. (1985). Four-month-old infants prefer to listen to motherese. *Infant Behavior and Development.* 8: 181–195.

Golestani, N., Paus, T., & Zatorre, R. J. (2002). Anatomical correlates of learning novel speech sounds. *Neuron.* 35: 997–1010. *This study demonstrated that people who are good at learning new language sounds show differences in the volume of certain brain regions when compared with people who are not as good at learning new language sounds. Adults were trained to be able to tell the difference between two Hindi syllables (the dental and retroflex sounds that differ in the place of articulation in the mouth), which sound the same to non-Hindi speakers. These same adults were then scanned with MRI. Adults who had been faster learners had more white matter (axon tracts) in the parietal regions of the left hemisphere than adults who had been slow learners, indicating that brain structure is related to language learning ability.*

Greenough, W. T. & Black, J. E. (1999). Experience, neural plasticity, and psychological development. In: *Proceedings of the 1999 Johnson & Johnson Pediatric Round*

*Table*: *The Role of Early Experience in Infant Development*. (Fox, N., Leavitt, L., & Warhol, J., eds.) 29–40. New Brunswick, NJ: Johnson & Johnson Consumer Companies.

Jacobs, B., Schall, M., & Scheibel, A. B. (1993). A quantitative dendritic analysis of Wernicke's area in humans: Gender, hemispheric, and environmental factors. *Journal of Comparative Neurology*. 327: 97–111.

Kuhl, P. K. (2004). Early language acquisition: Cracking the speech code. *Nature Reviews: Neuroscience*. 5: 831–843.

Kuhl, P. K., Tsao, F. M., Liu, H. M., Zhang, Y., & de Boer, B. (2001). Language/culture/mind/brain: Progress at the margins between disciplines. In: *Unity of Knowledge: The Convergence of Natural and Human Science*. (A. R. Damasio, ed.) 136–174. New York: The New York Academy of Sciences.

Neville, H. J., Coffey, S. A., Lawson, D. S., Fischer, A., Emmorey, K., & Bellugi, U. (1997). Neural systems mediating American Sign Language: Effects of sensory experience and age of acquisition. *Brain and Language*. 57: 285–308.

New Directions Institute for Infant Brain Development. (2006). S.T.E.P.S. Curriculum.

Petitto, L. A. (2000). On the biological foundations of human language. In: *The Signs of Language Revisited: An Anthology in Honor of Ursula Bellugi and Edward Klima*. (Emmorey, K. & Lane, H., eds). 447–471. Mahwah, NJ: Erlbaum.

Petitto, L. A., Holowka, S., Sergio, L., E., Levy, B., & Ostry, D. J. (2004). Baby hands that move to the rhythm of language: Hearing babies acquiring sign language babble silently on the hands. *Cognition*. 93: 43–73.

Petitto, L. A., Holowka, S., Sergio, L., & Ostry, D. (2001). Language rhythms in babies' hand movements. *Nature*. 413: 35–36.

Petitto, L. A. & Marentette, P. (1991). Babbling in the manual mode: Evidence for the ontogeny of language. *Science*. 251: 1483–1496.

Petitto, L. A., Zatorre, R., Gauna, K., Nikelski, E. J., Dostie, D., & Evans, A. (2000). Speech-like cerebral activity in profoundly deaf people while processing signed languages: Implications for the neural basis of human language. *Proceedings of the National Academy of Sciences.* 97(25): 13961–13966.

Spencer, P. (2005). Small talk: From first words to funny expressions, the surprising ways your child learns language. *Parenting Magazine.* August Issue: 136–142.

Tincoff, R. & Jusczyk, P. W. (1999). Mama! Dada! Origins of word meaning. *Psychological Science.* 10(2): 172–175.

Vouloumanos, A. & Werker, J. F. (2007). Listening to language at birth: Evidence for a bias for speech in neonates. *Developmental Science.* 10(2): 159–164.

Vukelich, C., Christie, J., & Enz, B. J. (2007). *Helping Young Children Learn Language and Literacy* (Second Edition). New York: Allyn-Bacon (Addison-Wesley-Longman).

Werker, J. F. & Tees, R. C. (2005). Speech perception as a window for understanding plasticity and commitment in language systems of the brain. *Developmental Psychobiology.* 46(3): 233–251.

## CHAPTER 14

Anderson, J. R. (2000). *Cognitive Psychology and Its Implications* (Fifth Edition). New York: Worth.

Balbani, A. P. & Montovani, J. C. (2003). Impact of otitis media on language acquisition in children. *Jornal de pediatria.* 79(5): 391–396.

Berman, S. (2001). Pediatricians need to help foster early brain development in children. *AAP News.* 19: 46.

Bloom, P. (2000). *How Children Learn the Meanings of Words.* Cambridge, MA: MIT Press.

Cheour, M., Shestakova, A., Alku, P., Ceponiene, R., & Näätänen, R. (2002). Mismatch negativity shows that 3- to 6-year-old children can learn to discriminate non-native speech sounds within two months. *Neuroscience Letters.* 325: 187–190. *In this study, researchers used EEG to measure brain responses in children before and after they began to learn a foreign language. Finnish children between the ages of three and six listened to two different French syllables, which sound the same to non-French speakers, while their brain responses were being recorded with EEG. A group of these children was then enrolled in a French school or day-care center for two months, while the rest remained in Finnish care environments. After two months, the children underwent the same EEG session while listening to the French syllables. Researchers examined the EEG data to see whether they could detect a mismatch negativity response (the brain's electrical change-detection response) when the children heard a change from one syllable to another. In the first EEG session, there was no mismatch negativity response; in other words, the children's brains did not perceive a change from one syllable to the other. However, in the second EEG session, the group that had been in French school or day care (and not the other group) displayed the mismatch negativity when they heard a switch from one syllable to the other. Interestingly, this difference in brain response was observed even though the children were not yet proficient French speakers. Although proficiency to hear non-native language sounds declines in the first year of life, thanks to neural plasticity, young children regain this ability very quickly.*

Christie, J., Enz, B., & Vukelich, C. (2006). *Teaching Language and Literacy: Pre-School through the Elementary Grades* (Third Edition). New York: Allyn-Bacon (Addison-Wesley-Longman).

Copeland, J. & Gleason, J. (1993). *Causes of Speech Disorders and Language Delays.* Tucson, AZ: University of Arizona Speech and Language Clinic.

Enz, B. J. (2003). The ABCs of family literacy. In: *Family Literacy: From Theory to Practice.* (DeBruin, A. & Krol-Sinclair, B., eds.) Newark, DE: International Reading Association.

Foreman, J. (2002). Two tongues better than one. *The Boston Globe.* September 10, 2002.

Friederici, A. D., Steinhauer, K., & Pfeifer, E. (2002). Brain signatures of artificial language processing: Evidence challenging the critical period hypothesis. *Proceedings of the National Academy of Sciences.* 99(1): 529–534.

Hart, B. & Risley, T. (1995). *Meaningful Differences in the Everyday Experience of Young American Children.* Baltimore, MD: Brookes.

Hoff, E. & Naigles, L. (2002). How children use input to acquire a lexicon. *Child Development.* 73(2): 418–433.

Johnson, E. K., & Newport, E. L. (1989). Critical period effects in second language learning: The influence of maturational state on the acquisition of English as a second language. *Cognitive Psychology*, 21: 60–99.

Jusczyk, P. W. (1999). How infants begin to extract words from fluent speech. *Trends in Cognitive Science*, 3: 323–328.

Jusczyk, P. W. (2002). How infants adapt speech-processing capacities to native-language structure. *Current Directions in Psychological Science*. 11(1): 15–18.

Kahneman, D. (1973). *Attention and Effort*. Englewood Cliffs, NJ: Prentice-Hall.

Liu, H.-M., Kuhl, P. K., & Tsao, F.-M. (2003). An association between mothers' speech clarity and infants' speech discrimination skills. *Developmental Science*. 6(3): F1–F10. *This study demonstrated that the quality of speech an infant hears can influence language skills. Researchers recorded infant-directed speech of mothers and measured the wideness of their vowel space. (Wider vowel space is associated with higher speech clarity and intelligibility.) Next, their infants (who were between six and twelve months of age) were given a test to see how well they could tell the difference between two similar-sounding syllables. The clearer the speech of the mother, the better the infant was at discriminating between the syllables, indicating that the use of parentese can be helpful for young children when learning the sounds of their native language.*

Mareschal, D., Powell, D., & Volein, A. (2003). Basic-level category discriminations by 7- and 9-month-olds in an object examination task. *Journal of Experimental Child Psychology*. 86: 87–107. *The research of Denis Mareschal and colleagues at the Center for Brain and Cognitive Development at Birbeck University in London has shown that eight-month-olds tend to categorize a group of objects by their perceptual features alone (all the big items go in one group and the small ones go in another), whereas nine-month-olds begin to group objects by the kind of object. They will start to place all the dogs together (whether big or small) and all the cats in another group.*

Mayberry, R. I. & Lock, E. (2003). Age constraints on first versus second language acquisition: Evidence for linguistic plasticity and epigenesis. *Brain and Language*. 87: 369–384.

McNealy, K., Mazziotta, J. C., & Dapretto, M. (2006). Cracking the language code: Neural mechanisms underlying speech parsing. *The Journal of Neuroscience.* 26(29): 7629–7639.

Mechelli, A., Crinion, J. T., Noppeney, U., O'Doherty, J., Ashburner, J., Frackowiak, R. S., & Price, C. J. (2004). Neurolinguistics: Structural plasticity in the bilingual brain. *Nature.* 431: 757. *This study showed that there are structural brain changes that occur in bilingual speakers as a result of learning a second language. After administering MRI and language proficiency tests to bilingual speakers, the researchers found that the more proficient the speaker is in the second language and the younger the age at which the speaker learned the language, the thicker the cortex in a part of the left parietal lobe. These results indicate that learning a second language produces changes not only in how the existing brain circuitry is used, but also in the structure of the brain itself.*

Perani, D., Abutalebi, J., Paulesu, E., Brambati, S., Scifo, P., Cappa, S. F., & Fazio, F. (2003). The role of age of acquisition and language usage in early, high-proficiency bilinguals: An fMRI study during verbal fluency. *Human Brain Mapping.* 19: 170–182.

Rakison, D. & Oakes, L. M. (Eds.) (2003). *Early Category and Concept Development: Making Sense of the Blooming, Buzzing Confusion.* New York: Oxford University Press.

Sanders, L. D., Neville, H. J., & Woldorff, M. G. (2002). Speech segmentation by native and non-native speakers: The use of lexical, syntactic, and stress-pattern cues. *Journal of Speech, Language, and Hearing Research* 45(3): 519–530.

Sanders, L. D., Newport, E. L., & Neville, H. J. (2002). Segmenting nonsense: An event-related potential index of perceived onsets in continuous speech. *Nature Neuroscience.* 5(7): 700–703.

Saffran, J. R., Aslin, R. N., & Newport, E. L. (1996). Statistical learning by 8-month-old infants. *Science.* 274: 1926–1928. *This was the first of many subsequent studies to show that infants as young as eight months of age can successfully learn to detect where word boundaries fall in a continuous stream of speech by calculating the statistical likelihood that sounds will occur together. In these studies, infants are exposed for just two and a half minutes to a continuous stream of nonsense speech containing no breaks, pauses, or prosodic cues such as stress pattern or pitch intonations (e.g., pabikutibudogolatudaropitibudo . . .). This speech contained four words ("pabiku," "tibudo," "golatu," and "daropi"). When later exposed to either "words" from within the speech stream or "partwords" formed by combining syllables from adjacent words (e.g., "tudaro," the last syllable of one word "golatu" and the first two of an adjacent word "daropi"), infants consistently display a novelty preference (i.e., they look longer toward the sound of the "partwords"). These results have been widely interpreted as demonstrating that infants are able to successfully calculate the statistical regularities between adjacent syllables to learn the words in the miniature artificial language.*

Sebastian-Galles, N. (2006). Native-language sensitivities: Evolution in the first year of life. *Trends in Neurosciences*. 10(6): 239–241.

Shevell, M. I. (2005). Outcomes at school age of preschool children with developmental language impairment. *Pediatric Neurology*. 32(4): 264–69.

Tibussek, D., Meister, H., Walger, M., Foerst, A., & von Wedel, H. (2002). Hearing loss in early infancy affects maturation of the auditory pathway. *Developmental Medicine and Child Neurology*. 44: 123–129.

Thiessen, E. D., Hill, E. A., & Saffran, J. R. (2005). Infant-directed speech facilitates word segmentation. *Infancy*. 7(1): 52–71.

Waseem, M., Aslam, M., Jones, M., Wilson, L., & Malis, D. (2006). http://www.emedicine.com/ped/topic1689.htm

Weber-Fox, C. & Neville, H. J. (2001). Sensitive periods differentiate processing of open- and closed-class words: An ERP study of bilinguals. *Journal of Speech, Language, and Hearing Research*. 44(6): 1338–1353.

## CHAPTER 15

Brambati, S. M., Termine, C., Ruffino, M., Danna, M., Lanzi, G., Stella, G., Cappa, S. F., & Perani, D. (2006). Neuropsychological deficits and neural dysfunction in familial dyslexia. *Brain Research*. 1113: 174–185.

Brown, W. E., Eliez, S., Menon, V., Rumsey, J. M., White, C. D., & Reiss, A. L. (2001). Preliminary evidence of widespread morphological variations of the brain in dyslexia. *Neurology*. 56(6): 781–783.

Bus, A., van Ijzendoorn, M., & Pellegrini, A. (1995). Joint book reading makes for success in learning to read: A meta-analysis on intergenerational transmission of literacy. *Review of Educational Research.* 65: 1–21.

Castro-Caldas, A., Petersson, K. M., Reis, A., Stone-Elander, S., & Ingvar, M. (1998). The illiterate brain: Learning to read and write during childhood influences the functional organization of the adult brain. *Brain.* 121: 1053–1063. *This study compared the pattern of brain activity in adults who could and could not read while they listened to and repeated aloud made-up non-words (like "gorp"). When listening to real words, literate and illiterate adults activated the same brain regions, as might be expected since the oral language skills are roughly the same in both groups of adults. However, when listening to the non-words, illiterate adults had trouble repeating them aloud and also did not use the same brain regions as did literate adults (they activated less in inferior frontal and anterior cingulated cortices), suggesting that knowing a written form of language and sound-letter correspondence interacts with how the brain processes auditory language. These results demonstrate that learning how to read and write in childhood affects the functional organization of the brain of adults.*

Christian, K., Morrison, F., & Bryant, F. (1998). Predicting kindergarten academic skills: Interaction among child-care, maternal education, and family literacy environments. *Early Childhood Research Quarterly.* 13: 501–521.

Christie, J., Enz, B., & Vukelich, C. (2006). *Teaching Language and Literacy: Pre-School through the Elementary Grades* (Third Edition). New York: Allyn-Bacon (Addison-Wesley-Longman).

Cloer, T., Aldridge, J., & Dean, R. (1981). Examining different levels of print awareness. *Journal of Language Experience.* 4(1&2): 25–34.

Cowley, F. (1997). The language explosion. *Newsweek: Your Child.* Spring/Summer: (special edition).

Dickinson, D. & Tabors, P. (2000). *Beginning Literacy with Language: Young Children Learning at Home and School.* Baltimore, MD: Paul H. Brookes.

Enz, B. & Scarfoss, L. (1996). Expanding our views of family literacy. *The Reading Teacher.* 49: 576–579.

Enz, B.J. & Stamm, J. (2003). The First Teacher Project. Paper presented at Association of Early Childhood International. Phoenix, AZ.

Gaillard, W. D., Balsamo, L. M., Ibrahim, Z., Sachs, B. C., & Xu, B. (2003). fMRI identifies regional specialization of neural networks for reading in young children. *Neurology*. 60(1): 94–100.

Goodman, Y. (1986). Children coming to know literacy. In: *Emergent Literacy: Writing and Reading*. (Teale, W. H. & Sulzby, E., eds.) 1–14. Norwood, NJ: Ablex.

Griffin, E. & Morrison, F. (1997). The unique contribution of home literacy environment to differences in early literacy skills. *Early Child Development and Care*. 127–128: 233–243.

Huttenlocher, J., Haight, W., Bryk, A., Seltzer, M., & Lyons, T. (1991). Early vocabulary growth: Relation to language input and gender. *Developmental Psychology*. 27(2): 236–248.

Koenig, M. A. & Woodward, A. L. (2007). Word learning. In: *Oxford Handbook of Psycholinguistics*. (G. Gaskell, ed.) Oxford, UK: Oxford University Press.

Kotulak, R. (1997). *Inside the Brain: Revolutionary Discoveries of How the Mind Works*. Kansas City, MO: Andrews McMeel.

Kuby, P., Aldridge, J., & Snyder, S. (1994). Developmental progression of EP recognition in kindergarten children. *Reading Psychology International Quarterly*. 15: 1–9.

Mason, J. (1980). When do children begin to read: An exploration of four-year-old children's letter and word reading competencies. *Reading Research Quarterly*. 15: 203–227.

Masonheimer, P., Drum, P., & Ehri, L. (1984). Does environmental print identification lead children into word reading? *Journal of Reading Behavior*. I: 257–271.

McGee, L., Lomax, R., & Head, M. (1988). Young children's written language knowledge: What environmental and functional print reading reveals. *Journal of Reading Behavior*. 20: 99–118.

McGee, L. & Richgels, D. (1996). *Literacy's Beginnings: Supporting Young Readers and Writers* (Second Edition). Boston, MA: Allyn & Bacon.

Morrow, L. (1983). Home and school correlates of early interest in literature. *Journal of Educational Research.* 76: 221–230.

Neuman, S. (1999). Books make a difference: A study of access to literacy. *Reading Research Quarterly.* 34(3): 286–311.

Parvainen, T., Helenius, P., Poskiparts, E., Niemi, P., & Salmelin, R. (2006). Cortical sequence of word perception in beginning readers. *The Journal of Neuroscience.* 26(22): 6052–6061.

Shaywitz, S. (2003). *Overcoming Dyslexia: A New and Complete Science-Based Program for Reading Problems at Any Level.* New York: Alfred A. Knopf.

Shaywitz, S. E. & Shaywitz, B. A. (2005). Dyslexia (specific reading disability). *Biological Psychiatry.* 57: 1301–1309.

Shaywitz, B. A., Shaywitz, S. E., Blachman, B. A., Pugh, K. R., Fulbright, R. K., Skudlarski, P., Mencl, W. E., Constable, R. T., Holahan, J. M., Marchione, K. E., Fletcher, J. M., Lyon, G. R., & Gore, J. C. (2004). Development of left occipitotemporal systems for skilled reading in children after a phonologically-based intervention. *Biological Psychiatry.* 55: 926–933. *Previous research has shown that dyslexic children do not activate the same regions in the back (posterior) portion of the left hemisphere during reading as do normal readers. This study used fMRI to compare the pattern of activity during reading of dyslexic children before and after one year of behavioral reading intervention. In the follow-up one year after the intervention had ended, the children had not only improved their reading fluency, but, importantly, showed a pattern of activation more like that of the control group participants (with increased activation in a posterior brain region known to be involved in reading, the occipitotemporal cortex, as well as other areas of the brain that are active in skilled readers). These results indicate that behavioral therapies for developmental dyslexia can lead to improved outcomes, likely by facilitating the use of more normative neural networks for reading.*

Shaywitz, B. A., Shaywitz, S. E., Pugh, K. R., Mencl, W. E., Fulbright, R. K., Skudlarski, P., Constable, R. T., Marchione, K. E., Fletcher, J. M., Lyon, G. R., & Gore, J. C. (2002). Disruption of posterior brain systems for reading in children with developmental dyslexia. *Biological Psychiatry.* 52(2): 101–110.

Shaywitz, S. E., Shaywitz, B. A., Fulbright, R. K., Skudlarski, P., Mencl, W. E., Constable, R. T., Pugh, K. R., Holahan, J. M., Marchione, K. E., Fletcher, J. M., Lyon, G. R., & Gore, J. C. (2003). Neural systems for compensation and persistence: young adult outcome of childhood reading disability. *Biological Psychiatry*. 54(1): 25–33.

Shaywitz, S. E., Shaywitz, B. A., Pugh, K. R., Fulbright, R. K., Constable, R. T., Mencl, W. E., Shankweiler, D. P., Liberman, A. M., Skudlarski, P., Fletcher, J. M., Katz, L., Marchione, K. E., Lacadie, C., Gatenby, C., & Gore, J. C. (1998). Functional disruption in the organization of the brain for reading in dyslexia. *Proceedings of the National Academy of Sciences*. 95: 2636–2641.

Simos, P. G., Fletcher, J. M., Bergman, E., Breier, J. I., Foorman, B. R., Castillo, E. M., Davis, R. N., Fitzgerald, M., & Papanicolaou, A. C. (2002). Dyslexia-specific brain activation profile becomes normal following successful remedial training. *Neurology*. 58(8): 1203–1213.

Sulzby, E., Teale, W., & Kamberelis, G. (1989). Emergent writing in the classroom: Home and school connection. In: *Emerging Literacy: Young Children Learn to Read and Write*. (Strickland, D. & Morrow, L., eds.) 63–79. Newark, DE: International Reading Association.

Tallal, P. (2004). Improving language and literacy is a matter of time. *Nature Reviews: Neuroscience*. 5(9): 721–728.

Turkeltaub, P. E., Gareau, L., Flowers, D. L., Zeffiro, T. A., & Eden, G. F. (2003). Development of neural mechanisms for reading. *Nature Neuroscience*. 6(6): 767–773. *In this study, researchers examined how the pattern of neural activity during reading changes as a function of age and reading skill. Participants between the ages of six and twenty-two underwent fMRI while viewing different words. The results showed that, as children get older and better at reading, there is increased activity in the middle portion of the temporal lobe and the inferior frontal lobe in the left hemisphere and decreased activity in the right temporal cortex. This type of study allows researchers to learn how changes in brain function are related to changes in acquired skills such as reading.*

Vukelich, C., Christie, J., & Enz, B. (2007). *Helping Young Children Learn Language and Literacy* (Second Edition). New York: Allyn-Bacon (Addison-Wesley-Longman).

Whitehurst, G.J., Epstein, J.N., Angel, A., Payne, A.C., Crone, D., & Fischel, J.E. (1994). Outcomes of an emergent literacy intervention in Head Start. *Journal of Educational Psychology*. 84: 541–556.

Woodward, A. L. (2004). Infants' use of action knowledge to get a grasp on words. In: *Weaving a Lexicon*. (Hall, D.G. & Waxman, S.R., eds.) 149–172. Cambridge, MA: MIT Press.

Woodward, A. L. (2003). Infants' developing understanding of the link between looker and object. *Developmental Science*. 6(3): 297–311.

## CHAPTER 16

Bengtsson, S. L., Nagy, Z., Skare, S., Forsman, L., Forssberg, H., & Ullen, F. (2005). Extensive piano practicing has regionally specific effects on white matter development. *Nature Neuroscience*. 8: 1148–1150.

Caine, J. (1991). The effects of music on the selected stress behaviors, weight, caloric and formula intake, and length of hospital stay of premature and low birth-weight neonates in a newborn intensive care unit. *Journal of Music Therapy*. 28: 180–192.

Costa-Giomi, E. (1999). The effects of three years of piano instruction on children's cognitive development. *Journal of Research in Music Education*. 47(5): 198–212.

de l'Etoile, S. K. (2006). Infant behavioral responses to infant-directed singing and other maternal interactions. *Infant Behavior and Development*. 29(3): 456–470. *This study investigated six- to nine-month-old infant responses to listening to mothers' singing and compared them to listening to recorded music and other mothers' actions such as playing with a toy and reading a book. While the babies were most physically responsive to the books and toys, they were the most vocal in response to infant-directed singing, and they far preferred the singing over listening to recorded music. This study provides support for what mothers have long known about the power of their own singing voices to capture their children's attention for soothing, bonding, and fun.*

Fujioka, T., Ross, B., Kakigi, R., Pantev, C., & Trainor, L. J. (2006). One year of musical training affects development of auditory cortical-evoked fields in young children. *Brain*. 129: 2593–2608. *The researchers in this study recorded the brain's response to auditory stimuli using a technique called magnetoencephalography (MEG) in four- to six-year-old children. One group of children received a year of music lessons and another group of children did not. During four MEG sessions throughout the year, both groups of children listened to violin tones and noise bursts, and their auditory cortical responses were compared. The children who received music lessons showed a larger and earlier waveform response in the left hemisphere to the violin tones than the children who did not receive lessons, and this difference was present only for the violin tones, not the noise bursts. These findings indicate that experience with music can influence how the brain processes and attends to sounds.*

Gaser, C. & Schlaug, G. (2003). Brain structures differ between musicians and non-musicians. *Journal of Neuroscience*. 23: 9240–9245.

Hetland, L. (2001). The relationship between music and spatial reasoning. In: Proceedings from "Beyond the soundbite: What the research actually shows about arts education and academic outcomes." (Winner, E. & Hetland, L., eds.) 55–70. Los Angeles: J. Paul Getty Trust.

Ho, Y.-C., Cheung, M.-C., & Chan, A. S. (2003). Music training improves verbal but not visual memory: Cross-sectional and longitudinal explorations in children. *Neuropsychology*. 17(3): 439–450.

Hutchinson, S., Lee, L. H. L., Gaab, N., & Schlaug, G. (2003). Cerebellar volume of musicians. *Cerebral Cortex*. 13(9): 943–949.

Jäncke, L., Schlaug, G., & Steinmetz, H. (1997). Hand skill asymmetry in professional musicians. *Brain and Cognition*. 34: 424–432.

Lee, D. J., Chen, Y., & Schlaug, G. (2003). Corpus callosum: Musician and gender effects. *NeuroReport*. 14: 205–209.

Norton, A., Winner, E., Cronin, K., Overy, K., Lee, D., & Schlaug, G. (2005). Are there pre-existing neural, cognitive, or motoric markers for musical ability? *Brain and Cognition*. 59: 124–134.

Overy, K. (2003). Dyslexia and music: From timing deficits to musical intervention. *Annals of the New York Academy of Sciences*. 999: 497–505.

Overy, K., Norton, A. C., Cronin, K. T., Gaab, N., Alsop, D. C., Winner, E., & Schlaug, G. (2004). After one year of musical training, young children show a left-hemispheric shift for melody processing. *Neuroimage*. 22S: S53.

Overy, K., Norton, A. C., Cronin, K. T., Winner, E., & Schlaug, G. (2005). Examining rhythm and melody processing in young children using fMRI. *Annals of the New York Academy of Sciences*. 1060: 210–218.

Rauscher, F. H., Shaw, G. L., Levine, L. J., Wright, E. L., Dennis, W. R., & Newcomb, R. (1997). Music training causes long-term enhancement of preschool children's spatial/temporal reasoning. *Neurological Research*. 19: 2–8.

Rauscher, F. H., Shaw, G. L., & Ky, K. N. (1993). Music and spatial task performance. *Nature*. 365: 611.

Rauscher, F. H. & Zupan, M. (2000). Classroom keyboard instruction improves kindergarten children's spatial-temporal performance: A field experiment. *Early Childhood Research Quarterly*. 15: 215–228.

Rauscher, F. H. (2002). Mozart and the mind: Factual and fictional effects of musical enrichment. In: *Improving Academic Achievement: Impact of Psychological Factors on Education*. (J. Aronson, ed.) 269–278. New York : Academic Press.

Saffran, J. R. (2003). Musical learning and language development. *Annals of the New York Academy of Sciences*. 999: 397–401.

Schellenberg, E. G. (2004). Music lessons enhance IQ. *Psychological Science*. 15(8): 511–514.

Schlaug, G. (2001). The brain of musicians: A model for functional and structural plasticity. *Annals of the New York Academy of Sciences*. 930: 281–299.

Schlaug, G., Jäncke, L., Huang, Y., & Steinmetz, H. (1995). In vivo evidence of structural brain asymmetry in musicians. *Science*. 267: 699–671.

Schlaug, G., Norton, A., Overy, K., & Winner, E. (2005). Effects of music training on brain and cognitive development. *Annals of the New York Academy of Sciences*. 1060: 219–230.

Shaw, G. L. (2000). *Keeping Mozart in Mind* (Second Edition). San Diego, CA: Academic Press.

Standley, J. (1998). The effect of music and multimodal stimulation on physiologic and developmental responses of premature infants in neonatal intensive care. *Pediatric Nursing Journal.* 21: 532–539.

Stewart, L. & Walsh, V. (2005). Infant learning: Music and the baby brain. *Current Biology.* 15(21): R882–883.

Tallal, P. & Gaab, N. (2006). Dynamic auditory processing, musical experience and language development. *Trends in Neurosciences.* 29(7): 382–390.

Vaughn, K. (2000). Music and mathematics: Modest support for the oft-claimed relationship. *Journal of Aesthetic Education.* 34 (3–4): 149–166.

Winner, E. & Hetland, L. (2000). The arts and academic achievement: What the evidence shows. *Journal of Aesthetic Education.* 34 (3–4).

Winner, E. & Hetland, L. (Eds.). (2001). Proceedings from "Beyond the Soundbite: What the Research Actually Shows About Arts Education and Academic Outcomes." Los Angeles: J. Paul Getty Trust.

www.musicianbrain.com/projects_children.html. *This Web site contains information about the NSF-funded longitudinal study, The Effects of Music Training on Children's Brain and Cognitive Development.*

## BRAIN BASICS:

Kandel, E. R., Schwartz, J. H., & Jessell, T. M. (2000). *Principles of Neural Science* (Fourth Edition). New York: McGraw-Hill Medical.

Purves, D., Augustine, G. J., Fitzpatrick, D., Hall, W. C., LaMantia, A.-S., McNamara, J. O., & Williams, S. M. (2004). *Neuroscience* (Third Edition). Sinauer Associates.

## FIGURES:

*Figure 1.* Reprinted by permission of John Mazziotta, M.D., Ph.D.

*Figure 2.* Reprinted by permission of the publisher from *The Postnatal Development of the Human Cerebral Cortex*, Vols. I–VIII, by Jesse LeRoy Conel. Cambridge, MA: Harvard University Press. Copyright © 1939, 1975 by the President and Fellows of Harvard College.

***Figures 3 and 4.*** Illustrations by Kurt A. Brown. All rights reserved. Reprinted by permission of Kurt A. Brown, Studio 44.

***Figure 5.*** Santrock, J. W. (1998). *Child Development* (Eighth edition). New York: McGraw-Hill Companies, Inc. Reprinted by permission of McGraw-Hill Companies, Inc.

***Figure 6.*** Reprinted by permission of New Directions Institute.

***Figure 7.*** From *Teaching with the Brain in Mind* (page 57), by Eric Jensen, Alexandria, VA: ASCD, 1998. Used with permission. The Association for Supervision and Curriculum Development is a worldwide community of educators advocating sound policies and sharing best practices to achieve the success of each learner. To learn more, visit ASCD at www.ascd.org.

***Figure 8.*** Reprinted by permission of Harry Chugani, M.D.

***Figure 9.*** Brillian Beginnings! Baby Brain Basics Guidebook: Birth to 12 Months, by Brilliant Beginnings, LLC. Copyright © 1999 by Brilliant Beginnings, LLC. Data from Hart, B. & Risley, T. (1995). *Meaningful Differences in the Everyday Experience of Young American Children*. Baltimore, MD: Brookes. Reprinted by permission of Brookes Publishing.

***Figure 10.*** Anderson, J. R. (2000). *Cognitive Psychology and Its Implications.* (Fifth Edition). New York: Worth. Copyright © 1980, 1985, 1995, 2000 by Worth Publishers and W. H. Freeman and Company. Used with permission.

***Figure 11.*** Reprinted from S. Shaywitz. *Overcoming Dyslexia: A New and Complete Science-Based Program for Reading Problems at Any Level.* New York: Alfred A. Knopf, 2003.

***Figures 12 and 13.*** Adapted from *Brain Facts: A Primer on the Brain and the Nervous System.* (2005). Washington, D.C.: The Society for Neuroscience. Copyright 2005 by The Society for Neuroscience. Reprinted by permission of the artist, L. Kibiuk, Society for Neuroscience.

***Figure 14.*** Petersen, S.E., Fox, P.T., Posner, M.I., Mintun, M., & Raichle, M.E. (1989). Positron emission tomographic studies of the processing of single words. *Journal of Cognitive Neuroscience*. 1:153–170. Reprinted by permission of the Massachusetts Institute of Technology.

*Figure 15.* Structural MRI images courtesy of the UCLA Ahmanson-Lovelace Brain Mapping Center. Reprinted by permission of Kristin McNealy.

*Figure 16.* Functional MRI image courtesy of the UCLA Ahmanson-Lovelace Brain Mapping Center. Reprinted by permission of Kristin McNealy.

*Figure 17.* Oertle, T., van der Haar, M. E., Bandtlow, C. E., Robeva, A., Burfeind, P., Buss, A., Huber, A. B., Simonen, M., Schnell, L., Brosamle, C., Kaupmann, K., Vallon, R., & Schwab, M. (2003). Nogo-A inhibits neurite outgrowth and cell spreading with three discrete regions. *The Journal of Neuroscience*. 23(13):5393–5406. Copyright 2003 by The Society for Neuroscience. Reprinted by permission of The Society for Neuroscience.

## RESOURCES
Zero-to-Three: www.zerotothree.org
Brain Connection: www.brainconnection.com
Parents Action for Children: www.parentsaction.org
The Society for Neuroscience: www.sfn.org
Child Trauma Academy: www.childtrauma.org
Ounce of Prevention Fund: www.ounceofprevention.org
Dana Alliance for Brain Initiatives: www.dana.org/braincenter.cfm
PBS Documentary: The Secret Life of the Brain: www.pbs.org/wnet/brain
New Directions Institute for Infant Brain Development:
    www.newdirectionsinstitute.org
Arizona's Children Association: www.arizonaschildren.org
Baby Brain Box: www.babybrainbox.com (1-800-707-1000)

# Index